4th – Adult

The Best Ever Book About

California Missions

AUTHOR
RANDY L. WOMACK, M.ED.

MISSION SKETCHES
RYDER RODRIGUEZ

PUBLISHED BY

"LEADING THE WAY IN CREATIVE EDUCATIONAL MATERIALS" ™

857 LAKE BLVD. ❖ REDDING, CALIFORNIA 96003
www.goldened.com

To Teachers and Parents

The Best Book Ever About California Missions is a comprehensive, easy-to-use format (like all of the books written by Randy Womack). The first section of the book has background information with maps, questions, and research activities. It is important for the students to understand this background information before they complete the sections on the individual mission. Although the mission sections can be used in any order, it is suggested that they are completed in order for two reasons: 1.) The *New Words to Learn* for each section are in order of appearance. 2.) The historical stories of the missions sometimes overlap or are references to the preceding section.

Each of the individual mission sections starts with a map of the mission chain, new words to learn (look up in the dictionary), and shows a diagram of the mission compound that the students have to label. These pages are followed by a fact sheet about the mission and then a short history about the founding of the mission. Wherever space allowed a crossword, word search, or other puzzle relating to the information in the section follows the history pages. After the puzzle comes "The Mission Today" page. At the end of each section there is a page of review questions, which also has bonus activities (research projects) for students to complete.

Thanks and Credits

Number one thanks to my lovely wife, Terry (Theresa — AKA: Lubby). She is the greatest.
Thanks for putting up with me and always being so supportive. Living with you, Lubby, is a hoot.

Dee Hill for giving me the initial idea of writing the book, and calling once a week for two years asking, "Is the missions book done, yet?" (And Linda, Dee's assistant, who called when Dee was out of town.)

Beth Watrous for giving me the idea to publish a *Best Ever...California Mission Poster* (which was way easier than this book).
My older son, Justin Womack, who drew all of the mission layouts, and completed a lot of the stuff I hate to do.

All of the personnel at the missions who were helpful answering questions.

Demery Rodriguez for reading through this manuscript numerous times, and for her advice — often saying "Randy, I don't think you want to write that."

My golfing buddy, Randy Rodriguez, who had to go solo several times until this book was complete. What a sacrifice! (Randy's some-number-of-great grandfather's wedding was the first held in Mission San Diego, making it the first wedding of non-natives in California. Pretty, cool, huh?)

Kendra Lee, the daughter who was "dragged" to every mission. (She did it for the children.)

Photographs of the missions in the 19th Century are used by permission of the Pacific Gas and Electric Company, San Francisco, California. They are from the Margaret E. Schlichtmann collection.

PUBLISHED BY GOLDEN EDUCATIONAL CENTER
857 LAKE BLVD. ❖ REDDING, CALIFORNIA 96003
1.800.800.1791 ❖ FAX 1.530.244.5939

ISBN 1–56500–048-X

California Missions

Section Contents

Vocabulary Words ❖ Questions ☆☆ Bonus Activities
are included in each section of the book.

California Missions
Spanish/Catholic

Name ______________________________

Date ______________________________

Section A
Historical Background

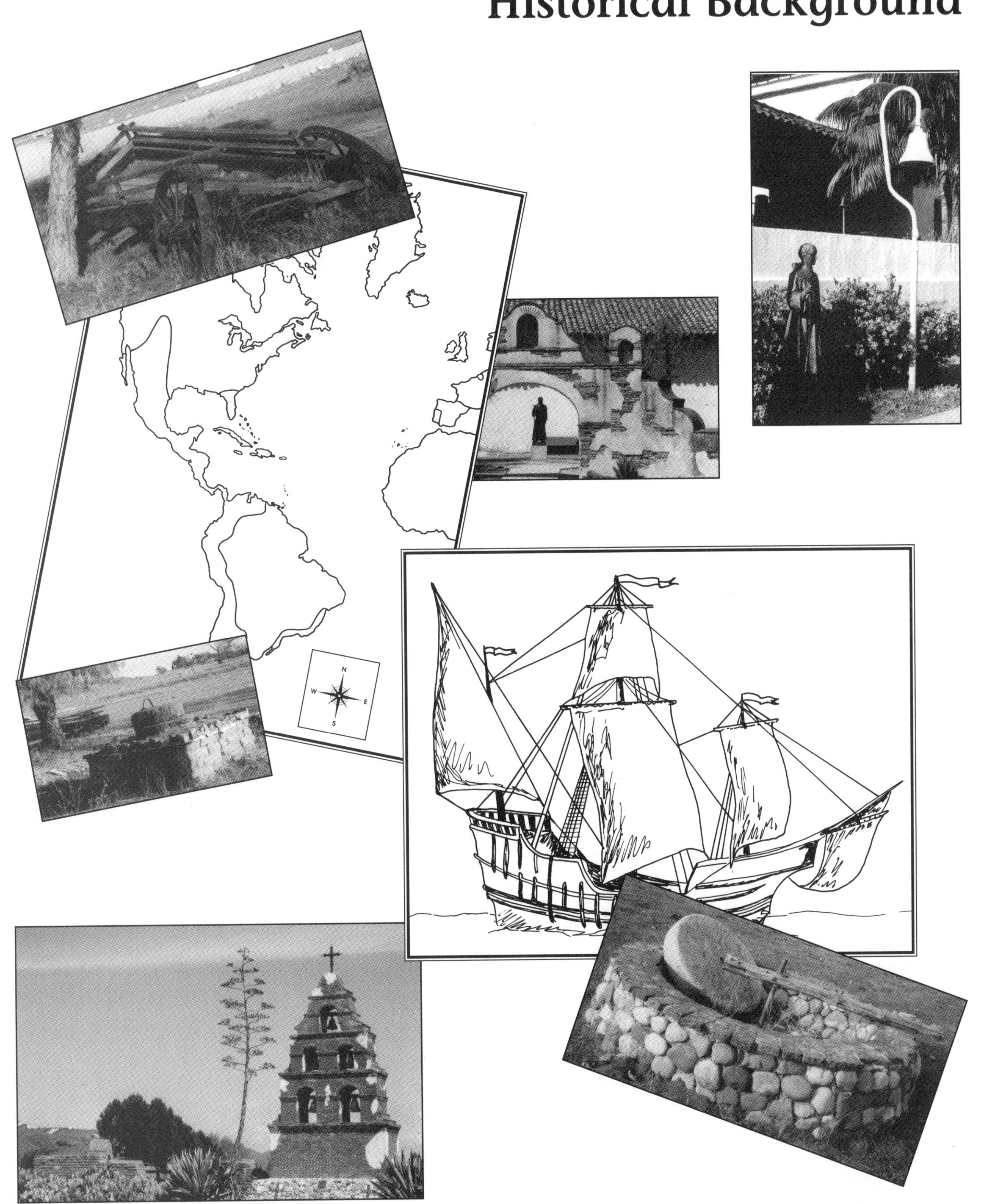

New Words to Learn:

Find the words in the glossary or a dictionary and write the meanings on the line.

1. **colonist**(s): ____________________
2. **crux:** ____________________
3. **desolate:** ____________________
4. **domain:** ____________________
5. **emancipation:** ____________________
6. **envy** (envied): ____________________
7. **expedition**(s): ____________________
8. **exterminate**(d): ____________________
9. **fertile:** ____________________
10. **Franciscan:** ____________________
11. **friar**(s): ____________________
12. **hemisphere**(s): ____________________
13. **hostilities:** ____________________
14. **Jesuit**(s): ____________________
15. **merchant:** ____________________
16. **missionary**(ies): ____________________
17. **padre:** ____________________
18. **peninsula:** ____________________
19. **philosophy:** ____________________
20. **plantation:** ____________________
21. **political**(ly): ____________________
22. **predominant**(ly): ____________________
23. **province:** ____________________
24. **reign**(ed): ____________________
25. **scurvy:** ____________________
26. **secular:** ____________________
27. **slave** (enslaved): ____________________
28. **turmoil:** ____________________
29. **viceroy**(s): ____________________
30. **yard:** ____________________

California Missions
Historical Background

Name ______________________

Date ______________________

In order to fully grasp some of the events, attitudes, conflicts, and situations discussed in this book about the missions it is important that we understand the historical context in which they occurred. The countries of Spain and Mexico and their **secular**, military, and religious leaders were most important in the history of the missions and California.

California first became occupied by Europeans in the summer of 1769. However, the beginnings of the missions movement can be traced back to 1493, just after Columbus discovered America. For almost 300 years (1493 to 1769) the mission system grew to be a **philosophy** of human rights advanced and defended by the religious leaders. The secular **colonists** and military leaders bitterly opposed the mission system.

The religious orders organizations had the belief that all men are brothers and that the newly discovered lands belonged first to the King of Spain and then to the original inhabitants. The secular military leaders believed that the natives were lower classed human beings and had no rights of private ownership. The two different philosophies had no common ground and this caused much division for the early explorers and colonists of California, an unknown wilderness at that time. The King of Spain played the parties against each other for the general advancement of the Spanish Empire.

When the **Franciscan Padre** Junípero Serra established the first California mission on July 16, 1769, the religious program for colonization seemed to be the winning philosophy. However, events in Europe and Mexico were already under way that would rob the Catholic church of its victory. The mission system that was just beginning in Alta California would pass out of existence in a very short 70 years.

In the 15th century, the Roman Catholic Church was very powerful, both financially and **politically.** The Catholic countries of Spain and Portugal, with their great fleets of ships, were leading world powers of the time. (It is important for us to remember that at this time in history most people believed the world was flat, not round.) Both Spain and Portugal used their great fleets to send explorers around the world and claim new lands for their respective countries. Many times the two countries would have conflicting territorial claims.

An ornate Catholic cross hanging on a stone wall at Mission San Carlos Borroméo de Carmel (Carmel Mission).

Both Spain and Portugal were **predominantly** Catholic, which in turn gave the Pope (the leader of the Catholic Church) a great deal of authority and power in the countries. In 1493, Pope Alexander VI made a decision to stop the disputed territorial claims of Spain and Portugal by giving them a declaration. Alexander divided the world into two **hemispheres** with Europe as the **crux.** He gave the right of exploration east of the "Line of Demarcation" to Portugal and west of the line to Spain. (See the map on page 8.) (No other Catholic European countries had developed colonial interests at the time of this declaration.) Alexander also declared that any exploration made by either Spain or Portugal must include God-fearing men in order to convert the inhabitants and instruct them in the Catholic faith. The King, and especially the Queen, of Spain (Ferdinand and Isabella) accepted the Pope's declaration in good faith. Before Isabella died she asked Ferdinand to respect the Indians and their liberties as the Pope had declared.

California Missions

Spanish Empire at its Height

Name ______________________

Date ______________________

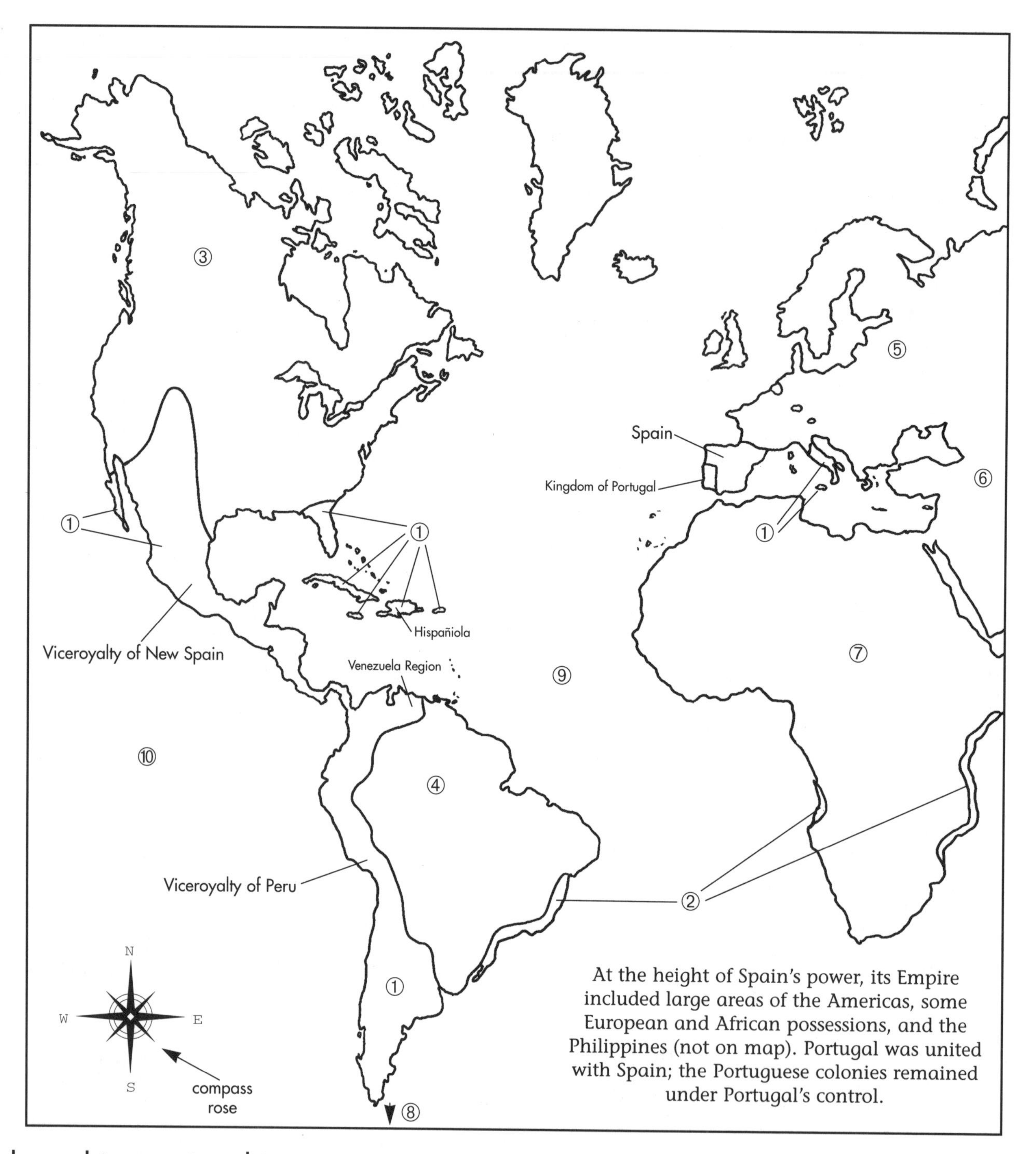

Do these things using this map.

1. Color the areas with ① red to show Spain's empire.
2. Color the areas with ② green to show the areas Portugal's colonies.
3. Write **North America** ③, **South America** ④, **Europe** ⑤, **Asia** ⑥, **Africa** ⑦, **Antarctica** ⑧, **Atlantic Ocean** ⑨, and **Pacific Ocean** ⑩ by the correct number.
4. Do your best job and color the rest of the map.

California Missions
Historical Background Continued

Name ___________________________

Date ___________________________

The first adventurers to explore the New World, however, did not care about the welfare of the Indians — ignoring the Pope's declaration. It was not until 1512 that a Dominican monk, Antonio de Montesino, brought word to King Ferdinand about the mistreatment of the Native Indians. With the help of Bishop Pedro de Córdova, Antonio de Montesino convinced the King of the injustices being done to the people in the new western colonies. They reported that in the islands of Hispañiola (now Haiti and the Dominican Republic) and Cuba the natives had been almost **exterminated.** In six short years after the Indians were **enslaved** by the colonists their population in Hispañiola had been cut in half.

King Ferdinand was impressed with the passion of Montesino and Córdova and allowed the bishop to establish a settlement on the coast of Venezuela. The settlement (mission) prospered until a crew of Spanish pearl-seekers raided an Indian village and kidnapped a tribal chief. The Indians thought the **missionaries** were part of the raid so they attacked and destroyed the mission. Enemies of the **friars** and their settlements prevented any more missionary efforts to the Indians until 1543.

Both Bishop Córdova and Antonio de Montesino had been working for the **emancipation** of the Indians. They succeeded in obtaining the support of King Charles V of Spain. The King issued mandatory requirements for the colonies in 1542 that were referred to as the *New Laws.* These *New Laws* contained five provisions that would eventually become the foundation of California's mission system. These were:

1. *Indians should be permitted to live in their own communities.*
2. *Indians should be permitted to choose their own leaders and counselors.*
3. *No Indian can be held as a slave.*
4. *No Indian can live outside his own village nor can any lay (a non religious leader) Spaniard live with an Indian for longer than three days, and then only if he were a* ***merchant*** *or ill.*
5. *Indians are to be instructed in the Catholic faith.*

Under the protection of the *New Laws* a small mission was established and prospered in Guatemala. When missionary groups in other areas faced the **hostilities** of **plantation** owners, they turned to the example of Guatemala for a formula of success. The **Jesuits** founded missions in what would become the areas of the wilderness of northern Mexico, as well as Paraguay. In these regions the authority of the padres was supreme, even over their military protectors. The Spanish plantation owners were opposed to the communities. However, the King of Spain and his **viceroys** looked upon them with favor. They were self-supporting and provided an inexpensive way of securing the frontiers against Great Britain and Russia.

A few locations of successful early Jesuit missions.

California Missions

Line of Demarcation

Name ______________________

Date ______________________

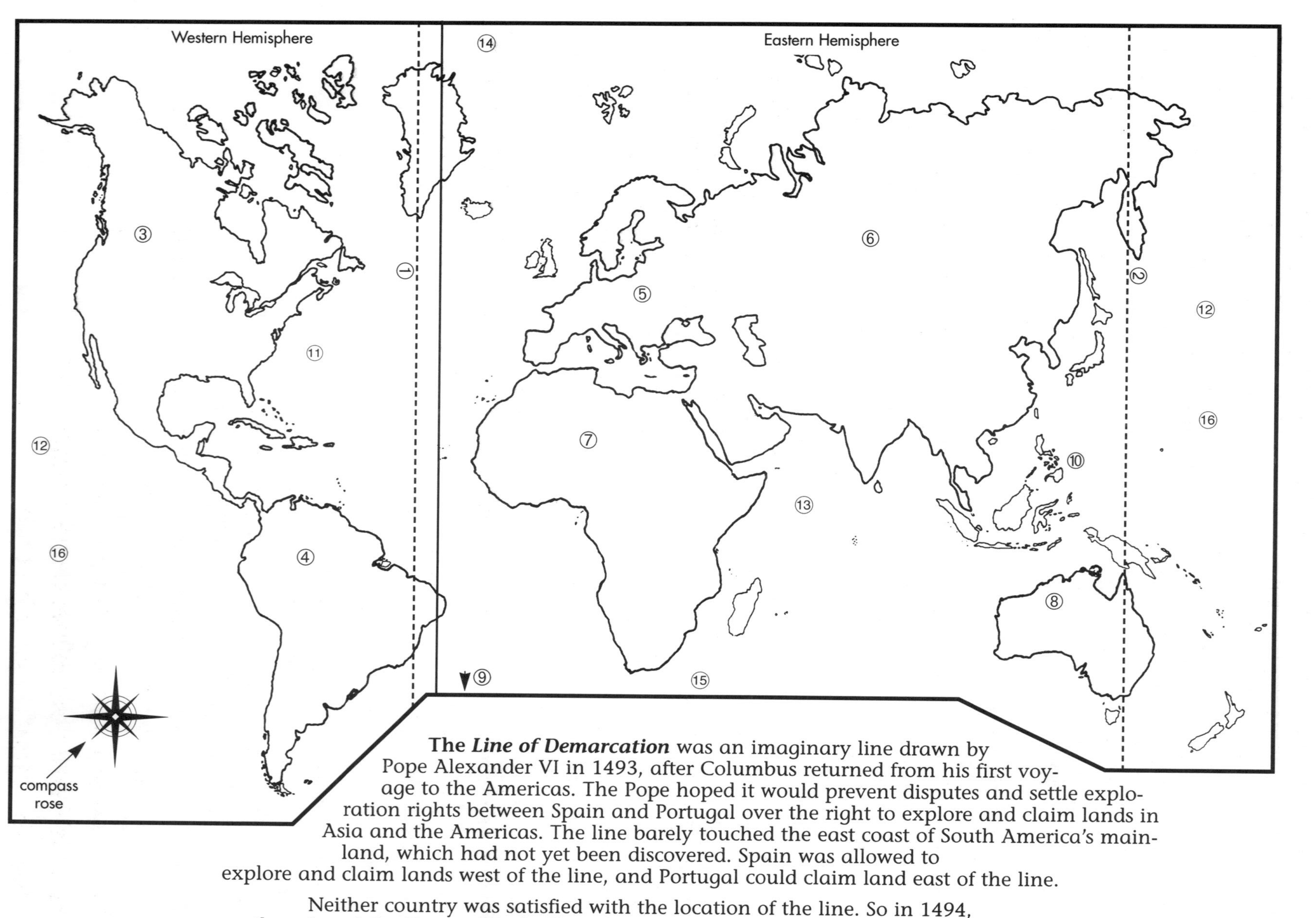

The *Line of Demarcation* was an imaginary line drawn by Pope Alexander VI in 1493, after Columbus returned from his first voyage to the Americas. The Pope hoped it would prevent disputes and settle exploration rights between Spain and Portugal over the right to explore and claim lands in Asia and the Americas. The line barely touched the east coast of South America's mainland, which had not yet been discovered. Spain was allowed to explore and claim lands west of the line, and Portugal could claim land east of the line.

Neither country was satisfied with the location of the line. So in 1494, they signed the *Treaty of Tordesillas*, which moved the line about 1,300 miles west.

As the Line of Demarcation continued around the earth and into the Eastern Hemisphere, it gave Portugal the right to claim the Philippine Islands as one of its colonies. Spain recognized Portugal's claim of the Philippines by signing the *Treaty of Saragossa* in 1529. Later, in other treaties with Spain, Portugal gave up its claim to the Philippines and received the rest of Brazil in return. (This is why Portuguese is the national language of Brazil and Spanish is the national language throughout the rest of Central and South America.)

California Missions

Historical Background Continued

Name ____________________________

Date ____________________________

The Spanish conquest of the Philippines made Philip II one of the wealthiest Kings in Europe. Spanish ships were bringing the rich treasures of the Philippines to Mexico by way of the Hawaiian Islands and the coast of California. These ships needed a safe harbor along California's coast where they could find fresh water and safety from English pirates and sea raiders. In attempts to locate safe harbors, Mexico sent a number of sea **expeditions** to explore the California coast. On December 16, 1602, the Spanish explorer Sebastian Vizcaíño, discovered the Bay of Monterey. In his journal he described the bay as *"...the best port that could be desired, for besides being sheltered from all of the winds, there is much wood and water, suitable for the masts and* ***yards****...this port is surrounded by the settlements of friendly Indians willing to give what they have, and would be pleased to see us settle in this country.... There are springs of good water; beautiful lakes covered with ducks and many other birds; most* ***fertile*** *pastures; good meadows for cattle, and fertile fields for growing crops...."*

In spite of the favorable report about the bay at Monterey, the expedition failed to establish a settlement along the coast of California. It took a century, as well as several costly and unsuccessful attempts to settle in Lower California (the **peninsula** below present-day San Diego and is part of Mexico) before the first settlement was established. This settlement was achieved by a group of rugged Jesuit priests at their own expense and terms.

The Jesuits gained the right of complete control over the Spanish military commanders who accompanied them. The soldiers and officers completely resented their being under the control of the priests. Most of the soldiers and military leaders came from the ranks of colonials who hated the Indians. They were shocked at the **desolate**, barren land and the lack of wealth in the area. In addition, the Indians lived in extreme poverty. The soldiers generally stole the wealth of the people they conquered. Since the Indians lived in poverty, no wealth could be had by conquering them. Because of their attitudes and the living conditions, Lower California gave the colonists only more reasons to resent the mission system and the padres getting the system started.

Do these things using the map provided on page 8.

1. Write **N**, **E**, **W**, and **S** in the correct place on the compass rose.
2. Write **Line of Demarcation 1493** on the solid black, vertical (No./So.) line.
3. Write **Treaty of Tordesillas 1494** on the line by ①.
4. Write **Treaty of Saragossa 1529** on the line by ②.
5. Write **North America** ③, **South America** ④, **Europe** ⑤, **Asia** ⑥, **Africa** ⑦, **Australia** ⑧, **Antarctica** ⑨, and **Philippine Islands** ⑩, by the correct number.
6. Write **Atlantic Ocean** ⑪, **Pacific Ocean** (two times) ⑫, **Indian Ocean** ⑬, and **Arctic Ocean** ⑭ by the correct number.
7. Write **Portuguese Zone of Influence** by ⑮.
8. Write **Spanish Zone of Influence** (two times) by ⑯.
9. If you color the map, do your best job.

California Missions

Routes of Early Explorers

Name ____________________

Date ____________________

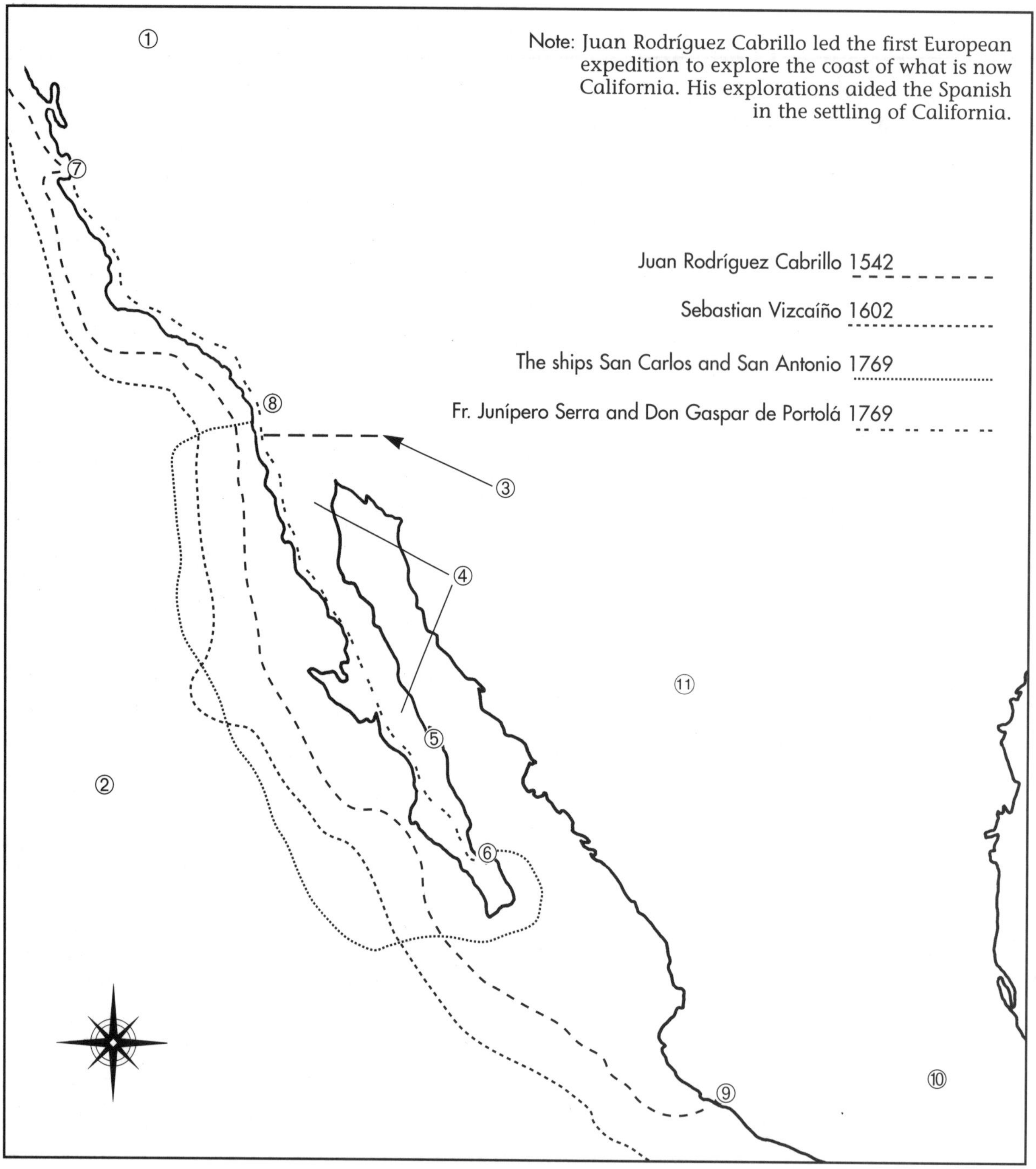

Note: Juan Rodríguez Cabrillo led the first European expedition to explore the coast of what is now California. His explorations aided the Spanish in the settling of California.

Juan Rodríguez Cabrillo 1542

Sebastian Vizcaíño 1602

The ships San Carlos and San Antonio 1769

Fr. Junípero Serra and Don Gaspar de Portolá 1769

Do these things using this map.

1. Write **N, E, W,** and **S** in the correct place on the compass rose.
2. Write **North America** ①, **Pacific Ocean** ②, **California/Mexico border** ③, **Lower (Baja) California** ④, **Loreto** ⑤, **La Paz** ⑥, **Monterey Bay** ⑦, **San Diego** ⑧, **Navidad** (near present-day Manzanillo) ⑨, **Mexico City** ⑩, and **New Spain (Mexico)** ⑪ by the correct number.
3. Trace over each explorer's route and line in the key with a colored pen, pencil, or crayon. Use a different color for each explorer.

California Missions
Historical Background Continued

Name ______________________

Date ______________________

The missions themselves proved to be the best thing about the system. Under the great leadership of the Jesuits, a little prosperity began to come from the land and its resources. After the early founders of the missions in Lower California died, a new group of missionaries emerged — the Franciscans, under the leadership of Fr. Junípero Serra.

At this time the Spanish rule was interested in discovering a group of islands that would be a good location for them to protect the Philippines from attack and possible conquest by other nations. However, these islands were never found. This made the Spanish government even more anxious to secure the coast of California for Spain. In 1763, England was victorious in gaining control of Canada. The Spanish heard rumors of Russia's approach from Alaska to expand its territory. This caused the Spanish Throne to look toward missions to establish strongholds of settlements in America.

Charles III became the King of Spain in 1759. In his attempt to establish Spain as a world power once again he made two decisions that would affect Alta (Upper) California's history forever. First, the mission system would be founded there by the Franciscans, not the Jesuits. Second, the missionary fathers would no longer have authority over the military. The King of Spain, as well as other leaders in Europe, seemed determined to take away power from the leadership of religious groups. The Jesuits were the first victims of these new rules, as they had become very strong and were **envied** for their wealth and position.

Don Gaspar de Portolá (the governor of Lower California) arrived in Loreto, Mexico in June 1767. With him, as replacements for the Jesuits, were the Franciscan fathers whose names are forever linked with California's history — Junípero Serra, Francisco Palou, Juan Crespi, and Fermín Lasuén. The Jesuits were sent away and along with them the missionary control. Governor Portolá placed a soldier in charge of each mission and limited the Franciscans only to religious duties. In a very short time, life in the missions was almost destroyed by the soldiers constantly searching for the buried treasures that they believed the Jesuits had been forced to leave behind.

Had Lower California been left alone, the missions could not have continued for long. King Charles III of Spain had sent two men to Mexico (a territory of Spain) with the intent of securing the Californias (Alta and Lower). They were General José de Galvez and Marques de Croix, the new viceroy. When Galvez arrived at Loreto in 1768, he became aware of the poor condition of the missions and restored the authority of the Franciscans to command over the military. Then, plans were made with Fr. Serra and Governor Portolá to extend Spanish **domain** in Alta California by using the mission system.

The priest and soldier divided the expedition into two sections and sent each to San Diego, one by land and one by sea. Three ships: the *San Carlos*, the *San Antonio,* and *San José*, carrying troops and four missionaries, sailed from La Paz, Lower California. The *San Carlos* sailed January 9, the *San Antonio* sailed February 15, and the *San José* sailed June 16, 1769. The *San Carlos* was driven off course by bad weather and arrived 20 days after the *San Antonio.* All of her crew but two (one sailor and the cook) got **scurvy** and many of the soldiers died. The *San Antonio* lost more than half of her crew from the same disease and the *San José* was lost at sea.

California Missions

European Colonization
of North America in 1790.

Name ____________________

Date ____________________

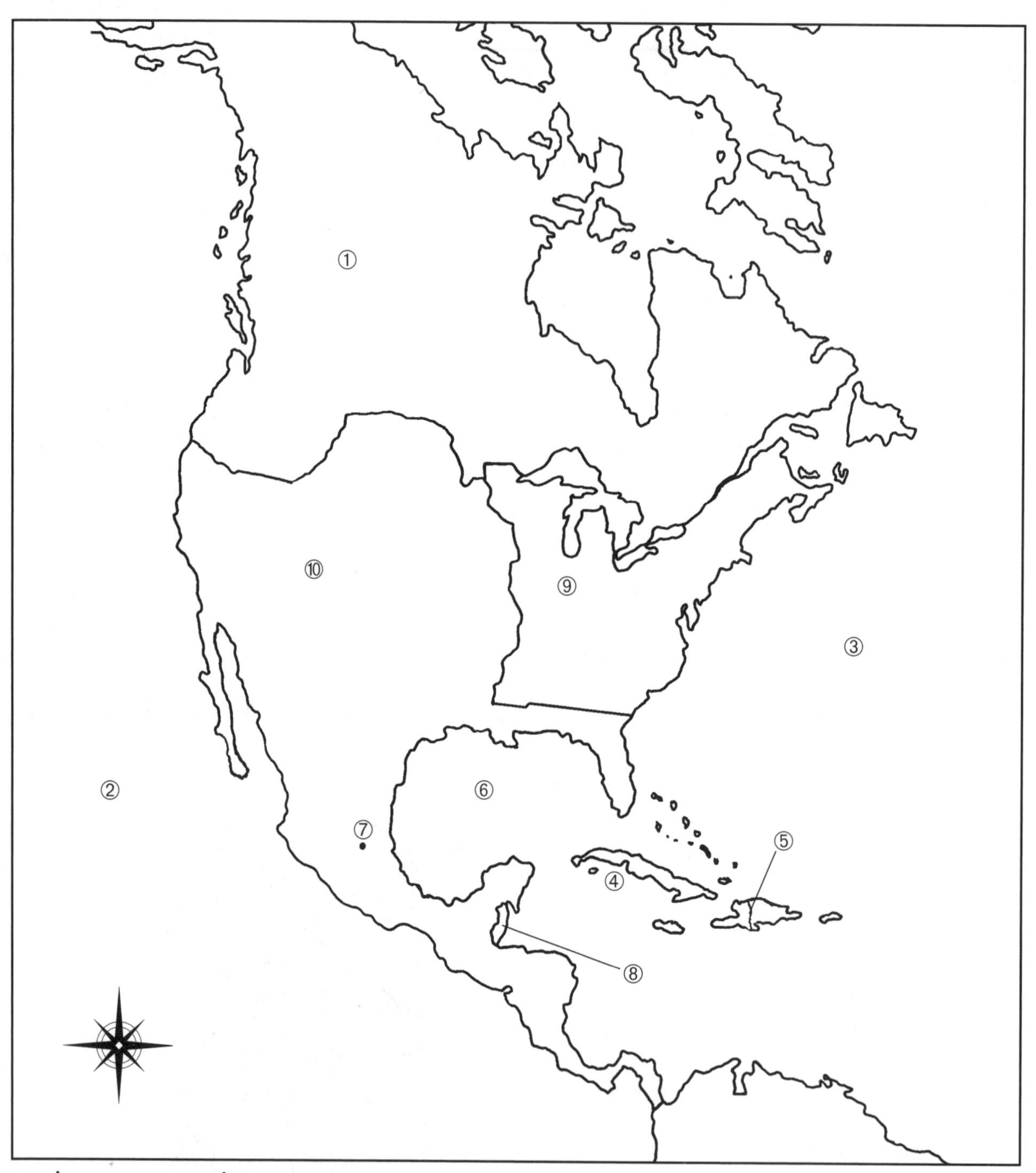

Do these things using this map.

1. Write **N**, **E**, **W**, and **S** in the correct place on the compass rose.
2. Write **British North America** ①, **Pacific Ocean** ②, **Atlantic Ocean** ③, **Cuba** ④, **Hispañiola** ⑤, **Gulf of Mexico** ⑥, **Mexico City** ⑦, **British Honduras** ⑧, **United States** ⑨, and **New Spain (Mexico)** ⑩ by the correct number.
3. Color the different colonization regions on the map.

California Missions
Historical Background Continued

Name ______________________

Date ______________________

The land expedition was divided into two divisions under Captain Fernando Rivera y Moncada and Governor Portolá. Captain Rivera led the advance division and Portolá followed with Fr. Serra. After many hardships, Portolá and Serra reached San Diego on July 1, 1769. There they found Rivera and his soldiers as well as the surviving members of the sea expedition. On July 16th Fr. Serra founded the first mission in California's history, as well as the work that he would do for the rest of his life.

The story of the founding of each of the missions is told later in the book. However, it is important to look ahead here and learn some of the factors that were destined to affect the fortunes of the missions, padres, and Indians living in them. The land that we see today with all of its wealth and prosperity was not the land that the first settlers encountered. For the most part it was a barren wasteland. The hardships undergone by the early settlers were worse than anything they imagined. The reports of the hardships sent back to Lower California and Mexico understandably did not bring a flood of new colonists. Soldiers often deserted and even some of the fathers, upon their arrival, would immediately write back to Mexico City asking for permission to return to Mexico.

In spite of all of the hardships and difficulties, the energy and determination of Fr. Serra and his closest associates, Fathers Palou, Lasuén, and Crespi, rooted the mission system and it slowly began to prosper. The fathers eventually lost their control over the military, which was there to protect them. The military leaders realized that the possession of the California coast was very important to Spain and they did their best to keep the padres happy.

Spain, however, was declining quickly as a world power. In 1797, its fleet came under the control of France, and the fortunes of that once great country declined rapidly. The Napoleonic Wars led to the total destruction of Spain's naval forces by Britain. In 1806, Napoleon invaded the peninsula of Spain, which completely disrupted Spain's government. This left Spain powerless to deal with the problems of its territory, Mexico. By 1810, the unrest in Mexico soon led to a revolt and open revolution. In 1821 Mexico won its independence from Spain. California became a **province** of Mexico in 1822. However, Mexico's social and political unrest continued in different degrees throughout the 1800s.

While **turmoil** and uncertainty **reigned** in both Mexico and Spain, the missions in California demonstrated that the new land was capable of supporting a rich and abundant agriculture. Great herds of sheep and cattle were seen by the colonists who came to find their fortunes. They saw that the greatest riches were controlled by the missions and the converted Indians, yet ignored the Franciscan beliefs that the lands belonged to the natives.

Statue of Father Junípero Serra, founder of the first mission in Alta California (Mission San Diego on July 16, 1769). He was the first president of the California Mission System.

California Missions
Historical Background Continued

Name ____________________

Date ____________________

In 1833, the Mexican Congress passed a bill ordering the immediate secularization (giving property to private citizens) of the missions in California. The intent of the act was to immediately transfer to the Indians living on the missions all of the wealth and property which had been accumulated by the missions. It was Governor José Figueroa's responsibility to oversee the transfer. In his opinion, the mission Indians were not capable of (or at least not interested in) assuming private ownership. He thought they needed a period of supervision and education before taking ownership. Therefore, he proposed to secularize only ten missions the first year. Half of these lands would be divided up among Indian families and they would not be allowed to sell, trade, or give them away. The other half would remain under the temporary control of the fathers who were to continue their religious work. If the Indians made good use of their land over a period of years, the rest of the mission's property, sheep, cattle, and so forth would be given to them. Eventually, under Figueroa's plan, the mission chapel would become the church in the center of an Indian community. However, Figueroa died in 1835 before he could implement his plans, and control of secularization fell into the hands of greedy politicians. These politicians ignored the interests of the Indians and divided the mission property among their friends and relatives.

With Spain's decline in power and importance, Alta California ceased to be one of Spain's colonies. It was hardly ever a part of Mexico, and this new country's social and political uncertainty led to the destruction of the mission system. Before Alta California could even consider being an independent nation, it had become part of the United States, as a result of the defeat of Mexico in the Mexican-American War. (The *Treaty of Guadalupe Hidalgo* was signed in 1848.)

Even though the mission system ceased over 150 years ago and was in place for a short 70 years, the impact of Spain, Mexico, and the Franciscan padres will always remain an important part of California's heritage. ❖

Do these things using this map.

1. Fill in the compass rose.
2. Fill in the map with the following: **British North America, Pacific Ocean, Atlantic Ocean, Cuba, Hispañiola, Gulf of Mexico, Mexico City, British Honduras, United States,** and **New Spain (Mexico).**

REVIEW QUESTIONS

Name ______________________________

Date ______________________________

Write the correct answer in the space provided.

1. King __________________________ and Queen __________________________ of Spain instructed explorers to respect the Native Indians, but many of them did not.

2. In 1493, a dividing "Line of Demarcation" permitted colonization by the countries of ______________________________ to the west and __________________________ to the east.

3. The first Spanish mission in the New World was founded by Dominican priests in the country of __________________________________ .

4. Spanish King Charles V established five provisions known as the ____________ _______________________________________ that upheld the rights of the Indians in the colonies.

5. Tension developed between _____________________________________ leaders and _______________________________________ leaders in the New World because of their different goals.

6. In the 1830s the Mexican government ordered the transfer of mission properties to native Indians, a process called ____________________________________ .

Matching: Write the correct letter on the correct line.

7. _____________ This disease is caused by lack of Vitamin C.

8. _____________ Who was the Spanish explorer who discovered Monterey Bay in 1602?

9. _____________ Who was the Franciscan priest who founded the first California mission?

10. _____________ The Spanish word for father or priest.

11. _____________ The Spanish governor of Alta California when the first missions were founded.

12. _____________ A representative of a king or queen who has the authority to act in the king or queen's name.

13. _____________ The first missions in Alta and Baja California were founded by what religion?

A. Junípero Serra
B. Vizcaíño
C. Portolá
D. Scurvy
E. Viceroy
F. Catholic
G. Padre

Name ______________________________

Date ______________________________

If these events happened today, what headlines might you read or hear?

Write the correct answer in the space provided.

Example: Portolá arrives from Spain with Franciscan priests to replace Jesuit missionaries.
Headline: "Jesuits Out – Franciscans In." or "Jesuits Get the Boot."

14. When three ships set sail for Alta California in 1769, most of the crewmen die and one ship is lost altogether.
Headline: ______________________________

15. Natives in Venezuela destroy a mission after their village is raided and their chief is kidnapped.
Headline: ______________________________

16. The Mexican government decides to transfer control of the mission properties to the Indians.
Headline: ______________________________

17. The military leaders realized controlling California's coast was important to Spain, so they tried to keep the padres happy.
Headline: ______________________________

18. Spain rapidly fell as a world power and couldn't deal with the problems which developed in Mexico.
Headline: ______________________________

19. If you were traveling to San Diego today, describe at least four ways your journey would be different from the Spanish expedition of Governor Portolá and Fr. Serra in 1769?

____
____
____
____
____
____

☆☆ Bonus Activity

Use another resource and write a report on one of the people or places mentioned in this *Historical Background Section*. Draw maps and pictures if appropriate for your report.

Mission #1

San Diego de Alcalá

Founded July 16, 1769

New Words to Learn:

Find the words in the glossary or a dictionary and write the meanings on the line.

1. **acre**(s): ______________________
2. **adobe:** ______________________
3. **basilica:** ______________________
4. **civilian:** ______________________
5. **era:** ______________________
6. **facade:** ______________________
7. **garrison:** ______________________
8. **granary:** ______________________
9. **impede**(d): ______________________
10. **parish:** ______________________
11. **presidio**(s): ______________________
12. **troughs:** ______________________

① ______________________

Mission #1 — Founded July 16, 1796

Layout of the Mission Grounds

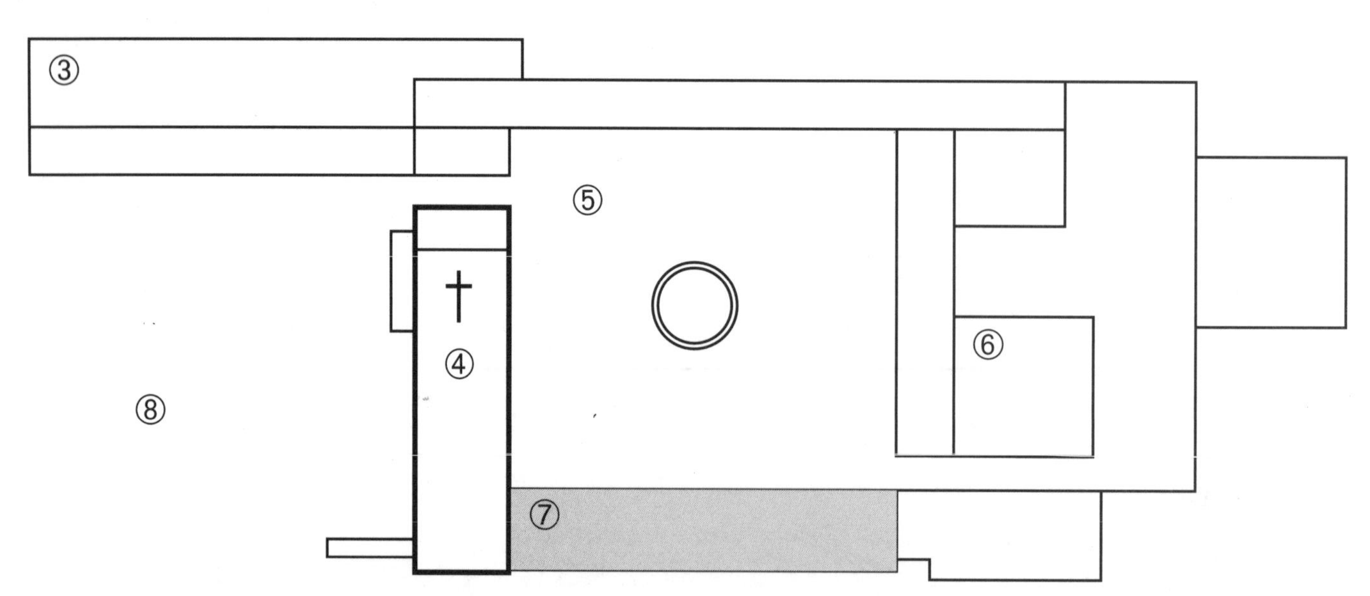

This is the layout of the mission **quadrangle** at the height of its prosperity.

San Diego de Alcalá

Named for Saint Didacus, who was born near Seville, Spain around the 1400s. He was born to poor parents. He was a hermit, a Franciscan missionary, and worked at the University of Alcalá in Castile, Spain.

Name ______________________

Date ______________________

The 1st of 21 Spanish/Catholic Missions

Design of the Mission

Church: (approximate outside measurements) 174 feet long, 35 feet wide, and 29 feet high. The church is built of **adobe** and has a tile roof.

Design:
It has a simple style, which set the standard for the *Mission Style*. The **facade** is plain, decorated with only a few flat ornamental columns to the side and above the front door entrance. There was an arched corridor that crossed the front of the original church, but it was not rebuilt during reconstruction. Short walls that act as buttresses (supports) extend from each side of the entrance.

Walls: The walls are 3 feet thick, roughly plastered, and have small windows near the ceiling.

Campanario:
A wall (called a *campanario*) extends like a wing from the front of the church. Five bells are hung in openings cut in this wall. The bells are arranged in three rows — one bell on top and two bells in the middle and bottom rows. The campanario is approximately 46 feet high and has a wooden cross on the top.

Mission Compound:
A square courtyard, 120 feet long on each side, was surrounded by the group of buildings that made up Mission San Diego. One corner of this square housed the church. Storage rooms, blacksmith and carpentry shops, a **granary**, living quarters, and a kitchen all faced the courtyard. Unlike the rest of the missions, most of the native Indians in the area remained in their own villages with just a few actually living at Mission San Diego.

Mission Grounds:
Mission San Diego had 50,000 **acres** of land. The mission had grazing land for its 20,000 sheep, 10,000 cattle, and 1,250 horses. Agricultural crops at the mission included wheat, barley, corn, beans, and grapes. The mission had a reputation for producing fine wines.

Water System:
In 1807, the Diegueno Indians helped the mission padres build a dam six miles up the river from the mission. Cement **troughs** carried the water to the mission. This system relieved the problem Mission San Diego always had of getting water.

Santa Ysabel:
The Franciscans of Mission San Diego built a sub-mission about 60 miles east of the main mission, in the Santa Ysabel Valley. The first building was erected there in 1818. A few years later an adobe church was built .

Do these things using the map provided. (Use the map on page 18.)

1. Write **Mission San Diego de Alcalá** ①, **cattle brand** ②, **workshops** ③, **church** ④, **patio** ⑤, **storage** ⑥, **padres' living quarters** ⑦, and **cemetery** ⑧ by the correct number.
2. Do your best job if you color the map.

San Diego de Alcalá

Name ______________________

Date ______________________

The 1st of 21 Spanish/Catholic Missions

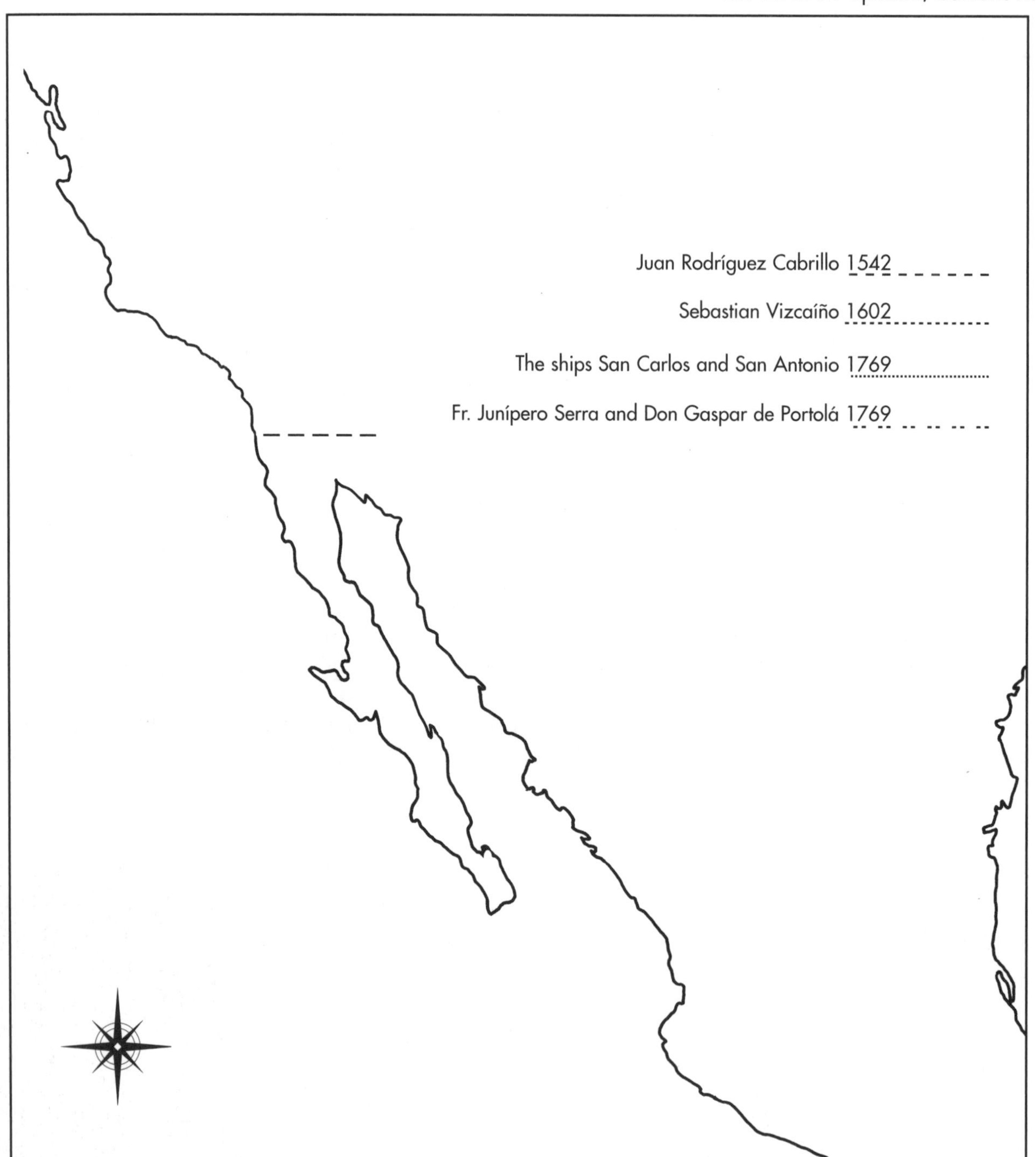

Do these things using this map.

1. Write **N**, **E**, **W**, and **S** in the correct place on the compass rose.
2. Label the map showing the location of the following:
   North America, **Pacific Ocean**, **California/Mexico border**, **Loreto**, **Baja California**, **La Paz**, **Alta California**, **Monterey Bay**, **San Diego**, **Mexico City**, **New Spain (Mexico)**, and **Navidad** (near present day Manzanillo).
3. Draw each explorer's route with the same type of line as above. You can use different colored pencils or pens for each explorer, but make the key correspond to your colors.

San Diego de Alcalá

Also known as "Mother of the Missions"

Name ______________________

Date ______________________

The 1st of 21 Spanish/Catholic Missions

Early History

Don Gaspar de Portolá was sent to New Spain in 1767 to be governor of the Californias. In 1769, he organized an expedition to Alta California to establish missions and **presidios**. Portolá and Fr. Junípero Serra led one of two land divisions on the northward march, while three ships set sail from La Paz, Mexico. The land divisions and the ships were to meet on the shores of a harbor which the Spanish explorer Vizcaíño had named San Diego.

The first ship, the *San Carlos*, set out January 9, but storms at sea drove her off course and she arrived 20 days after the *San Antonio*, which sailed February 15. A third ship, the *San José*, set sail June 16, but was lost at sea because of violent weather. All of the crew of the *San Carlos*, except for the cook and one sailor, suffered from scurvy and many of the 219 men aboard died from sickness and disease. The ones who survived arrived weak, sick and totally exhausted by the long journey.

Arriving July 1, Governor Portolá considered the stop in the San Diego area only a rest stop on his way to the Bay of Monterey, a few hundred miles north of San Diego. He allowed the men to rest for two weeks. Then he gathered the men strong enough to continue and marched north to find the Bay of Monterey. He sent the *San Antonio* back to New Spain (Mexico City) for additional supplies. He took Frs. Crespi and Gomez with him on the march. He left Fr. Junípero Serra behind with the task of founding a mission at the new settlement.

Fr. Junípero Serra and the men who were able built a small, crude brushwood chapel with a wooden cross erected on a hill overlooking the bay. The first mission bell was hung on a tree. On July 16, 1769 Fr. Serra dedicated this mission site. This became the first Christian church in California.

The Indians were slow to come to the settlement. They watched the development of the settlement with wonder, distrust, and caution. Fr. Serra and his Franciscan followers tried to make friends with the native Indians. However, the Indians were indifferent to their attempts at friendship and came around only to steal whatever was not defended by the Franciscans. Because Fr. Serra wanted their salvation and friendship, the use of any guns was strictly forbidden until an Indian attack on the settlement left him no alternative. The superior arms of the Franciscans soon ended the harassment. These early missionary efforts saw very little progress.

Campanario at Mission San Diego

Meanwhile, unable to locate the Bay of Monterey, Portolá returned to the settlement at San Diego after six months. Little was done while he was gone except the marking of 19 new graves. He returned to find that food and supplies were dangerously low. The fathers prayed for the arrival of the supply ship *San Antonio*, and Portolá sent some of his men overland to Loreto for help. By Portolá's calculations, the Catholic settlement could only survive until the middle of March, 1770.

San Diego de Alcalá

Name ______________________

Date ______________________

The 1st of 21 Spanish/Catholic Missions

The little ship *San Carlos,* unable to sail because of the death of most of her crew, was still in San Diego Harbor. Portolá was going to sail to the north to find the Bay of Monterey if help did not arrive. Frs. Crespi and Serra talked to the captain of the *San Carlos* about their desperate need of provisions. They decided that they would sail northward on the small vessel to find Monterey no matter what Portolá decided to do. Whoever they could persuade to come with them was welcome.

As fate would have it, the *San Antonio* was sighted far out at sea just one day before they were to sail to Monterey. The sighting was enough to persuade Portolá that a delay of a few days would be beneficial. Three days later the *San Antonio* put into the harbor with the much needed provisions.

Three weeks later, Governor Portolá and his expedition again set out overland in hopes of finding the harbor in Monterey. Fr. Crespi went with Portolá because he was stronger and in better health than the other friars. Fr. Serra headed for Monterey Harbor aboard the *San Antonio.* He had an infected leg, which had been hurt during the overland trip to Loreto for supplies. This injury would bring him near death on several occasions during his later journeys along the El Camino Real.

Fr. Serra left two priests, three workmen, and eight soldiers in San Diego in hopes that they could carry on the missionary work at the settlement. After a year of struggle against the hostile Indians and illness, the two returned to Mexico. Fathers Jáyme and Dumetz replaced them. Seeing that the situation was critical, Fr. Dumetz immediately set out to Baja California for supplies. When he returned a few months later with food and a small flock of sheep, the mission had already received help from the new establishment in Monterey. From then on the need for supplies was never again so critical.

Even though supplies were no longer a problem, other problems began to wear on the mission fathers. Portolá returned to Mexico and he was replaced by Pedro Fages as the new military comandante. Lieutenant Fages soon began demanding that the Franciscans submit themselves to the control of his office. Fr. Serra went to Mexico to complain about Lt. Fages' demands. With the help of Fr. Serra's Franciscan friends in the capital, Lt. Fages was removed from his office. However, the problem of *who's the authority on the missions* — the friars or the military — remained throughout the mission **era**.

The ships, *San Antonio* and *San Carlos*, looked similar to the one pictured here.

San Diego de Alcalá

Name ____________________

Date ____________________

The 1st of 21 Spanish/Catholic Missions

While Fr. Serra was in Mexico on the Fages matter, the missions of Baja California were transferred to Alta (upper) California. Ten new Franciscan friars, including Frs. Palou and Lasuén, arrived in Alta California. Fr. Palou was made acting president of the mission during Fr. Serra's absence. In 1774, he moved the mission site six miles inland, on the San Diego River. He did this in order to have better soil and more water. He also wanted to be further from the soldiers at the presidio because of all of the problems the soldiers were causing. Many of the white Spanish soldiers were cruel and abusive to the American Indians — especially the women. The Indians often did not trust the missionaries, who were also white and Spanish, because of how cruelly the Spanish soldiers treated them. The cruelty of the Spanish soldiers hindered the work of converting the Indians to Catholicism.

On November 4, 1775, a large force of Indians attacked the unprotected mission. A short and bloody fight took place where Fr. Jáyme, a blacksmith, and a carpenter were killed. The log buildings were burned beyond use. Because it was so far from the presidio, the conflict went unnoticed by the soldiers who could have beaten the Indians easily with their superior weapons.

This uprising **impeded** further development of the missions. The fathers were forced back to the military fort on the bay. At this time, Mission San Juan Capistrano was in the process of being founded. This was temporarily abandoned and the **padres** were brought back to San Diego. A new military commander, Rivera y Moncada, was determined to make an example of the leaders of the uprising, and saw no immediate reason to rebuild the mission. Rivera's brutal attitude toward the Indians was strongly opposed by Fr. Serra. After several months of delay, Fr. Serra won out and returned to the valley site in July 1776.

A temporary church was finished in October. The church building, constructed in the style we recognize today as mission style, was not completed until November 12, 1813 — 29 years after the death of Fr. Serra. He never saw the large tile roofed buildings which serve as reminders of his stamina and energy.

After the early 1780s, the Franciscan missions enjoyed peaceful years. At its peak of prosperity, Mission San Diego de Alcalá owned more than 20,000 sheep, 10,000 cattle, and 1,250 horses. It covered an area of 50,000 acres. The mission was noted throughout the region for making great wine.

The decline of the mission began in 1824 with the growth of **civilian** settlements in the region. Following the Mexican Revolution of 1830, the authorities took the properties away from the Franciscans and transferred them to the government. The mission buildings began to decay and fall apart after 1834, when they were no longer occupied by the Franciscan missionaries. In 1846, the mission was sold to Santiago Arguello for "services to the government." It was not until 1862 that the United States Congress gave 22 acres back to the Catholic Church. For the 15 years before the U.S. Congress gave back the acreage to the church, it was used as a military **garrison** for the United States Army. In the 1890s the site was used for an Indian school run by Father Anthony Ubach, who was interested in restoring the mission. However, little was done after 1900, and soon all that remained was the front of the church. ❖

San Diego de Alcalá

Name ______________________________

Date ______________________________

The 1st of 21 Spanish/Catholic Missions

The Mission Today

Serious restoration did not begin until 1931, with the rebuilding of the campanario with its five bell niches. Care was taken to rebuild the tower as an exact duplicate of the original. A few of the original bells were found. The largest bell in the campanario is the 1,200 pound *Mater Dolorosa* ("Mother of Sorrows") forged in 1884 in San Diego, reportedly from the lead of the original bells that came to the San Diego settlement in 1796 from New Spain (today's Mexico). Restoration of the church was completed as accurately as possible, without very many pictures or descriptions available. In 1941, the completely restored mission became an active **parish** church. In 1976, Pope Paul VI named the church a "minor **basilica**" because of its historical importance.

Only a small part of the padres' quarters remains of the quadrangle. Excavation of more foundation was completed in the 1960s by university students. The mission has five graves of Franciscan friars, including Fr. Jáyme who died there in 1775. It also has graves of many native Americans who were an integral part of the mission's success and history. There is a small museum, as well as, the articles relating to Fr. Serra (the mission's founder) are in the Serra Museum on Presidio Hill. There, where the Mission was first established, is a large cross and a plaque. The palm trees that Fr. Serra planted on the hill are no longer there. ❖

Mission Basilica
San Diego de Alcalá
10818 San Diego Mission Rd.
San Diego, CA 92108
Phone: 619.283.7319

San Diego de Alcalá

Name ______________________

Date ______________________

Crossword Puzzle

The 1st of 21 Spanish/Catholic Missions

Across

2. Spanish word meaning *upper.*

6. This Catholic order of priests founded the mission system in Alta California.

8. At first was called *New Spain.*

10. The name of the present-day city where the first Franciscan mission was founded in California.

12. The country that Mexico won its independence from.

14. The bay to the north of San Diego that Governor Portolá was trying to locate on his early land expeditions.

16. Mission San Diego de Alcalá was noted for making this beverage.

18. This Franciscan padre is considered the "Father" of the California Mission system.

19. Mission San Diego de Alcalá was named after this saint.

20. The Governor of Lower California who organized the expedition to Alta California in order to establish missions and presidios.

Down

1. A Spanish word for a wall where bells usually hung.

3. Many mission walls were built with these in order to add strength and support to them.

4. The town north of La Paz, Mexico, where the Franciscan replacements for the Jesuit priests first arrived. (See *Historical Background Section* or map on page 20.)

5. Spanish word meaning *lower.*

7. The ship that was sent back to Mexico for supplies.

9. One of the padres Portolá took with him on his expedition to find the bay at Monterey.

11. These native Indians helped the padres build a dam for the mission's water supply.

13. A fortified place or military post.

15. The people of Spain and Portugal were primarily this religion.

17. This padre went with Portolá on his expedition to find the harbor at Monterey because he was stronger and in better health than the other friars.

San Diego de Alcalá

Name ______________________

Date ______________________

Review Questions

Write the correct answer in the space provided.

1. The first mission founded in Alta California was ____________. It is also called the "______________ of Missions." It is named for Saint ______________ of Spain.

2. The founder of the first mission was Father ________________, a priest of the ________________ Order.

3. In its prosperous years, the mission covered ________________ acres and was noted for making good ________________ .

4. In 1941, the restored mission became a ________________ church. In 1976, Pope Paul VI named it a minor ________________ .

5. Explain some of the hardships the first settlers in Alta California experienced.

____

____

____

____

____

____

6. Explain why the mission was moved six miles inland in 1774.

____

____

____

____

____

7. Why did the early missionary efforts have very little progress?

____

____

____

____

____

☆☆ Bonus Activity

Use another resource and write a report on Fr. Serra, Governor Portolá, Lt. Fages, the Franciscan Order, Jesuit Order, Catholicism, the Dieguena Indians, Saint Didacus, Spain, Portugal, or Mexico. Draw maps and pictures if appropriate for your report.

Mission #2

San Carlos Borroméo de Carmelo

Founded June 3, 1770

Print the name of the mission on the correct line. (You may need to look back at a previously finished section/map.)

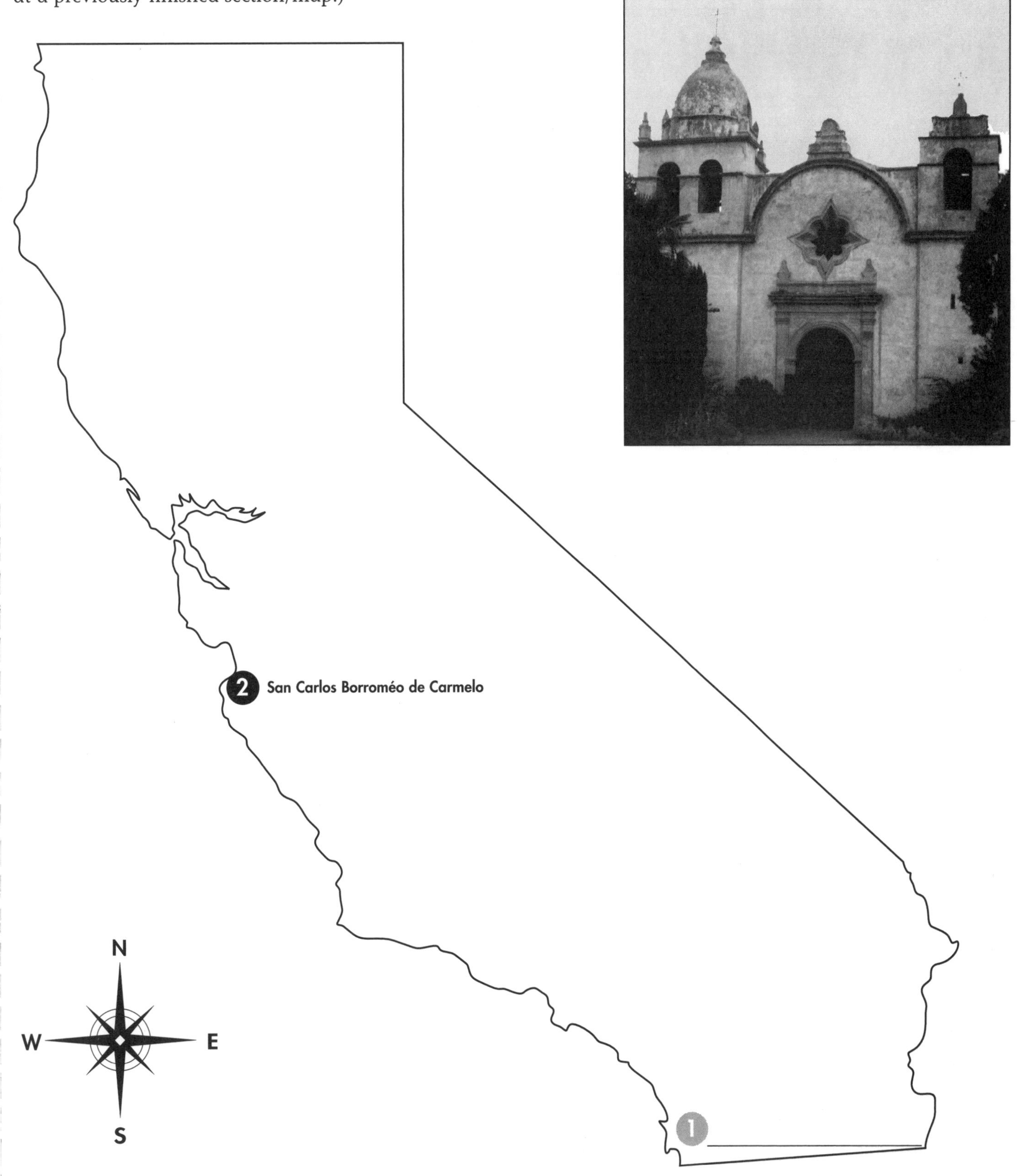

New Words to Learn:

Find the words in the glossary or a dictionary and write the meanings on the line.

1. **abalone:** ____________________
2. **altar:** ____________________
3. **authentic:** ____________________
4. **belfry:** ____________________
5. **devote**(d): ____________________
6. **flourish:** ____________________
7. **limestone:** ____________________
8. **Moor**(ish): ____________________
9. **mortar:** ____________________
10. **quadrangle:** ____________________
11. **sandstone:** ____________________
12. **Virgin:** ____________________

① ____________________

Mission #2 — Founded June 3, 1770

Layout of the Mission Grounds

MR ②

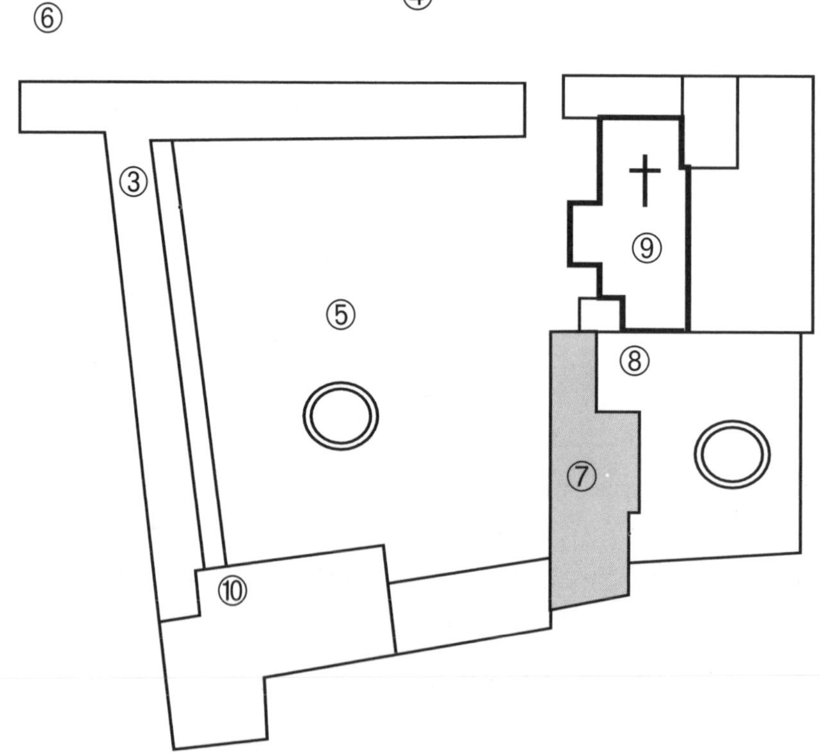

The layout of the mission compound.

San Carlos Borroméo de Carmelo

Name ______________________________

Date ______________________________

Named for Saint Charles Borroméo (born in Italy in 1538), the first great leader of the Counter-Reformation.

The 2nd of 21 Spanish/Catholic Missions

Design of the Mission

Church: (approximate outside measurements) 167 feet long, 39 feet wide, and 26 feet high.
The church is constructed of native yellow **sandstone** blocks. The blocks are held together with **mortar** made from lime in **abalone** shells found on the ocean's beach. It has a roof made of tile.

Design:
The church was designed by a master mason from Mexico City named Manuel Ruíz, who also designed the Royal Chapel in Monterey. He used some **Moorish** architectural elements in the design, including the "star window" above the entrance. The window is made from a combination of a circle and a square placed at an angle. The walls of the church taper inward to form an arched ceiling. The restored ceiling is made of wood and has been painted to look like stone.

Walls: The walls are five feet thick at the base and become wider as they rise, so that the walls curve inward. The windows are placed high on the walls.

Campanario:
The two towers are different from each other in design. The larger tower has a Moorish dome on top, and it holds eight bells with an outside staircase which gives access to the **belfry**. The smaller tower has only one bell.

Mission Compound:
The workshops and living quarters were built around a **quadrangle** like most of the other missions. Carmel Mission's quadrangle differs from the other missions, however, because it is irregularly shaped. The front section of the quadrangle is shorter than the back section. A beautiful fountain and olive trees throughout the gardens add beauty to the compound. A stone wall of the courtyard is carved with the coat of arms of the Dominicans and Franciscans, with statues of their founders St. Dominic and St. Francis.

Mission Grounds:
Mission San Carlos Borroméo did not have large herds of livestock or production of agricultural goods. The Eslenes tribe (native to the region) were fewer in number than native people living near other missions along the El Camino Real, so there was not a need for large-scale farming. A small canal brought water from the Carmel River to the mission compound for irrigation and daily use.

Do these things using the map provided. (Use the map on page 28.)

1. Write **Mission San Carlos Borroméo de Carmelo** ①, **cattle brand** ②, **workshops** ③, **ovens** ④, **patio** ⑤, **tannery** ⑥, **padres' living quarters** ⑦, **cemetery** ⑧, **church** ⑨, and **soldiers' living quarters** ⑩ by the correct number.
2. Do your best job if you color the map.

San Carlos Borroméo de Carmelo

Name ______________________

Date ______________________

Also known as "Carmel Mission"

The 2nd of 21 Spanish/Catholic Missions

Early History

On the first day of June, 1770, the Spanish ship *San Antonio* sailed into the beautiful harbor of Monterey. It had taken the ship over a month to travel more than 400 miles from San Diego. Fr. Junípero Serra led the ship's passengers ashore where they were greeted by the men of Governor Portolá's land expedition. Governor Portolá and his men left the southern mission in San Diego after the *San Antonio* set sail to Monterey. However, they arrived a week before. While waiting for the *San Antonio,* Portolá realized that he had camped on the shores of Monterey on his last journey, but never recognized it.

Both parties joined in on a joyous religious ceremony in celebration of arriving in Monterey. They raised the Spanish flag, claiming the land for Spain, and erected the presidio first. On June 3, 1770 Fr. Serra founded the Mission San Carlos Borroméo which began having church services in one of the storerooms of the presidio.

Portolá soon sent news of the occupation to the authorities in Mexico. Within a few short weeks, a church was erected and the military presidio was established. The shores were thick with forests which provided the logs needed to construct housing. Fr. Serra enjoyed the mild climate and beauty of the land so much that it became his favorite mission and the headquarters of the mission chain. This mission was intended to be the northernmost mission in the chain built along the *El Camino Real* — "the King's Highway."

In July, 1770, Governor Portolá turned his command over to his lieutenant, left the region and departed forever from California's history pages. Lt. Fages, the new military commander was unlike the easy-going Portolá. Fages immediately began to get involved in the affairs of the padres and missions. It did not take Fr. Serra long to realize that the mission was more likely to prosper away from the presidio where Lt. Fages was in command. In 1771, he moved the mission five miles south to a pasture along the Carmel River. However, the church at the Monterey Presidio continued in use for the soldiers until 1794, when it was replaced by the building which is still in use as a place of worship.

After the new mission had been settled along the river, the people often had to wait long periods of time for supplies to arrive from Mexico. However, in the late 1770s agricultural efforts began to **flourish** at the mission. Even though the mission often lacked provisions in its early years, it boasted of 165 Indians converted to Catholicism by the end of 1783.

Today, statues of Father Serra and bells (pictured here) can be seen along El Camino Real (*The King's Highway*).

San Carlos Borroméo de Carmelo

Name ______________________________

Date ______________________________

The 2nd of 21 Spanish/Catholic Missions

In 1774, Fr. Serra returned to Carmel after a journey to Mexico which had lasted about one and a half years. He lived in a little hut next to the mission where he administered the affairs of the growing mission chain. While he was in Mexico meeting with the Mexican leader, he succeeded in having Lt. Fages removed. However, Rivera y Moncada, who followed Fages, was even more difficult. When Rivera was removed and sent to Loreto, the Monterey Governor, Felipe de Neve was even worse to get along with.

Monterey became the capital city of California. Governor Felipe de Neve was made governor of the capital by Mexico's leaders. This gave de Neve a lot of power and authority. Not only did he distrust the native Indians, he was not personally interested in their welfare and regarded the missions as merely an outpost of the Spanish empire. De Neve wanted to make California's mission establishments into thriving communities well-populated with Spaniards. To accomplish this, he encouraged immigration from Mexico and began forcing the Franciscan friars out of economic and political authority. Fr. Serra strongly opposed de Neve, and defeated the governor's acts against the established missions. However, the struggle for authority over the missions caused a long delay in expansion. Only one new mission was founded between 1777 and December, 1786.

The people responsible for the establishment of the early missions were beginning to die off. Fr. Crespi, the man who wrote in detail about the beginning days of the missions, died in 1782. A year later, Fr. Junípero Serra, at the age of 70, made his last journey down El Camino Real. He returned to Carmel and died August 24, 1784. Fr. Serra had **devoted** 54 years to the Franciscan way of life. He did not live to see the missions' prosperity and the grand structures we see today. However, he remains the single most important person in their history.

After Fr. Serra died, Carmel remained the "parent" mission. Fr. Palou became president of all the missions until he retired to Mexico in 1785. At age 49, Fr. Fermín Lasuén followed as president of the California missions. He actively guided the missions for about 20 years. It was under his guidance that the missions reached their greatest prosperity. He lived at Carmel during most of this period. Carmel succeeded and grew, but not as much as some of the later missions.

Because Carmel was in the shadows of the governor's office, it was always the first mission to experience the new rules and regulations imposed by the government. Following the Mexican Revolution of 1830, the authorities took the properties away from the Franciscans and transferred them to the government. Eventually even the mission buildings were not owned by the church.

From 1836 until 1862, when the property was given back to the church by the United States, the mission was totally abandoned and left to decay. In 1882, an effort was made to preserve the existing ruins, but nothing else was accomplished until 1924, when part of the structure was restored. ❖

View of bell tower from Carmel Mission courtyard.

San Carlos Borroméo de Carmelo

Name ____________________

Date ____________________

Crossword Puzzle

The 2nd of 21 Spanish/Catholic Missions

Note: You will have to read page 33 in order to answer all of the questions in this puzzle.

Across

2. The first one in California was at Carmel Mission.
4. California was under the control of this government during the mission period.
6. Fr. Serra intended Carmel to be the ________ mission along El Camino Real.
8. He became president of the mission system after Fr. Serra.
10. He is the single-most important person in the history of California Missions.
12. Fr. O'Connell opened the mission as a ________ in 1933.
14. A building layout where work shops and living quarters are built around a courtyard.
16. This architectural influence is only found in the Carmel Mission.
18. Church services were first held in the ________ of the presidio.

Down

1. *The King's Highway.*
3. The Mission was moved five miles south of the original site to a pasture along this river.
4. This substance holds brick and block together.
5. The Franciscan padre who wrote detailed accounts of the early mission days.
7. This settlement became the first capital of California.
9. In the 1770s, the work in this industry began to flourish.
11. This man replaced Governor Portolá as commander of the military in Alta California.
12. A military fort.
13. Carmel was made the ________ of the mission chain by Fr. Serra.
15. ________ seashells were ground up and mixed with lime to make the mortar for building the mission.
17. This master mason was from Mexico City and designed Mission Carmel.

San Carlos Borroméo de Carmelo

Name ______________________

Date ______________________

The 2nd of 21 Spanish/Catholic Missions

The Mission Today

True restoration did not begin on the mission until the 1930s. Two men, Father Michael O'Connell and Harry Downie, deserve most of the credit for the restoration of the mission. Fr. O'Connell opened the mission as a parish church in 1933. At the time, Mr. Downie was one of the leading authorities on mission architecture and restoration. The first thing he did on the mission was to replace the shingle roof with a replica of the original tile roof. His expertise made the restoration of this mission the most complete and **authentic** of any of the missions along El Camino Real. He also supervised the replacement of the entire quadrangle based on the original foundations.

An old wooden door leads visitors into the mission where historical items are carefully displayed. A number of implements and garments give visitors an accurate description of what mission life might have been like. One room of the historical landmark was constructed showing a complete reproduction of an early mission kitchen. Other rooms are filled with mission tools and examples of amazingly beautiful handcrafted basketry made by natives of the region. Visitors show special interest in a small room where Fr. Serra lived. It contains simple furniture — a board bed, single blanket, wood table and chair, chest, and candlestick. The mission also boasts of having California's first library, once containing about 1,500 books. It still has books that belonged to Fr. Serra. There is a small chapel with a statue of the **Virgin Mary** which Fr. Serra brought to Mission San Diego and then to Mission Carmel.

The beautiful stone church was built under the direction of Fr. Lasuén in 1797. The use of **limestone** for the construction, shared only by three other churches in the mission chain, represents a departure from the less durable adobe structure. However, the Moorish architectural influence is only found at Mission Carmel. The remains of Frs. Junípero Serra, Juan Crespi, Fermín Lasuén, and Julian Lopez are all buried at the foot of the church's **altar**.

Today, Mission San Carlos de Borroméo de Carmelo remains one of the most beautiful and interesting historical landmarks on the coast of California. ❖

Mission San Carlos Borroméo de Carmelo
P.O. Box 2235;
3080 Rio Road
Carmel, CA 93921
Phone: 831.624.3600

San Carlos Borroméo de Carmelo

REVIEW QUESTIONS

Name ____________________

Date ____________________

Write the correct answer in the space provided.

1. The second Alta California mission, founded on ____________ ____________ years ago, and known as ____________.

2. The ship, *San Antonio*, sailed over ____________ miles and longer than a ____________ to reach the harbor at Monterey.

3. The architecture of this mission, with its ____________ window, makes it different from all the other missions.

4. Father ____________, the founder of this mission, loved it above all the others and made it his headquarters. He is buried here, along with Frs. ____________, ____________ and ____________.

5. The road along which the padres built the missions was called ____________ ____________, or *The King's Highway*.

6. Today, Carmel Mission is one of California's most ____________ and ____________ historical landmarks.

7. Why was Mission Carmel usually the first mission to experience the new laws and regulations?

____

8. Why is Carmel the most complete and authentic of any of the missions?

____

____

____

____

9. Explain why only one mission was founded between the years of 1777 and 1786.

____

____

____

☆☆ **Bonus Activity**

Use another resource and write a report on one of the padres buried under the altar, Saint Charles Borroméo, Italy, Catholicism, the Counter-Reformation, Saint Dominic and/or the Dominican Order, or Moorish architecture. Draw maps and pictures if appropriate for your report.

Mission #3

San Antonio de Padua

Founded July 14, 1771

Print the name of the mission on the correct line. (You may need to look back at a previously finished section/map.)

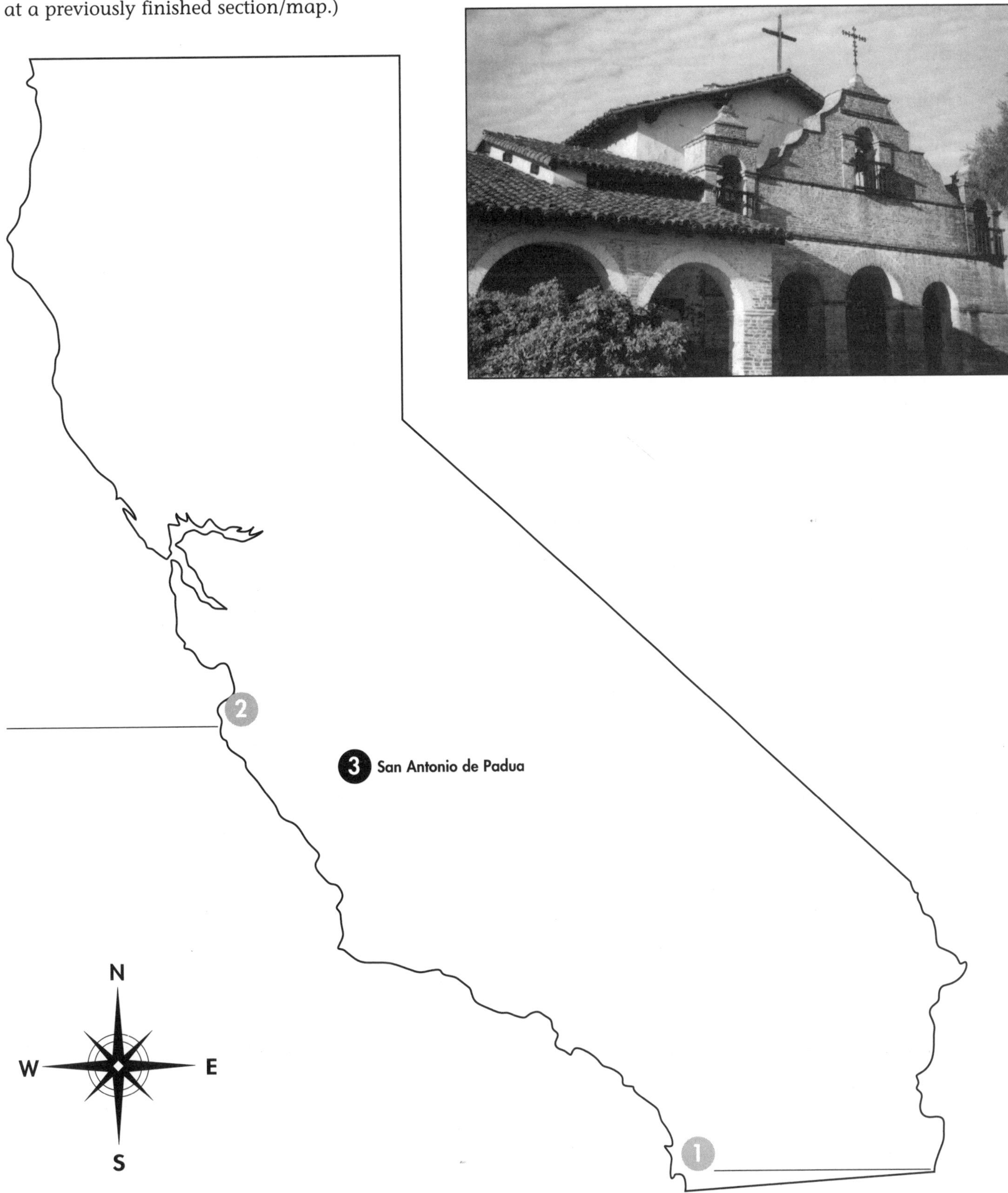

New Words to Learn:

Find the words in the glossary or a dictionary and write the meanings on the line.

1. **aqueduct**(s):______________________________
2. **cobblestone:** ______________________________
3. **disintegrate**(d):______________________________
4. **dormitory:** ______________________________
5. **dwelling**(s): ______________________________
6. **gentile**(s):______________________________
7. **primitive:** ______________________________
8. **reservoir**(s):______________________________
9. **shale:**______________________________
10. **thresh**(ed):______________________________
11. **vault:** ______________________________

① ______________________________

Mission #3 — Founded July 14, 1771

Layout of the Mission Grounds

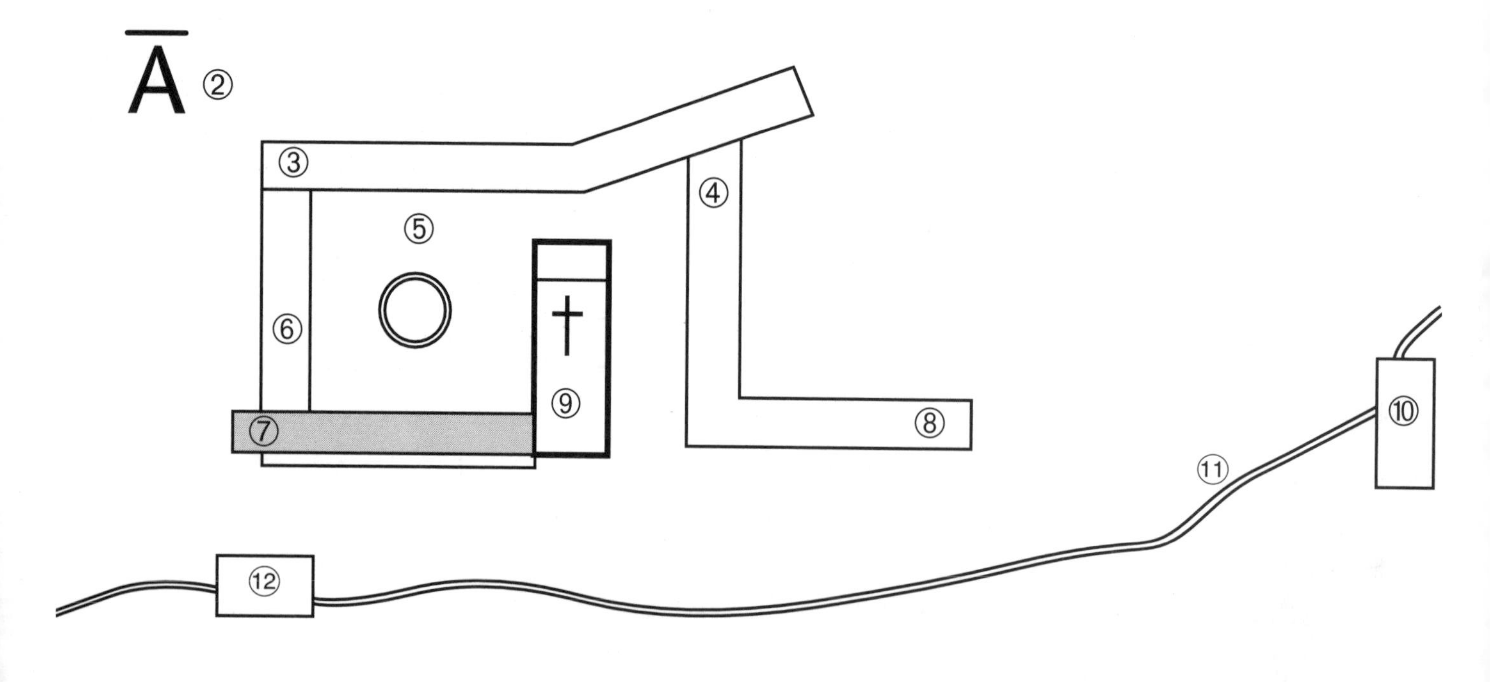

This layout is taken from a drawing in the mission's museum.

San Antonio de Padua

Name ______________________________

Named for St. Anthony, born in Lisbon, Portugal in 1195. He was a famous preacher and miracle worker who became a defender of the poor. He is buried at Padova (Padua) in northern Italy.

Date ______________________________

The 3rd of 21 Spanish/Catholic Missions

Design of the Mission

Church: (approximate outside measurements) 200 feet long, 40 feet wide, and 26 feet high.
The walls are made of adobe brick. The roof is made of tile, representing the first use of tile on a church in California.

Design:
It has a plain exterior, but is noted for its campanario that decorates the front and the barrel **vault** that leads to the entrance of the church. Most of the missions had tile floors, however, Mission San Antonio had a floor made from **cobblestone** covered with plaster. The vaulted wooden ceiling is painted blue with stars decorating the area over the altar. Native Indian art decorates the interior walls.

Walls: The walls are six feet thick at the bottom and taper to five feet thick at the top.

Campanario:
The bell tower with arched openings for the three bells is made of burnt brick. It is connected to the church by a *barrel vault* (an enclosed passageway with an arched roof) also made of brick.

Mission Compound:
As in most of the missions, a quadrangle of buildings is built around a courtyard. The buildings include the padres' living quarters, **dormitory** rooms, workshops for the weavers and other craftsmen and women, a winery, granary, and storerooms.

Mission Grounds:
The native Salinan tribe lived near the mission compound while they helped in the construction of the buildings. Large vineyards, olive groves, and wheat fields surround the mission. The wheat was **threshed** at the mission and then ground into flour at the **grist** mill. (This was the first water-powered grinding mill in California.) The mission was famous for the quality of horses which it raised. At one time it had more than 800 horses.

Water System:
The padres and natives built dams on the San Antonio River about three miles from the mission. The water was brought to the mission through **aqueducts** (the first in California) and stored in **reservoirs**. The aqueducts were made from 750 clay pipes on a bed of tile, covered with **shale**. The water turned a waterwheel that operated the grist mill. There were also pools of water for laundry and bathing.

Do these things using the map provided. (Use the map on page 36.)

1. Write **Mission San Antonio de Padua** ①, **cattle brand** ②, **workshops** ③, **kitchen** ④, **patio** ⑤, **granary** ⑥, **padres' quarters** ⑦, **dormitory** ⑧, **church** ⑨, **reservoir** ⑩, **aqueduct** ⑪, **grist mill** ⑫, and **native dwellings** ⑬ by the correct number.
2. Do your best job if you color the map.

San Antonio de Padua

Name ______________________

Date ______________________

The 3rd of 21 Spanish/Catholic Missions

Sometimes "de las Robles" (of the oak tree) is added to the name.

Early History

On July 14, 1771, a small party of Spanish missionaries, headed by Fr. Junípero Serra and two other Franciscan padres, walked into a beautiful valley covered with oak trees. The valley was located near the coastal region of central California. After the small party pitched their camp they began to prepare for the devotional services. It was their custom to have devotionals before the day was done. A large bronze bell was lifted from the back of a mule and secured to a lower branch of an oak tree. The friars were careful in their preparations because they knew this was no overnight campsite. This was to be the site of the new (third) mission along El Camino Real. It was named in honor of Saint Anthony of Padua. After the bell was in place, an aging Fr. Serra rang the bell with all his energy to officially dedicate Mission San Antonio de Padua.

The first written record found about the mission in 1774 shows San Antonio doing fairly well with 178 Indian converts and property increasing to 68 cattle, 7 horses, a number of new buildings, and a modest harvest of corn and wheat. In 1776, the mission was visited by de Anza on his second journey overland from Mexico to California. With Juan Bautista de Anza came Father Pedro Font who wrote in his diary very detailed accounts of the daily life within the religious settlement.

Fr. Pedro Font's diary also clearly indicated that he did not care for or about the newly converted Indians of San Antonio. He found them to be "dirty, not pleasantly formed, and embarrassingly **primitive** in their mode of dress." Unlike Fr. Font, Fr. Serra cared about the souls of the Indian **gentiles**.

The padres of San Antonio de Padua concentrated on building operations from the start. During the year 1776, the church was roofed with mortar and tile and adobe Indian dwellings were built. Storerooms, sleeping quarters, warehouses, and shops were also completed. Irrigation ditches were also dug to carry water to the fields from the San Antonio River.

A building 133 feet long was begun in 1779 and was completed in 1780. This building was used as the church and **sacristy**. Records also show that a new church was built in 1813. A few years before the completion of the new church, a water-powered mill for grinding grain had been built. As the Indian community steadily grew, improvements at the mission did the same. Wells were dug and a reservoir and aqueduct were built. In 1825, the region of San Antonio received so much rainfall that several buildings collapsed, but they were replaced by larger and stronger structures.

A close up photo of the bell on the left side of the campanario.

San Antonio de Padua

Name ____________________

Date ____________________

The 3rd of 21 Spanish/Catholic Missions

As Mission San Antonio prospered and improved, so did the appearance of the Indians who converted to Catholicism (at least in the opinion of the Spanish leaders and padres). In 1782, the usually quick-to-anger Lt. Fages was back in California for another term as governor. He commented on the great industry of the mission and the good manners of the converted Indians. In 1830, the valley contained more than 8,000 cattle and 12,000 sheep. It produced large amounts of grain. Wine and basket making were thriving industries. In spite of the great success of the mission, the number of Indians was declining each year as the result of disease.

After 1834, the mission rapidly **disintegrated** because of the secularization of the missions. (Secularization followed the Mexican Revolution in the 1830s when government leaders took the properties away from the Franciscans and transferred them to the government. Eventually, even the mission buildings were not owned by the church.) President Abraham Lincoln signed an order in 1862 that gave the mission back to the church, but not until after 1882. By this time the last priest living on the mission had died and the buildings were left to decay in the weather. In 1949, it was discovered that a railroad station was completely roofed by the tiles taken from the mission. The railroad station had purchased the tiles from an antique dealer. ❖

This is a picture of what remains of the first aqueduct built in California. The water flowed from the San Antonio River through the aqueduct (smaller left structure) and was stored in the reservoir (the larger brick structure). This method of supplying and storing water had been used for centuries in other countries.

San Antonio de Padua

Name ______________________________

Date ______________________________

WORD SEARCH PUZZLE

The 3rd of 21 Spanish/Catholic Missions

Note: You will have to read page 41 in order to find some of the words that fit into the clue sentences below.

Write the answers from the clue sentences by the corresponding numbers **before** you complete the puzzle.

1. ______________________________
2. ______________________________
3. ______________________________
4. ______________________________
5. ______________________________
6. ______________________________
7. ______________________________
8. ______________________________
9. ______________________________
10. ______________________________
    ____
11. ______________________________
12. ______________________________
13. ______________________________
    ____
14. ______________________________
15. ______________________________
16. ______________________________

```
G M X U Q U P C W R S E V J R O H S L C
Q E U H S D Y Q B R J S H A N M T H I A
J C N T H P B S A Z K W J L N C G Q P L
D A O T S V D B Y X Z T O O U Q P W N I
S W V B I U U M Y M I C I D F Z C N B F
D K P L B L N F I S N T E Q O A T X G O
V T X Z G L E S D I C U H X F B N I J R
E D C W H M E S L U Q W R Z M X Z Z I N
A R T E J K S S R A N H F E N B H U R I
X J N J V L S T T D G Y D S E Z R B R A
L N R V U E S Y E O I R I L X J D O I C
L M S O S N T B A X N S I U U I C P G D
A K S R O S K X F F Y E E S K P W R A Y
W J O C I H B U W W D K I A T P F R T R
L H E R K Y W M D O R B K B S T P I I Z
W R C E P I B W U D R C W F A E H Y O L
M A M H K J X O H L V N K X Z R Y I N Q
S T F P N K N U G X X Y Q U J V R T R W
R N N O X L N E A R T H Q U A K E E M D
F R A N C I S C A N S Y W E I I V D L O
```

1. An enclosed passageway with an arched roof is called a ________ vault.
2. The first ________ mill in California was built at Mission San Antonio de Padua.
3. Father Serra cared about the ________ of the native Indians.
4. President ________ signed an order which gave the mission back to the Catholic church.
5. The number of native people living at the mission declined each year as a result of ________ .
6. The room adjoining the church where the sacred vessels were kept is called the ________ .
7. Father Serra called the native people ________ because they were not of the Catholic faith. (Jews call all non-Jewish people ________ .)
8. A lot of progress on restoring the mission was made until the great ________ of 1906 hit the mission.
9. Mission San Antonio is mostly a ________ of an earlier mission, rather than a preserved ruin.
10. Father Buenaventura ________ spent 37 years putting the native ________ language into writing.
11. Mission San Antonio was famous for the ________ it raised.
12. Since 1948 the ________ have lived at the mission.
13. Water was brought to the mission through ________ , which were the first ones built in ________ .
14. Unlike most other missions that had tile floors, Mission San Antonio had floors made from ________ .
15. Mission San Antonio de Padua was the ________ mission built along El Camino Real.
16. ________ ditches were dug to carry water to the fields from the San Antonio River.

Name ______________________________

Date ______________________________

The 3rd of 21 Spanish/Catholic Missions

The Mission Today

In 1903, Congressman Joseph Knowland was a leader in forming the California Historic Landmark League. The first project chosen by the league was the restoration of Mission San Antonio de Padua. A lot of progress was made until unusually stormy weather and the great earthquake of 1906 hit the mission. The elements and tremors damaged most of the mission beyond repair. After a few years only a front section and a few arches remained intact.

It was not until 1948 that further restoration was attempted. The effort received a $50,000 grant from the William Randolph Hearst Foundation for mission restoration. The Franciscan Order also contributed to the restoration efforts. When this second attempt to restore the mission was undertaken, the existing structures were in such disrepair that they had to be leveled to the ground. As a consequence, Mission San Antonio is mostly a reconstruction of an earlier mission, rather than a preserved ruin. A complete rebuilding of the church and quadrangle was made.

The process was supervised by Harry Downie, who was aided by some descendants of local people who had helped to build the original mission. He employed several of the techniques used by the original mission builders in his reconstruction. The small hills of earth that once formed the adobe brick of the original walls were reformed using the same technique as the padres and natives used 150 years before. Every piece of timber in the new structure was cut and shaped using a tool similar to one the first woodcutters used. New adobe bricks were made from the ruins of the mission's old walls. The exterior shows no sign of modern tools being used in the construction. Only electric lights and radiant heat reveal the modern world's contribution to its restoration.

The restored padres' quarters has been turned into a museum. There is also an area showing visitors how the founding mission workers made adobe bricks and tiles. Part of the original reservoir and aqueduct can be seen nearby.

Father Buenaventura Sitjar spent 37 years at the mission, and completed the tedious task of putting the native Mutsun language into writing. He compiled a book of grammar and a dictionary which is on display at the mission.

Mission San Antonio de Padua is currently an active parish church, serving the people of the area. Since 1948 the Franciscans have lived at the mission. The one remaining bell, called *Osquila,* rings out over the area just as it did in 1821. The restoration of Mission San Antonio de Padua extends beyond the buildings. It is the only mission along El Camino Real whose surroundings remain as they were when it was first founded. The valley is still beautifully natural, with very few inhabitants to be seen nearby. Only the parking lot shows signs of the modern world. ❖

San Antonio de Padua Mission
P.O. Box 803;
Mission Creek Road
Jolon, CA 93928
Phone: 831.385.4478

An old grinding wheel at Mission San Antonio.

San Antonio de Padua

Name ______________________

Date ______________________

REVIEW QUESTIONS

Write the correct answer in the space provided.

1. Founded in ______________, the third California mission was named ______________________________.

2. Fr. Serra called worshippers to the first church service by ringing a bell he had hung in an ______________________________.

3. Features of this mission include the first California ______________ for irrigation and for powering a ______________ for grinding grain.

4. The design of this mission differs from the others in its ______________ floor and its arched passageway, called a ______________.

5. About 50 years ago it was discovered that a ______________ had been roofed by the tiles taken from the mission.

6. Explain what special techniques workers used in restoring this mission.

7. Explain why you think the mission grew bigger and more prosperous as the Indian population at the mission grew.

8. What did Fr. Font's diary reveal about his heart toward the native people?

☆☆ **Bonus Activity**

Use another resource and write a report on one of the people mentioned in this section, horses and/or breeding them, aqueduct history and/or construction, or the history and/or process of casting bronze bells or statues. Draw maps and pictures for your report.

Mission #4
San Gabriel Arcángel
Founded September 8, 1771

Print the name of the mission on the correct line. (You may need to look back at a previously finished section/map.)

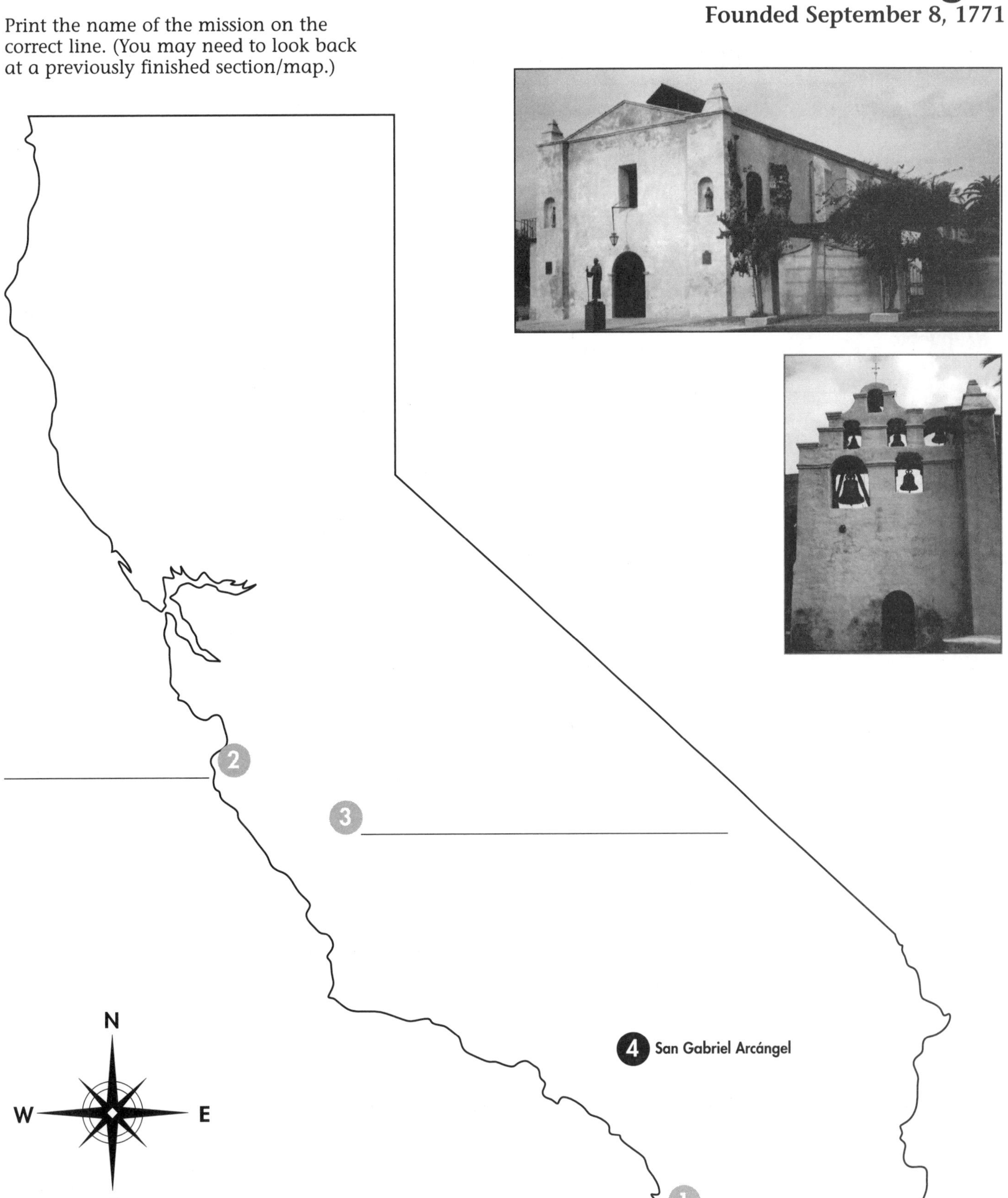

New Words to Learn:

Find the words in the glossary or a dictionary and write the meanings on the line.

1. **baptism:** ____________________
2. **corrupt:** ____________________
3. **decree**(s): ____________________
4. **devastate**(d): ____________________
5. **font:** ____________________
6. **Mass:** ____________________
7. **moral**(ly): ____________________
8. **pageantry:** ____________________
9. **pueblo:** ____________________
10. **republic:** ____________________

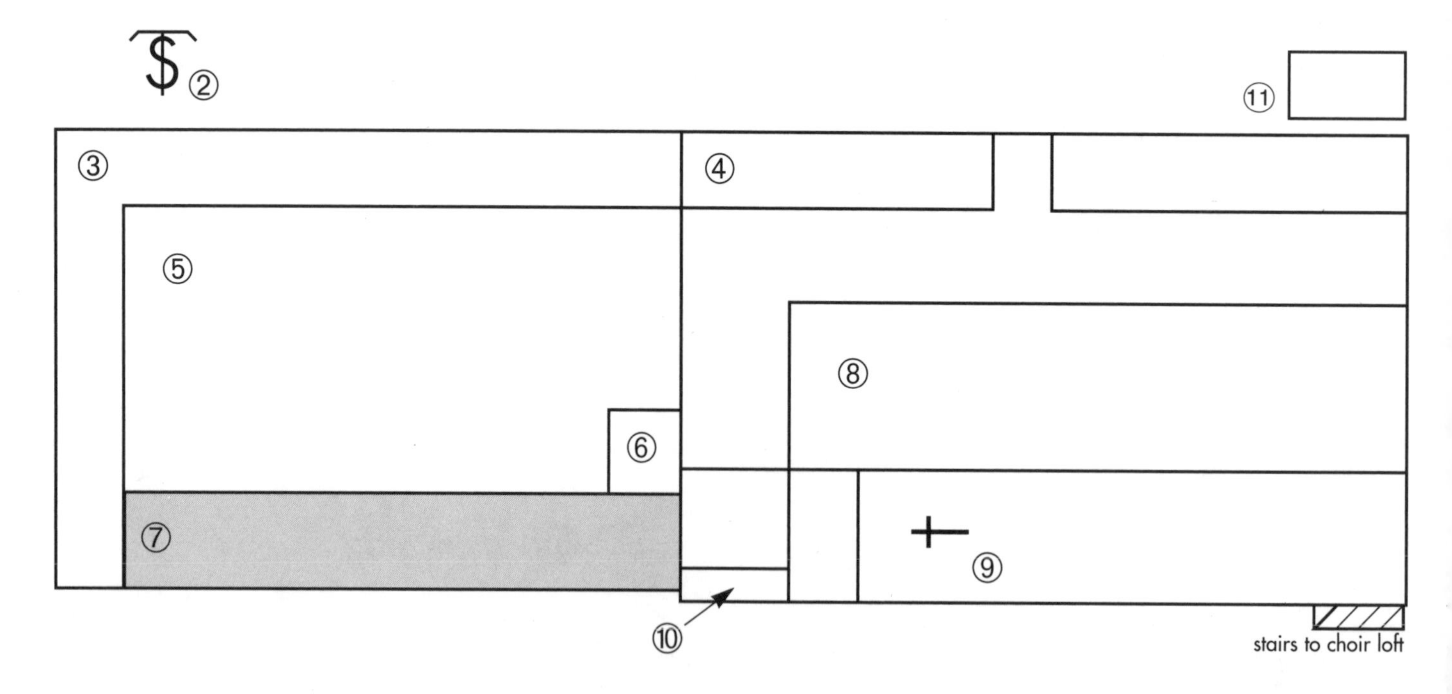

Layout of the mission grounds.
The cemetery is located above the laundry.

San Gabriel Arcángel

Named for the Archangel Gabriel, who was the messenger to Mary, the mother of Jesus; one of three California missions named for angels.

Name ______________________

Date ______________________

The 4th of 21 Spanish/Catholic Missions

Design of the Mission

Church: (approximate outside measurements) 172 feet long, 35 feet wide, and 30 feet high.

The church is made of stone and concrete up to the windows and of burnt brick above that point. The roof was made of vaulted concrete until it was replaced in 1804 with a flat roof made of brick and mortar. It was replaced with pitched roof tiles in 1812, and finally with shingles in 1886.

Design:

Mission San Gabriel is built in a fortress style, with capped buttresses (supports) along the outside walls. It has long and narrow windows. The style was copied from the Cathedral of Córdova located in Spain. Fr. Antonio Cruzado of Córdova was in charge of the construction. The outside stairway leads to the inside choir loft.

Walls: The walls are between four and five feet thick, the buttresses are seven feet thick.

Campanario:

The original bell tower at the northeast corner of the church was destroyed in the 1812 earthquake. It was replaced in 1828 by a campanario (bell wall) at the south end of the church. Six bells of various sizes hang in spaces cut to fit each bell. There are three rows of bells, one on top, three in the middle, and two on the bottom. The oldest bell was made in 1795 in Mexico City; two others are from the original set; and two were made in 1828 when the wall was built. The largest bell was made in 1830 and weighs 2,000 pounds. The campanario extending from the side wall of the church with the uniquely capped buttresses, the outside stairs, and a door make this side wall the front of the church.

Mission Compound:

There were two quadrangles covering several acres with buildings for sleeping, workshops, storerooms, and kitchens. The Indians working on the mission were skilled in weaving, leather work, and making soap. The mission supplied the soap to all of the other missions. A winery was begun in 1771, and at one time was the largest in California. There were eight brandy stills and three wine presses. It produced about 50,000 gallons of wine per year.

Mission Grounds:

Called the *Mother of California Agriculture,* Mission San Gabriel produced more wheat than any other mission. It also produced barley, corn, beans, peas, lentils, many different fruits, as well as grapes for wine. It raised more than 20,000 cattle, sheep, and goats. An **aqueduct** brought water from a nearby lake. Gardens were enclosed by fences made from very tall cactus.

Do these things using the map provided. (Use the map on page 44.)

1. Write **Mission San Gabriel Arcángel** ①, **cattle brand** ②, **workshops** ③, **kitchen** ④, **patio** ⑤, **winery** ⑥, **padres' living quarters** ⑦, **cemetery** ⑧, **church** ⑨, **bell wall** ⑩, and **laundry** ⑪ by the correct number.
2. Do your best job if you color the map.

San Gabriel Arcángel

Also known as the "Pride of the Missions."

Name ______________________

Date ______________________

The 4th of 21 Spanish/Catholic Missions

Early History

In 1771, ten Franciscan missionaries (padres) arrived at Fr. Serra's headquarters in Monterey. With the arrival of these padres the plans of Fr. Serra gained momentum. He immediately began implementing his plan to close the long gap between his own San Carlos Borroméo de Carmelo near Monterey and the southernmost mission San Diego. During the summer, two new missions were to be established. One of these was to be a day's journey (by walking or horseback) to the south of Carmelo. This one was to be called San Antonio de Padua (see last section). The second mission to be established in 1771 was to be a day's journey to the north of San Diego. This second mission — which is actually the fourth built in the chain along El Camino Real — was to be called San Gabriel Arcángel.

Late in the summer of 1771, Fr. Serra sent two Franciscan friars to the proposed site on the Rio de los Temblores, which is now called the Santa Ana River. Once they arrived at the proposed site, however, they decided they could find a more appropriate location. They crossed the San Gabriel River and selected a site near the present-day city of Montebello. On September 8, 1771, Mission San Gabriel Arcángel was founded.

Unlike other missions, the Native Indians were attracted to Mission San Gabriel Arcángel by the **pageantry** of the Franciscan **Mass**. They were eager to participate in the religious ceremonies and the building of the mission walls. The ultimate goal of the Franciscan fathers was the conversion of the Indians to the Catholic (Christian) faith through **baptism**. Baptisms of the newly converted Indians began on the second day of the mission's existence. Because of this, Mission San Gabriel Arcángel was considered an instant success by the padres.

This photo shows the "Pride of the Missions" in the late 1880s.

The good faith and trust that was established between the friars and the Indians was soon interrupted by the actions and attitudes of some of the **morally corrupt** Spanish soldiers. For one example, a soldier forcibly took a chieftain's wife and shot him when he objected. This incident aroused the Indians and only quick actions by the padres stopped a bloody fight between the Spaniards and the native people. The guilty soldier was quickly sent to another presidio. After a short time the friendship and acceptance that existed between the fathers and their native converts was completely restored.

San Gabriel Arcángel

Name ______________________

Date ______________________

The 4th of 21 Spanish/Catholic Missions

The first land link between the mission and Mexico was established when Juan Bautista de Anza and his party arrived on March 22, 1774. By establishing a land route to the mission, the long and dangerous sea journey around the peninsula of Baja California could be avoided. The importance of San Gabriel as the chief point of contact with Mexico greatly increased with de Anza's arrival. In 1776, the padres moved their mission five miles to the northwest. There they rebuilt the mission on the broad fertile plain where it still stands. Construction of the buildings seen today began in 1796.

San Gabriel grew to become the wealthiest and most prosperous of all the missions. The major difficulty came from the secular colonists who established residence at the nearby **pueblo** of Nuestra Señora la Reina de Los Angeles de Porciúncula — now America's second largest city, Los Angeles.

The military and political figures of the rapidly growing civilian colony in Los Angeles were land-hungry and greedy. The people were attracted to the colony by the mission's power, property, and wealth. They knew Spain had been cut off from its colonies in the New World because its naval forces were **devastated** in Europe's Napoleonic wars. The people of Mexico discovered they could get along without the help of their mother country, Spain. Mexico became a **republic** after gaining independence from Spain. However, it was not a strong republic, and the policies of the legislature were changing almost weekly.

Because of the unrest in Mexico, the Californians in authority and power welcomed the **decrees** of secularization. The decrees initially gave the Indians nominal possession of most of the mission lands. However, the more powerful Californians soon discovered that the Indians did not care much about private ownership of the land. It did not take long for the land ownership of the Indians to shift into the hands of military leaders and civilian authorities.

In November 1834, Mission San Gabriel was taken from the Franciscans and turned over to a civilian administrator. At this time the inventory included more than 16,500 cattle. In less than six months, however, all but about one hundred were taken from the Franciscans. In 1843, when the Franciscans were allowed to temporarily return to Mission San Gabriel, everything of any value had been removed from the mission (actually stolen from the Franciscans). Ten years later, in 1853, the Franciscan fathers left the mission for the last time because California's Governor, Pio Pico, had arranged the sale of the mission. However, the sale was prevented by the arrival of United States troops. In 1862, the mission buildings and part of the surrounding properties were returned to the Catholic Church by the American Congress. ❖

San Gabriel Arcángel

Name ____________________

Date ____________________

Word Search Puzzle

The 4th of 21 Spanish/Catholic Missions

Note: You will have to read page 49 in order to find some of the words that fit into the clue sentences below.

Write the answers from the clue sentences by the corresponding numbers **before** you complete the puzzle.

1. ____________________
2. ____________________
3. ____________________
 ____
4. ____________________
 ____
5. ____________________
6. ____________________
7. ____________________
 ____
8. ____________________
9. ____________________
10. ____________________
11. ____________________
12. ____________________
13. ____________________
14. ____________________
15. ____________________

G	Q	L	B	M	S	O	A	P	R	M	W	N	C	D	Y	W	X	Z	P
G	A	C	W	U	O	A	M	J	A	O	X	I	Z	Q	I	K	E	H	U
Z	W	R	Z	P	T	R	J	W	A	P	Y	W	H	C	L	K	L	N	O
M	I	O	D	I	M	T	A	D	K	N	F	W	D	K	O	Z	O	W	J
Y	N	U	W	E	B	O	R	L	M	J	P	P	G	T	W	Q	I	C	J
C	E	G	H	Y	N	R	N	E	L	C	G	A	E	G	D	M	P	I	W
G	R	D	E	W	J	S	E	T	S	Y	A	K	P	D	I	T	Y	W	U
E	Y	P	A	W	V	Y	F	P	E	S	Z	C	T	K	B	T	T	N	W
B	G	D	T	N	T	O	J	F	U	B	E	G	T	T	P	W	Z	I	H
Y	G	G	V	I	J	G	X	T	O	B	E	S	T	U	A	V	J	W	O
T	K	M	M	X	Z	M	A	L	D	K	L	L	Y	J	S	R	E	I	S
U	T	Q	N	Q	V	G	N	I	D	Y	Y	I	L	N	E	K	R	S	T
P	C	R	I	D	U	L	K	K	C	V	Q	L	C	O	A	A	E	P	K
F	G	L	N	Z	J	F	W	U	U	Y	C	Z	Z	U	N	R	U	R	G
R	L	J	Q	X	G	T	A	D	C	Q	T	F	Q	A	T	R	E	N	O
E	D	S	D	C	H	L	F	E	A	Z	F	H	P	R	R	H	I	C	R
L	X	P	A	E	J	I	O	W	N	B	T	M	O	O	T	V	I	Q	C
I	O	A	D	Y	D	W	I	Y	G	R	A	F	C	A	A	X	A	B	J
C	K	I	S	H	I	Y	U	G	A	C	K	Q	E	E	E	X	K	A	V
S	N	N	L	H	C	E	Y	E	S	S	L	L	W	M	Z	K	S	D	T

1. The mission is located near the present-day city of ________ .
2. The ________ of 1812 destroyed the original campanario.
3. Native Indians working on the mission were skilled in ________ , making soap, and ________ work.
4. The trust between the friars and Indians was interrupted by the actions and attitudes of some of the ________ ________ Spanish soldiers.
5. Mission San Gabriel is built in a ________ style.
6. The walls have capped ________ along the outside of the walls to add strength to them.
7. Large ________ were used to form a tall fences around the ________ .
8. Mission San Gabriel possesses one of the best collections of mission ________ in existence today.
9. More ________ was grown at San Gabriel Arcángel than any other mission.
10. Mission San Gabriel supplied all of the ________ used by other the other Franciscan missions.
11. Mexico won its independence from ________ .
12. The oldest bell in the campanario was made in what country? ________
13. At one time the mission had the largest ________ in California.
14. Mexico became a ________ after it gained its independence.
15. The ________ was then, and remains today, the visual identity of Mission San Gabriel.

San Gabriel Arcángel

Name ______________________

Date ______________________

The 4th of 21 Spanish/Catholic Missions

The Mission Today

The campanario at Mission San Gabriel Arcángel.
(Note the capped buttress to the right of the bells.)

In 1908 the mission was turned over to the Claretian Missionary Fathers, who continue to maintain it even today. They restored much of quadrangles and patios. They also continue to use it as a parish church. The Camposanto (cemetery) was first used in 1778 and is still used today by the Claretian Fathers as a burial ground.

The church was in great condition until the earthquake of 1987. This earthquake caused so much structural damage that the church and museum had to be closed to tourists for several years. The building had to be shored up until money became available to fix the structural damage. During this time, only the cemetery and parts of the patios were open to visitors.

From its founding, Mission San Gabriel has always had a great number of visitors. It was founded at the crossroads of three main trails. Two trails ran north-south connecting Mexico to upper California, the other ran east-west connecting the eastern part of the United States to the Pacific Ocean.

Mission San Gabriel possesses one of the finest collections of mission relics in existence. In the museum (which was originally the winery) is a series of 14 paintings of the Stations of the Cross. These Indian paintings are considered one of the oldest examples of native California church art in the world. Also included in the mission's collection is the hammered copper baptismal **font**, a gift of King Carlos III of Spain in 1771, and six altar statues brought from Spain in 1791.

The original bell tower was destroyed by an earthquake in 1812. In the reconstruction, the builders differed from the traditional mission bell tower and built the strikingly beautiful campanario (bell wall) which presently displays the ancient and massive bells. This campanario was then, and remains today, the visual identity of Mission San Gabriel Arcángel. ❖

Mission San Gabriel
537 West Mission Drive
San Gabriel, CA 91776
Phone: 626.457.3048

San Gabriel Arcángel

Name ______________________

Date ______________________

REVIEW QUESTIONS

Write the correct answer in the space provided.

1. Mission San Gabriel is also known as ______________________.
2. The first mission site chosen was by the ______________________ River.
3. By establishing a ______________________ to the mission, the long and dangerous ______________________ around Baja California could be avoided.
4. What was the ultimate goal of the Franciscan friars? ______________________ ______________________.
5. San Gabriel grew to become the ______________ and ______________ ______________ of all the missions.
6. Mission San Gabriel is a ______________________ north of Mission San Diego.
7. In ______________ the mission buildings and part of the surrounding land was returned to the ______________________ by the American Congress.
8. Explain why Mission San Gabriel was considered an instant success.
9. Explain why the authorities of California welcomed secularization.
10. Explain why Mission San Gabriel Arcángel always had lots of visitors.

☆☆ **Bonus Activity**

Use another resource and write a report on one of the people mentioned in this section, Catholic Mass, Los Angeles, aqueduct history and/or construction, or the history and/or process of casting bronze bells or statues. Draw maps and pictures for your report.

Mission #5

San Luís Obispo de Tolosa

Founded September 1, 1772

Print the names of the missions on the correct lines. (You may need to look back at a previously finished section/map.)

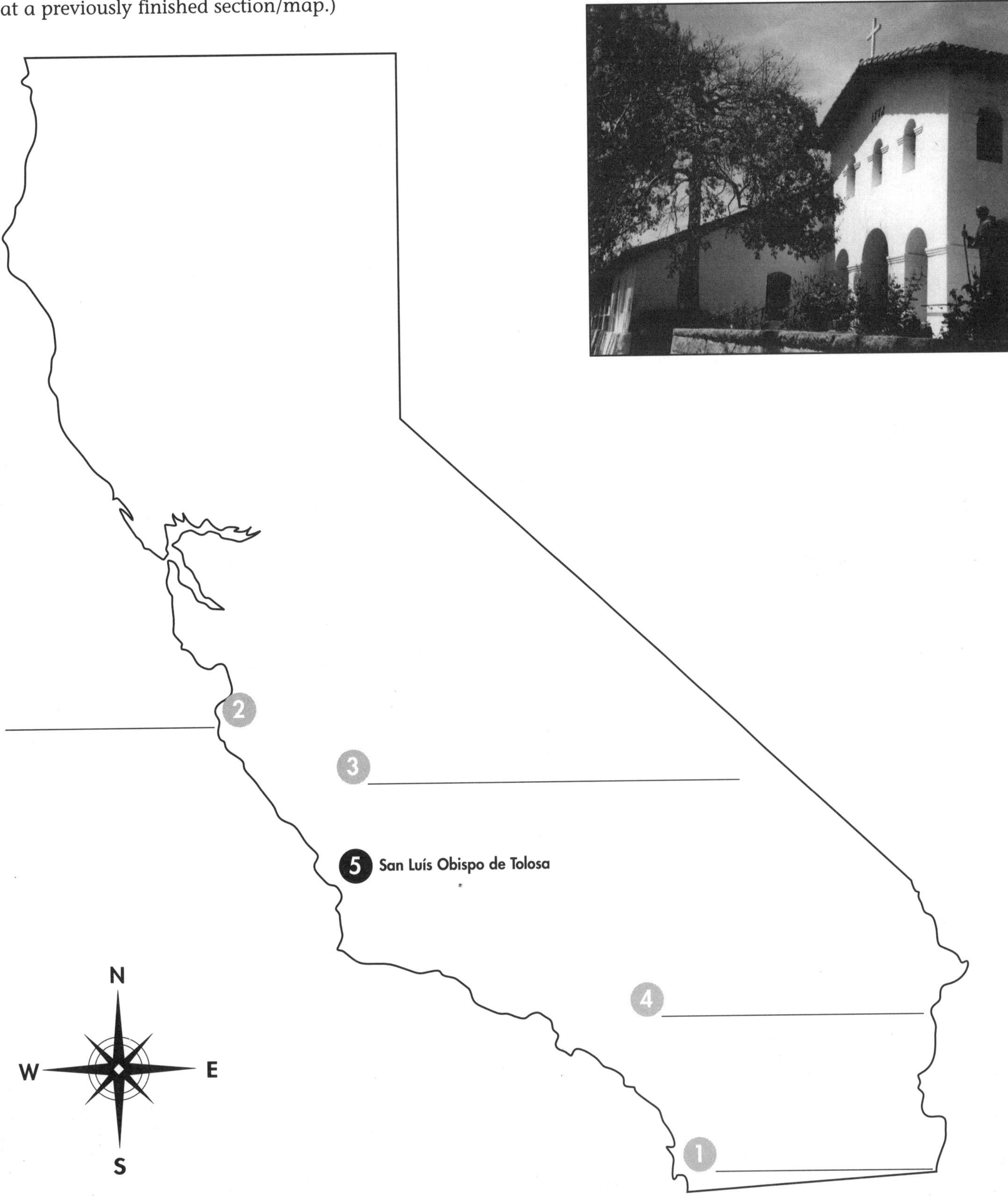

New Words to Learn:

Find the words in the glossary or a dictionary and write the meanings on the line.

1. **annual:** ______
2. **arbor**(s): ______
3. **hostage:** ______
4. **kiln:** ______
5. **mezcla:** ______
6. **retreat**(s): ______
7. **sarcasm** (sarcastic): ______
8. **serape**(s): ______
9. **thatch**(ed): ______

① ______

Mission #5 — Founded September 1, 1772

Layout of the Mission Grounds

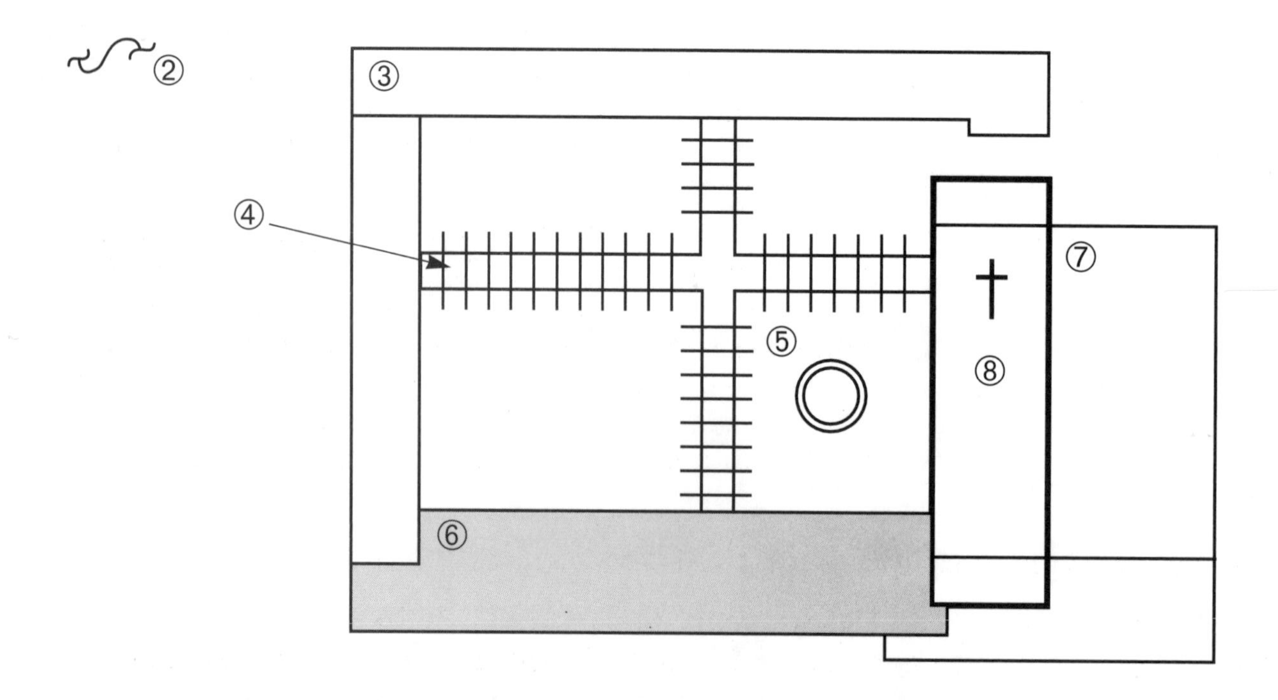

This was the layout of the mission compound at the height of its prosperity.

San Luís Obispo de Tolosa

Name ______________________

Named for St. Louis, Bishop of Toulouse, France. Born in1274 in southern France and died at the age of 27. He was held **hostage** in Barcelona, Spain 7 years, and instructed there by Franciscan friars.

Date ______________________

The 5th of 21 Spanish/Catholic Missions

Design of the Mission

Church: (approximate outside measurements) 153 feet long, 34 feet wide, and 26 feet high.

The church building is constructed with adobe walls and a tile roof. The floor is made from stone and mortar called *mezcla*.

Design:

The style is the simple "mission" style with a church and quadrangle for shops, living quarters, and so on, which surround a courtyard or patio. Mission San Luís Obispo is noted for its belfry and vestibule (entry hall). The courtyard has porches with rounded pillars with square openings, which is unlike any of the other missions along El Camino Real.

Walls: The walls are adobe, covered with plaster and whitewash.

Campanario:

The three bells were made in 1818 in the South American country of Peru, and were recast in 1878. They hang in uniformly arched openings all on the same level. The campanario (bell tower) also serves as an entrance to the church.

Mission Compound:

The mission compound is built around the traditional patio, which is divided uniquely into four sections by grape **arbors**. The church is built on the north side of the quadrangle, the priests' living quarters are on the east side, workshops are on the west side, and storerooms are on the south side.

Mission Grounds:

Water came from a nearby stream and was used to power a grist mill. Mission San Luís Obispo was noted for its wines, olive oil, and the fruits and vegetables it grew. It was also known for the fine quality of cloth it produced and even more for roofing tiles. Large flocks of sheep produced wool which was spun into yarn and then woven into cloth. Heavy wool blanket material was used to make **serapes**. It also produced lightweight cloth for making clothing for the other missions.

Even though the red roofing tiles, which became a symbol of the California Missions, were first used at Mission San Antonio de Padua, San Luís Obispo gets credit for establishing their use. The process was perfected and the tiles were produced on a large scale by Mission San Luís Obispo. The roofing tiles were patterned after the ones used in Spain, which some of the padres had remembered. Water and local clay was mixed by having horses walk around in circles through the clay, which was then formed over curved wooden molds, dried in the sun and then baked in a **kiln**. The tiles were about 22" long and between 12" to 20" wide.

Do these things using the map provided. (Use the map on page 52.)

1. Write **Mission San Luís Obispo de Tolosa** ①, **cattle brand** ②, **workshops** ③, **grape arbors** ④, **garden** ⑤, **padres' living quarters** ⑥, **cemetery** ⑦, and **church** ⑧, by the correct number.
2. Do your best job if you color the map.

San Luís Obispo de Tolosa

Name ______________________

Date ______________________

The 5th of 21 Spanish/Catholic Missions

Early History

On September 1, 1772, Fr. Junípero Serra founded Mission San Luís Obispo de Tolosa. It was the fifth in the chain of Franciscan stations (missions) along El Camino Real. Don Gaspar de Portolá named the location the *Valley of the Bears* on his first northward expedition from San Diego in search of Monterey Bay in 1769.

On their slow march in hopes of finding Monterey Bay, Portolá and his soldiers encountered bears between the mouth of the Santa María River and the present site of San Luís Obispo. The historical diaries of Frs. Juan Crespi and Francisco Gomez record that they were amazed at the large number of bears in the region. The fathers also recorded that at one time the early settlers were threatened with starvation. Portolá sent out a hunting party that returned with more than 9,000 pounds of bear meat. A few months later Mission San Luís Obispo was founded at the scene of the hunt.

In August 1772, Fr. Serra received word at his headquarters in Monterey that the two ships *San Carlos* and *San Antonio* had arrived in San Diego from Mexico with supplies. The two captains of the ships decided not to go farther north with any of the supplies, because of the difficulty they had on their previous sailings to Monterey. Word was sent to Fr. Serra about their decision and it was suggested that the supplies be taken north overland from the southern port. Fr. Serra set out from Monterey in hopes of persuading one of the captains to bring the supplies north.

Mission San Luís Obispo as it looked near the turn of the century

Fr. Serra took another friar on his trip south to San Diego. He gave this Franciscan the responsibility of establishing the mission at San Luís Obispo. Fr. Serra was reluctant to leave only one padre at the new mission. He thought the military might interfere and cause trouble with the mission personnel and Indian converts. However, the military did not interfere and the mission grew. The early contact with the native Indians went very well. The Spanish had been generous with the Indians months earlier when they shared some of their bear meat.

Prior to 1774, Mission San Luís Obispo de Tolosa was attacked by hostile Indians on three different occasions. The Indians burned the **thatched** roofs of the mission on each separate attack. (Up until this time, most of the missions were built out of adobe with thatched roofs.) As a result of many fires destroying the mission roofs, the padres at San Luís Obispo developed a roof tile to protect their buildings. It did not take long for the other four missions in the chain to replace their thatched roofs with the more durable tile.

San Luís Obispo de Tolosa

Name ______________________

Date ______________________

The 5th of 21 Spanish/Catholic Missions

In 1782, the King of Spain imposed a tax on all of the Franciscans in California to raise money for his war efforts against England. Even though San Luís Obispo was one of the smallest of all the missions, it sent its share of the tax, which was $107, to Spain.

From 1794 to 1809, the building and expansion of the mission and its operations were extensive. In 1804, the number of Indians living at the mission reached a peak of 832. The number of recorded baptisms showed a total of 2,074. There were also 1,091 recorded deaths. In May of 1807, Mission San Luís Obispo de Tolosa was designated as one of six in which the California Padres could take their **annual retreats**. For nine years, beginning in 1811, the mission fathers built numerous dwellings for the Indians. They also made many improvements and additions to the mission during those years. In 1819, construction of the quadrangle was completed. A year later, two large bells made in Lima, Peru were hung at the mission.

Following Mexico's revolt against Spain in 1810, all of the California missions were forced to contribute food and clothing to the Spanish army. At San Luís Obispo, Father Luís Martinez often found himself and the native Indians lacking the ordinary necessities of life because of the constant demands of the military.

Fr. Martinez' good sense of humor won him widespread fame in the early days of the settlement. However, his **sarcastic** comment about the soldiers being idle and lazy in 1816 stirred up trouble with the army. Two years later he led a company of native Indians to Santa Barbara and San Juan Capistrano — many miles apart — to help defend the missions against two shiploads of South American pirates. These efforts restored him to the soldiers' good graces. Legend has it that on one occasion an important general came to visit the mission and Fr. Martinez had all of the animals in the barnyard march past the general to entertain him.

Unfortunately, Fr. Martinez had a quick temper and often openly criticized the governor. This led to some difficulties for the padre. Eventually, his enemies gained enough power within the government to drive him from the country. In 1830, after 34 years of missionary service, he was forced to leave San Luís Obispo. The records tell how sorrowful he was at his departing. However, only a short five years later the mission became the property of the military and civilian leaders through the laws of secularization. He might have had a happier termination than the one that secularization would have brought him.

The story of the destruction and ruin of San Luís Obispo de Tolosa under the Mexican governors is similar to that of the other missions of California. The ruin of this mission has been fully documented. It is interesting to note that the Spanish occupation of California was one of the best documented colonizing efforts made by any nation. The number of records, accounts, **census** figures, and personal diaries produced by the early Californians is amazing, considering the primitive nature of their surroundings. From the very first years of colonization, reports were constantly sent to Mexico City, to the viceroy, to the Franciscan College of San Fernando, and to friends. The volume of information was so large that a conflict over who would pay the postage arose between the civil and religious leaders. No doubt some of the accounts were written to each group's superiors in order to inform them of a different interpretation of issues that were in dispute. ❖

San Luís Obispo de Tolosa

Name ____________________

Date ____________________

The 5th of 21 Spanish/Catholic Missions

Crossword Puzzle

Note: You will have to read page 57 in order to answer all of the questions in this puzzle.

Across

2. The ________ of Mexico was appointed by the Crown in Spain, had his headquarters in Mexico City, and received reports about Spanish colonization efforts in California.

4. Mission San Luís Obispo showed a total of 2,074 ________ from 1794 to 1809.

6. Fr. Martinez called the Spanish soldiers ________ and....

7. From the very first years of ________ , reports were constantly sent back to Mexico City.

9. Don Gaspar de Portolá named the region *Valley of the* ________ .

11. California was a colony of ________ .

12. The simple mission style had a church and ________ which surrounded a patio or courtyard.

13. Two shiploads of ________ from South America were defeated by the help of Fr. Martinez and a company of native Indians.

14. The people at the mission often found themselves lacking the necessities of life because of the constant demands of the ________ .

16. The campanario also serves as the ________ to the church.

Down

1. For nine years, beginning in 1811, the mission fathers built numerous ________ for the Indians.

3. The King of Spain imposed a tax on all of the ________ in California to fund Spain's war against England.

4. Mission San Luís Obispo's is noted for the design of its ________ and entry hall.

5. The three bells hanging in the campanario were made in ________ , South America.

7. Fr. Martinez often openly ________ the governor of California, which led to some difficulties for the padre.

8. The traditional patio is divided into four sections by grape ________ .

10. The word for entry hall is ________ .

15. Fr. Martinez not only called the Spanish soldiers idle, he called them ________ .

17. The natives and padres living at the mission perfected the process of making roofing ________ .

18. Mission San Luís Obispo was also known for producing high quality, lightweight ________ .

San Luís Obispo de Tolosa

Name ______________________

Date ______________________

The 5th of 21 Spanish/Catholic Missions

The Mission Today

In the 1880s, a parish priest tried to make Mission San Luís Obispo look like a New England church. (Why anybody would ever want to do this puzzles the author as well as many other people!) He had wooden siding placed over the adobe walls, and had a steeple added to the building. He destroyed the bell tower and vestibule by having them torn down. On the inside, he covered the original mezcla floor with wood flooring. It took over 50 years before anybody began undoing this man's mistakes.

Authentic restoration was started in 1933 under the leadership of Father John Harnett. He had the wood siding, floor, and steeple all removed. He had both the campanario (bell tower) and vestibule rebuilt, and returned the three bells to their niches.

Restoration of the interior of the church continued during the 1940s. The goal of the restoration was to return the interior to its original 1794 condition. The workers uncovered the original beamed ceiling. The altar which was used in the early days is still there, as well as the original statue of Saint Louis above the altar and the original baptismal font.

Mission San Luís Obispo serves as a parish church to many of the Catholics in the area. A large wing has been added to the original church, which doubles the seating capacity. The original padres' quarters has been restored into an excellent museum. The museum contains a great collection of early photographs and other items which depict the way of life in California before the turn of the century.

The city of San Luís Obispo calls itself "The City with a Mission," in honor of its beginnings as a Spanish mission/settlement. A town plaza faces the restored mission church, and each year the city holds a fiesta to celebrate the founding of the mission. ❖

Mission San Luís Obispo de Tolosa
P.O. Box 1461;
728 Monterey Street
San Luís Obispo, CA 93401
Phone: 805.543.6850

San Luís Obispo de Tolosa

Name ______________________

Date ______________________

Review Questions

Write the correct answer in the space provided.

1. The fifth California mission, founded in __________, was ______________ ______________________________.

2. Because of repeated fires, the padres started making ______________ to use for roofing instead of thatch.

3. The appearance of this mission was altered in the 1880s to make it look more like a church in ______________. Authentic restoration was begun under the leadership of Father ______________ in __________.

4. The mission's museum contains early ______________ and items depicting life in California before the turn of ______________.

5. Explain why the missions were taxed.

6. Explain how we know details of the Spanish colonization of California.

7. Explain why Mission San Luís Obispo gets credit for using tile roofing.

8. Explain why the padres and neophytes were sometimes short of food.

☆☆ **Bonus Activity**

Use another resource and write a report on one of the people mentioned in this section, Spain, Spanish Armada, Peru, bears, the history or process of making clay roofing tiles, or native people to the area. Draw maps and pictures for your report.

Mission #6

San Francisco de Asís

Founded October 9, 1776

Print the names of the missions on the correct lines. (You may need to look back at a previously finished section/map.)

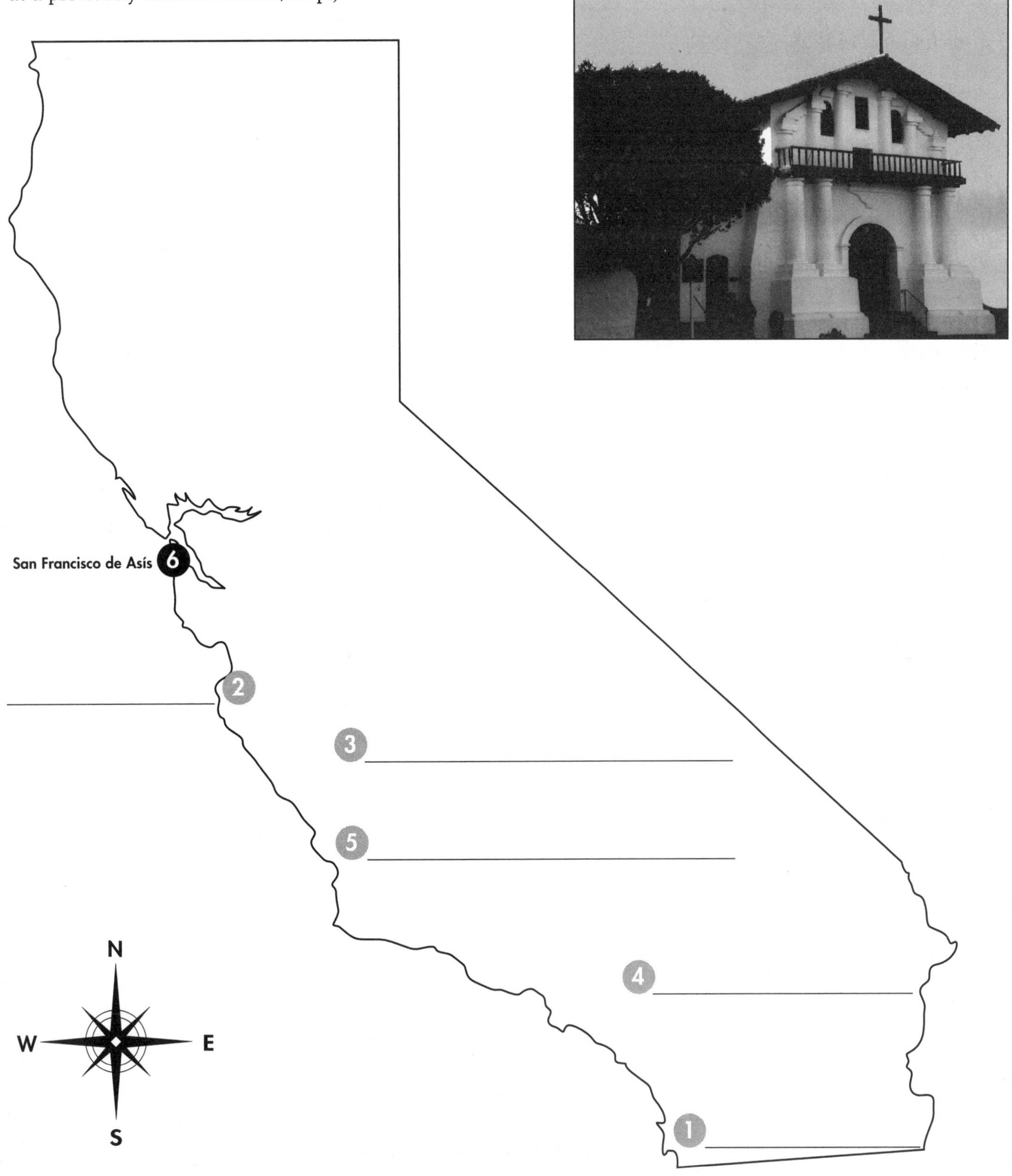

New Words to Learn:

Find the words in the glossary or a dictionary and write the meanings on the line.

1. **chastity:**____
2. **compromise:**____
3. **debate:** ____
4. **distinguish**(ed):____
5. **domesticate**(d):____
6. **infirmary:** ____
7. **susceptible:** ____
8. **symmetry** (symmetrically):____
9. **tallow::**____
10. **trestle:**____
11. **vow**(s):____

① ____

Mission #6 — Founded October 9, 1776

Layout of the Mission Grounds

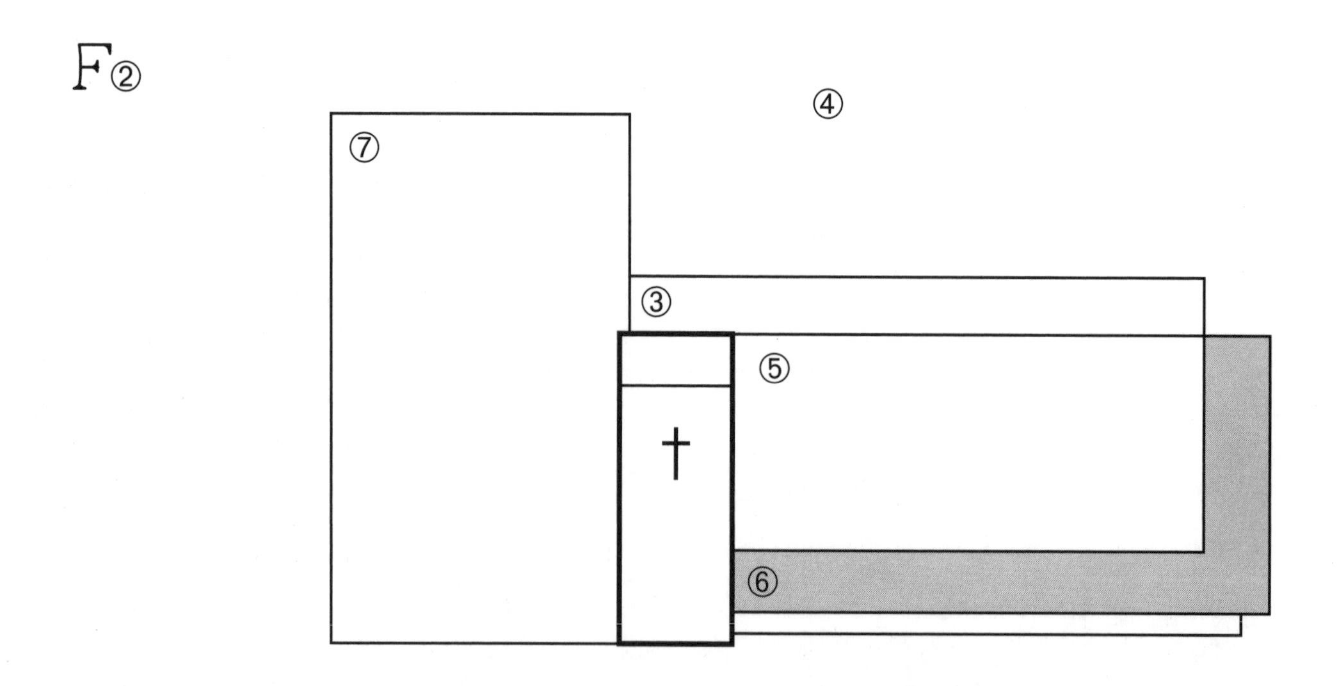

This shows the mission compound after 1810.

San Francisco de Asís

Name ______________________

Date ______________________

Named for St. Francis of Assisi, Italy, born in 1182. He was a son of wealthy parents, but gave wealth up for **vows** of poverty, obedience, and **chastity**; thereby starting the Franciscan Order.

The 6th of 21 Spanish/Catholic Missions

Design of the Mission

Church: (approximate outside measurements) 145 feet long, 33 feet wide, and 26 feet high. The church is made of adobe walls, with a tile roof and tile floors.

Design:

The style of Mission San Francisco de Asís (most often called *Mission Dolores*) is simple with clean lines. There is an exterior balcony that crosses the front and is supported by four Corinthian columns. The four columns are **symmetrically** spaced, with two on each side of an arched entrance. Mission Dolores has no bell tower, but the three original bells still hang in niches in a loft above the entrance. The bells were cast in Mexico, one in 1792 and the other two in 1797. Strips of rawhide are used to hang the bells as well as to lash together the interior ceiling beams. The designers of Mission Dolores **distinguished** it from the others by extensive use of redwood in the interior. The redwood ceiling beams are decorated with brightly painted native art and designs, and the wooden columns are painted to look like marble. Like Mission San Gabriel, the original church had outside stairs that led to the choir loft.

Walls: The walls are four feet thick.

Campanario:

There is no separate bell tower at Mission San Francisco de Asís.

Mission Compound:

The mission was built in the typical quadrangle style, with a patio in the middle of the buildings. The buildings provided living quarters, storerooms, workshops, and a granary that was 150 feet long. There was also an **infirmary** at the mission because the native workers were very **susceptible** to illnesses brought to the area by European settlers. The compound also included dwellings for the mission workers.

Mission Grounds:

Mission Dolores had little space and the soil and weather were poor for growing crops. This is part of the reason the mission did not prosper like most of the other missions. Weaving was an important activity on the mission. It provided the blankets for the soldiers at the nearby presidio. The most important activity of the mission was that it was a shipping center. Hides and **tallow** from other missions were sent to Mission Dolores, where the staff administered the trading of these products with ships from Spain and New England. Mission women were very skilled in tanning the hides that were being exported to Spain and New England. The cemetery at the mission grew at a staggering rate because of the high number of illnesses. More than 5,000 native Californians are buried there.

Do these things using the map provided. (Use the map on page 60.)

1. Write **Mission San Francisco de Asís (Dolores)** ①, **cattle brand** ②, **workshops** ③, **garden** ④, **patio** ⑤, **padres' living quarters** ⑥, and **cemetery** ⑦ by the correct number.
2. Do your best job if you color the map.

San Francisco de Asís

Also known as "Mission Dolores"

Name ______________________________

Date ______________________________

The 6th of 21 Spanish/Catholic Missions

Early History

In late June 1776, Fr. Francisco Palou and Lt. José Moraga, along with 16 Spanish soldiers with their wives and children, arrived on the shores of San Francisco Bay. Some families of Spanish-American settlers (convinced by Juan Bautista de Anza to move to the new colony) were also with the party. In addition, some **domesticated** Indians herded about 200 tired cattle onto the shores of the bay.

Most of the supplies for the land expedition had been sent on the ship *San Carlos*. The ship and the expedition both left Monterey at the same time. As usual, the overland marchers arrived several days before the ship. Fr. Palou and Lt. Moraga wasted no time in laying out the plans for the new settlement. The site selected for Mission San Francisco de Asís was on the border of a small inlet. The Spanish explorer Juan Bautista de Anza had discovered the little inlet earlier in the year. He named it Laguna de Nuestra Señora de los Dolores. (The laguna became so well identified with Fr. Palou's mission that even today the mission is far better known as Mission Dolores than San Francisco de Asís.)

On August 18, 1776, the *San Carlos* arrived in the laguna and construction moved quickly. Permanent mission buildings were completed by September 1st. However, Fr. Palou and Lt. Moraga postponed the dedication of the mission because Captain Rivera was not there. The Captain opposed the founding of another mission, but his view was not shared by the viceroy of Mexico. They had seen a letter sent to Fr. Serra in which the viceroy had expressed the hope of two more missions being established. He wanted one to be dedicated to San Francisco and the other named after Santa Clara. The fathers were convinced that Captain Rivera would approve their project after learning the wishes of the viceroy (his superior).

They waited several weeks for Captain Fernando Rivera y Moncada to send word of his arrival. After no word was received, they decided that formal dedication of Mission San Francisco de Asís would take place in October. Within a year Fr. Palou sent another padre to establish the seventh mission in the chain at Santa Clara while he remained at Dolores. After the death of Fr. Serra in 1784, Fr. Palou briefly served at Carmel as president of the Franciscan missions in California. He retired to Mexico City and wrote a detailed historical account of the California missions.

The mission at Laguna de los Dolores soon became popular with the local natives of the San Francisco region. The mission system offered them food and protection from their enemies. These natives were the least gifted of all of the coastal Indians in the area of survival and they also left much to be desired as converts to the Catholic religion. They did not seem to understand the complex social and religious concepts of the Spaniards nor did they seem concerned with them.

At Dolores, many of the supposedly converted Indians would leave the mission without any apparent reason. The padres never knew whether their Indian workmen would perform their tasks or flee. The Indians were torn between the nearby presidio and the self-indulgent life of other Indians living in the region. The manner in which the fathers handled the runaway Indians is the basis of many charges of cruelty brought against the Franciscans.

San Francisco de Asís

Name ______________________

Date ______________________

The 6th of 21 Spanish/Catholic Missions

At Dolores, the desertion of the converted Indians, as well as other circumstances, threatened the very existence of the mission. In addition to the problem of the runaway workers, the mission was built on a narrow peninsula. The nearby ocean produced recurring fog and this placed limitations on the size and nature of crops the mission could produce. Also, the steady growth of the nearby civilian pueblo cut off growth to the north. To the south were mud flats and the missions of Santa Clara and San José, which also hindered its expansion. Dolores never prospered agriculturally or financially like other missions in the chain. In addition to the above problems, disease — especially measles — killed many of the Indians living at the settlement. This left surviving Indians wondering if they were really supposed to be at the mission.

The military officers got tired of constantly sending soldiers out to retrieve the runaway Indians. After a time this caused bitterness to grow between the padres and the presidio. Both sides realized that something had to be done about the behavior of the Indians. A mission rancho (*asístencia* in Spanish) was set up on the north side of the bay near San Rafael. The climate and soil at the San Rafael rancho was better than that on the peninsula. A Franciscan father who had a knowledge of medicine was placed in charge of the rancho.

Later, an impatient Franciscan father proposed to abandon both Dolores and the San Rafael asístencia and move to a third location at Sonoma. The governor approved the idea immediately and the move was under way before the president of the California missions, Father Vincent Sarría, discovered what was happening. He was astonished and pointed out that the action taken was beyond the authority of even the governor. After much **debate**, it was decided that all three sites would remain as missions. It was also decided to give the Indians their choice as to which mission they would like to live on. In this way, Mission San Rafael Arcángel and Mission San Francisco de Solano in Sonoma came into being as the northernmost and last of the California missions chain.

From the time of the compromise to 1834, Dolores met with misfortune after misfortune. By the time the land reforms were put into effect, there was hardly anything left of the mission except the buildings. When California became part of the United States, Mission San Francisco de Asís (Dolores) was given back to the Catholic Church. It did not take long for the settlement of Yerba Buena, now called San Francisco, to grow around the mission. Several years later a forceful earthquake hit San Francisco. All of the buildings around the mission were in ruins while Dolores remained untouched. ❖

Mission Dolores about 1782.

San Francisco de Asís

Name ______________________

Date ______________________

QUOTEFALLS PUZZLES

The 6th of 21 Spanish/Catholic Missions

Here's how to complete these puzzles.

Write the letters in the squares below them in order to solve the *Quote Falls Puzzles* correctly. One sentence from the pages of this mission was used to create each of the puzzles. We tried to use exact quotes, but most often had to omit or add certain words, or combine a couple sentences together in order to make the puzzles shorter and/or fit correctly. Cross off the letters as you use them in order to keep track of the ones you have not used. Note that a gray square separates words, and some words are continued onto the next line.

Puzzle #1

Puzzle #2

		A		V	E	N				M	E	N	T	S			
M	S	S	I	P	O	I	Y	D	O	L	P	R	E	E	R	N	T
S	I	H	S	I	P	R	N	G	I	C	O	O	R	T	A	W	A

Puzzle #3

I	C	K	E		E	R			E	T		R			F	I	S	A	I	C	I	S				
D	O	U	L	T	U	S	A	N	O	Y	H	E	R		M	O	N	S	N	R	N	A		A	G	
L	I	L	O	R	T	H	E	L	L	V	E	O	R	P	R	I	S	P	E	O	E	D	L	L	Y	R

Puzzle #4

T		E		M	I			N	A	N		T	Y	S		E			O		A	N	E					
E	C	L	O	O	N	L	F	R	O	T		V	H	S	T	F	M	E	D	F	M	E	D	E	P		O	T
E	H	T	I	C	A	S	S	I	O	M	I	S	E	E	I	R	O	O	N	E	F	I	R	S	D	R	T	H

Puzzle #5

	E		G				E			R	F			O		T	A					B		S			
T	I	N	N		V	H	W	H	N	S	A	S	C	Y	A	V	E	E	U	P	R	W	E	R	L	T	N
C	F	O	A	T	D	O	R	S	A	O	T	N	P	G	V	E	H	N	Y	O	O	D	E	D	T	E	H
S	A	I	R	N	T	F	C	A	F	C	I	I	T	I	S	C	R	T	R	E	B	Y	E	A	I	A	R

Name ______________________________

Date ______________________________

The 6th of 21 Spanish/Catholic Missions

The Mission Today

Most of the buildings of the mission compound have been destroyed over the years, but the mission church has changed very little since the 1790s, in spite of the drastic changes all around it. It is the oldest standing building in San Francisco, but the church and part of the cemetery are all that remain of the original mission compound.

As early as 1876 the chapel was considered too small to serve as a parish church because of the rapid growth of the city of San Francisco. A large Victorian-style church was built right next to the old mission church. The earthquake of 1906 didn't damage the mission church, but the larger church, known as Mission Dolores Basilica, was destroyed and had to be rebuilt. Unlike most of the other missions, Mission Dolores has never had to be restored, and what remains has been preserved in almost its original state. However, in 1917 steel beams covered with cement were added to strengthen the exterior, with steel **trestle** supports shoring up the roof. The earthquake of 1989 weakened the structure and $2.5 million was spent to stabilize the building, restore the interior, and repair the gravestones in the historic cemetery. ❖

The above picture shows the typical room of the Franciscan padres.
As you can see, most of them lived modestly with very few worldly possessions.

Mission San Francisco de Asís
(Mission Dolores)
3321 16th Street
San Francisco, CA 94114
Phone: 415.621.8203

San Francisco de Asís

Name ______________________

Date ______________________

REVIEW QUESTIONS

Write the correct answer in the space provided.

1. The sixth California mission, founded in ____________, was ____________ ______________________. It was named for ____________ ______________________, but is better known by its nickname, Mission ______________, which means "sorrows".

2. Features at this mission include an ______________ where sick native Indians were cared for, and a ______________, where more than 5,000 Indians were buried.

3. This mission was a center of trade being a shipping point for goods such as ______________ and ______________ back to Spain and England.

4. The mission church withstood the ______________ of 1906, but the larger church known as ______________ was destroyed.

5. Explain why this mission did not prosper as the others did.

____

____

____

____

6. Describe what the campanario looked like at Mission Dolores.

____

____

7. Explain why the native people were not good converts to Catholicism.

____

____

____

____

8. List some of the misfortunes that happened to Mission Dolores.

____

____

☆☆ Bonus Activity

Use another resource and write a report on one of the people mentioned in this section, ship building, the Franciscan Order, Spain, St. Francis of Assisi, the history or process of making leather, or native people to the area. Draw maps and pictures for your report.

Mission #7

San Juan Capistrano

Founded November 1, 1776

Print the names of the missions on the correct lines. (You may need to look back at a previously finished section/map.)

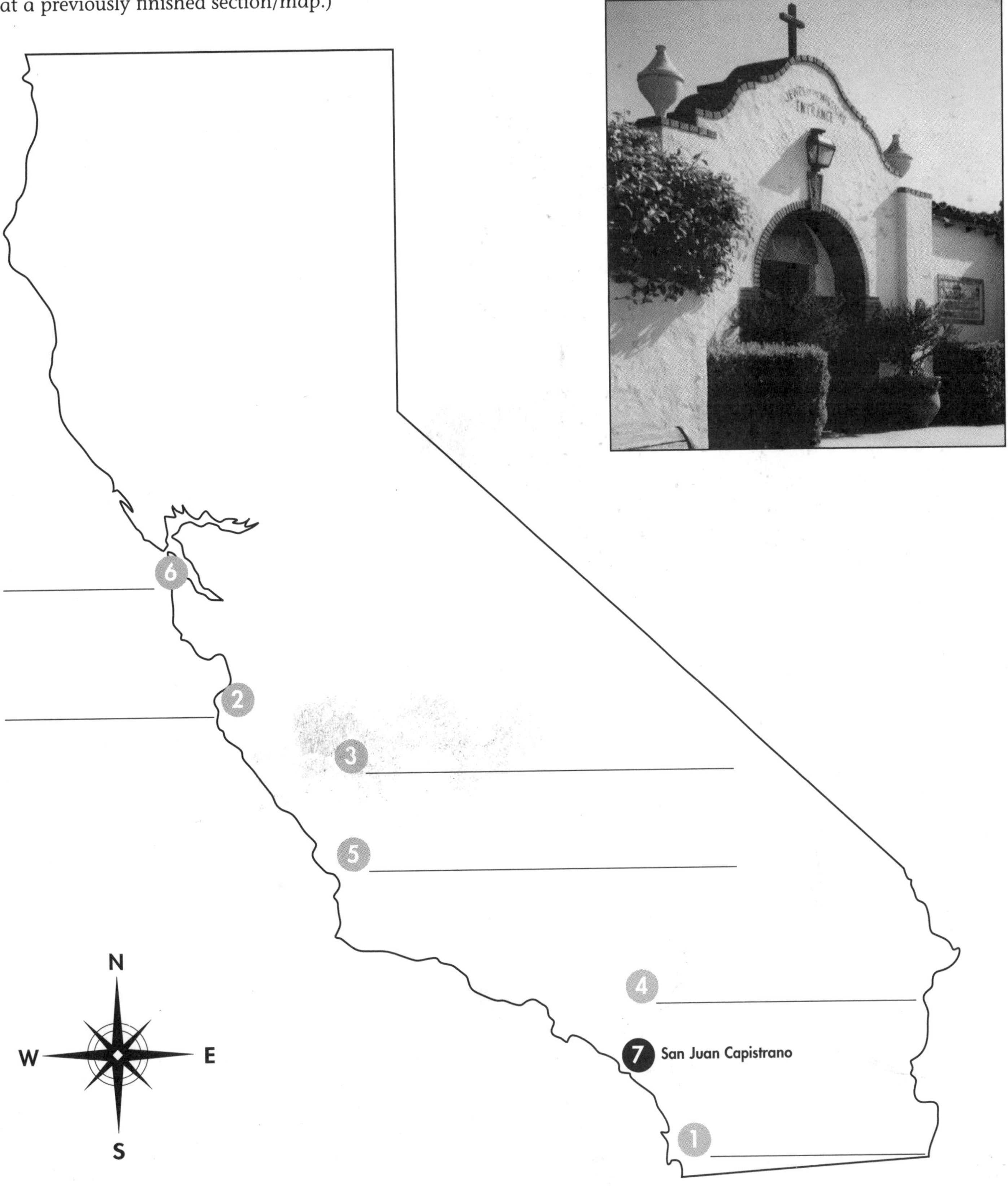

New Words to Learn:

Find the words in the glossary or a dictionary and write the meanings on the line.

1. **barracks:** ______________________________
2. **cruciform:** ______________________________
3. **crusade:** ______________________________
4. **economy:** ______________________________
5. **erosion:** ______________________________
6. **feeble:** ______________________________
7. **gild**(ed): ______________________________
8. **nave:** ______________________________
9. **noble:** ______________________________
10. **transept:** ______________________________

① ______________________________

Mission #7 — Founded November 1, 1776

Layout of the Mission Grounds

CA ②

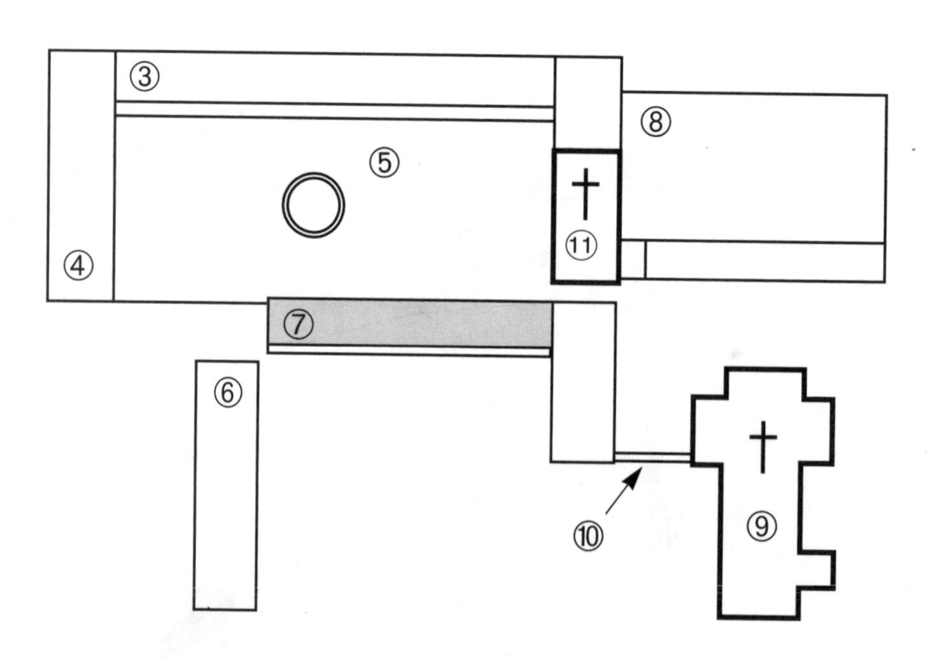

This was likely the layout of the mission compound before the earthquake of 1812.

San Juan Capistrano

Name ______________________

Date ______________________

Named for Saint John of Capistrano, Italy. He was born in 1385 of **noble** birth, studied law, and was named governor of the village. He organized a **crusade** against the Turks and turned them back at Belgrade.

The 7th of 21 Spanish/Catholic Missions

Design of the Mission

Church: (approximate outside measurements) 180 feet long and 30 feet wide.

Mission San Juan Capistrano is also known as the *Great Stone Church.* It is made of sandstone brought in from a distance of six miles. The sandstone is held together with limestone mortar.

Design:

The church is a Cathedral-like style with a **cruciform** or cross design. (Only one other mission along El Camino Real has a similar design.) The roof was constructed using seven masonry domes, five over the long **nave** of the church and one over each wing of the **transept**. The expert stonemason from Mexico, Isidor Aguilar, was in charge of the sophisticated design and construction of elaborate stone. This huge stone church took nine years to complete, and is the most impressive building in the whole mission chain.

Walls: The walls are as much as seven feet thick in various places.

Campanario:

At one time, the Great Stone Church had a massive bell tower. It was 120 feet tall with a **gilded** rooster weather vane on top. It held four bells cast in 1796 and 1804. These bells (two large and two smaller) now hang in a low campanario.

Mission Compound:

An irregularly shaped compound — each side had a different length — was built around a patio. The compound covered about an acre of land. There were living quarters, buildings for storage of ammunition and other goods, and workshops where candles, blankets, hats, shoes, and soap were made. There was a **barracks** for the soldiers who protected the mission. There was also a jail on the compound.

Mission Grounds:

From its beginning Mission San Juan Capistrano was prosperous with its fields of grain, vegetables, and fruit. The climate was moderate, and water was easy to get from the nearby streams. Twenty thousand head of cattle and sheep grazed on the mission's eight ranchos (covering what is now Orange County). The selling of hides to New England shoe factories provided much of the mission's wealth. The stiff hides were thrown down from the top of the cliffs to the beach 280 feet below, where they were loaded on to cargo ships and sent to New England.

Do these things using the map provided. (Use the map on page 68.)

1. Write **Mission San Juan Capistrano** ①, **cattle brand** ②, **workshops** ③, **storerooms** ④, **patio** ⑤, **soldiers' barracks** ⑥, **padres' living quarters** ⑦, **cemetery** ⑧, **Great Stone Church** ⑨, **bell wall** ⑩, and **Serra Church** ⑪ by the correct number.
2. Do your best job if you color the map.

San Juan Capistrano

Also known as "Jewel of the Missions"

Name ______________________

Date ______________________

The 7th of 21 Spanish/Catholic Missions

Early History

San Juan Capistrano is the only mission that was founded twice. The first occasion was in 1775, after Fr. Junípero Serra, president of the missions, convinced Captain Rivera that a mission was needed between San Diego and San Gabriel, which was more than a day's journey by walking or horseback. Fr. Serra sent Fr. Fermín Lasuén from Serra's headquarters in Carmel to San Juan Capistrano. With the help of a small band of soldiers from San Diego, they set up a cross and dedicated the new mission on October 30, 1775.

Eight days after the dedication, news arrived from Mission San Diego which halted the mission's brief existence. Indians had attacked and killed one of the San Diego padres. Such information in the early days of the colonization of California was very serious because any hostile Indian attacks could have destroyed established outposts and ended Spanish occupation. As a safeguard, Fr. Lasuén and his party buried the bells, took the rest of their goods, and rushed back to the presidio in San Diego.

It took a year before the padres decided it was peaceful enough to return to Capistrano. This time Fr. Serra headed the founding party. When they arrived at the former site, Fr. Serra was pleased to see the cross still standing. The party recovered the bells, hung them from a tree, and mission life began again. The date of the second founding is given as November 1, 1776. A year later, the first adobe church was built. In 1791, the bells were removed from the tree on which they hung and were placed in a tower.

By 1797, the growth of the mission led to plans for a larger church. Isidor Aguilar, an expert stonemason from Mexico, was hired to supervise the construction. He incorporated a design into the structure which has not been found in any other mission. Instead of the usual flat roof, the San Juan Capistrano church ceiling was divided into six huge domes. To provide stone for the construction, the converted Indians spent endless days dragging boulders from the surrounding area. Limestone was gathered and crushed into powder to make a mortar which proved to be more resistant to **erosion** than the stone itself.

It took nine years to complete the church. Unfortunately for the mission, Aguilar died three years before the completion. The padres and Indians carried on the work. However, without experienced supervision, irregular measurements of the walls and ceiling resulted, (forcing the addition of a seventh dome) detracting from the workmanship.

Mission San Juan Capistrano campanario.

San Juan Capistrano

Name ________________________

Date ________________________

The 7th of 21 Spanish/Catholic Missions

The church was finished in 1806, but the inhabitants living on the mission were unable to enjoy their building for long. In 1812, a huge earthquake brought the church to the ground and killed 40 converted Indians. The disappointed and exhausted missionaries never attempted to rebuild the fallen building. They returned to the original little church for worship. From then on, only construction that was absolutely necessary was performed.

In 1818, Mission San Juan Capistrano was visited by California's only pirate, Bouchard. He had two ships that were used to attack missions along California's coast. Bouchard attacked California because of Spain's occupation in the region. He fought in the name of a South American province that was engaged in a revolt against Spain. In reality, his connection with the revolution provided him with a convenient excuse for attacking the settlements. News of the attacks reached Padre Geronimo Boscano at the mission. He led the Indians living at the settlement inland and out of danger. The few guards left at the mission made a **feeble** attempt to hold off the pirates. This angered the pirates even more, and as a result, they did greater damage. When the party returned from their escape, the padres blamed the soldiers more than the pirates for the damage they found.

After the arrival of the new Mexican Governor Echeandia in 1824, a difficult period began. He issued a statement (decree of secularization) advising the Indians that they did not have to follow the commands of the Franciscans. Thus, the discipline at Mission San Juan Capistrano began to break down — and the mission's **economy** depended on strict rules and regulations. When California's new Governor Figueroa chose the mission at Capistrano as the site for a pueblo of free Indians in 1833, mission activity had all but ended.

Though the governor's attempt to give the Indians an opportunity to be independent was genuine, no legal safeguards were provided which would allow them time to make the appropriate adjustments necessary. Had he lived long enough, the governor might have been successful in protecting the Indians' share of mission properties, but he died less than three years after establishing the pueblo. The mission land soon fell into the hands of white settlers. The last of Mission San Juan Capistrano's property was disposed of in 1845 when California's Governor Pio Pico sold it to his brother-in-law and a partner. ❖

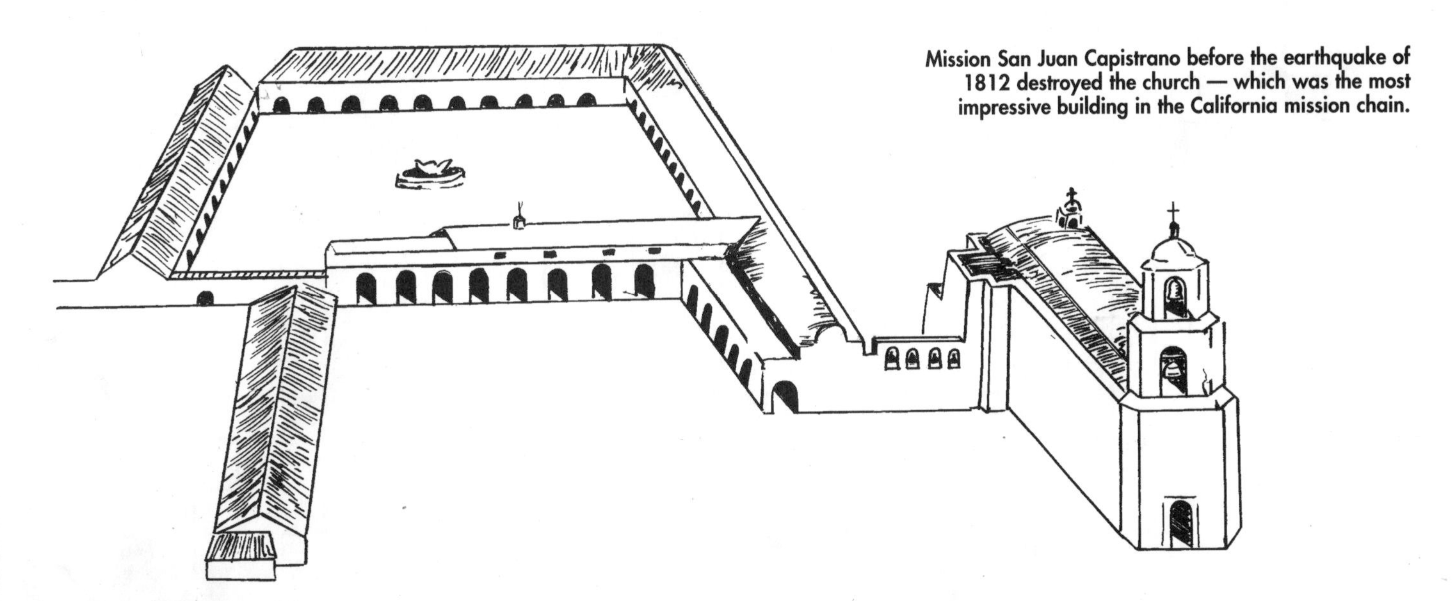

Mission San Juan Capistrano before the earthquake of 1812 destroyed the church — which was the most impressive building in the California mission chain.

San Juan Capistrano

Name ____________________

Quotefalls Puzzles

Date ____________________

The 7th of 21 Spanish/Catholic Missions

Here's how to complete these puzzles.

Write the letters in the squares below them in order to solve the *Quote Falls Puzzles* correctly. One sentence from the pages of this mission was used to create each of the puzzles. We tried to use exact quotes, but most often had to omit or add certain words, or combine a couple sentences together in order to make the puzzles shorter and/or fit correctly. Cross off the letters as you use them in order to keep track of the ones you have not used. Note that a gray square separates words, and some words are continued onto the next line.

Puzzle #1

T	E	E		C		A	N	A		H	A	D				G		O			T		R	
B	S	L	E	R		W	E	A	N	A	R	R	V	A	H	E	L	D	N	E	O	U	P	
O	H	T	L	S	A	M	P	D	T	H	E	I	O	A	N	E	I	L	D	F	D	O	R	O
t	h	e	■	sa										■					■					■
					■				■				■		■							■		
					■												■			■				■

Puzzle #2

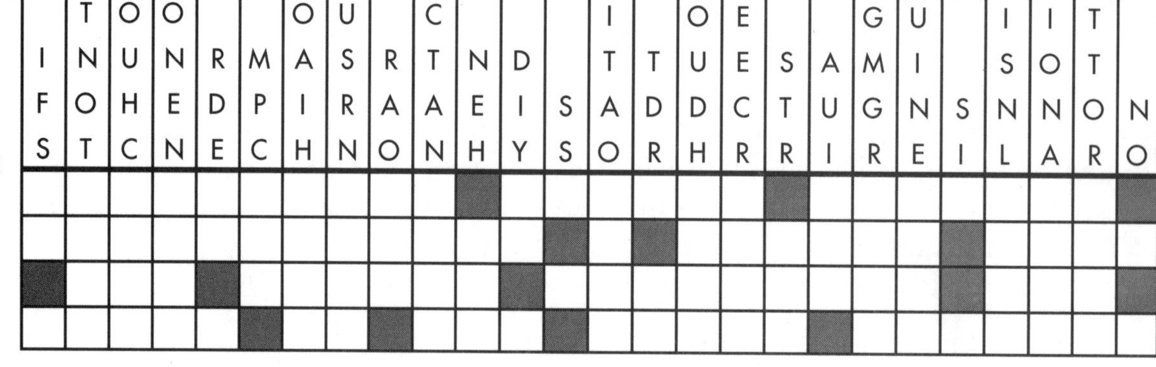

	T	O	O			O	U		C				I		O	E			G	U		I	I	T	
I	N	U	N	R	M	A	S	R	T	N	D		I	T	U	E	S	A	M	I		S	O	T	
F	O	H	E	D	P	I	R	A	A	E	I	S	A	D	D	C	T	U	G	N	S	N	N	O	N
S	T	C	N	E	C	H	N	O	N	H	Y	S	O	R	H	R	R	I	R	E	I	L	A	R	O
										■							■								■
												■		■							■				
■				■							■										■				■
					■			■				■						■							

Puzzle #3

		H		O				E			T	F	D		N			A	T										
N	N	D	O	T	N	I	F	O	S		D	H	I		R	I	D	S	E	T	N		K	N	D		T	I	O
L	E	E	H	S	T	D	A	O	F	N	A	D	T	E	M	A	S	R	I	S	A	C	A	I	C		K	I	E
E	I	G	W	L	Y	E	L	Y	U	I	N	E	E	A	P	S	T	H	E	O	D	E	D	E	D	A	T	H	L
					■					■						■				■									
	■								■								■									■			
■						■								■								■				■			
			■				■			■				■							■	■	■	■	■	■	■	■	■

Puzzle #4

	H			S	S		T			L		C	E	M	H		T			K					
N	H	E		M	T	S	T			C	P	M	P	S	S	I	O		A	B	U	L	I	D	
T	Y	E	A	L	O	O	N	O	I	C	O	U	R	L	I	T	E	E	R	E	A	I	L	N	E
T	G	E	A	R	O	N	G	E	E	M	H	R	A	C	E	N	V	O	O	N	D	N	I	S	I
			■						■							■				■					
■						■			■									■				■			■
			■					■											■						
		■						■			■							■					■	■	

Name ______________________

Date ______________________

The Mission Today

In 1865, part of the former mission holdings were returned to the Catholic Church and some attempts were made to stop the decay of the buildings. However, the results were ineffective and deterioration of the mission continued until 1895, when Charles Fletcher Lummis set up more permanent protection of the historical landmark. (Lummis was founder of The Landmarks Club.) No attempt has ever been made to rebuild the Great Stone Church, and its ruins have changed little over time.

In 1910, with the arrival of secular Father O'Sullivan, the restoration of Mission San Juan Capistrano truly began to take hold. He realized how historically important the mission was to the people of the area, the Catholic Church, and California. He worked untiringly to make a great monument out of the former mission. In 1922 he discovered the original adobe church which had been used as a granary and storeroom. Fr. O'Sullivan's restoration efforts produced the beautiful church that stands in the grounds today. This little church is the only one left in existence where Fr. Junípero Serra is known to have conducted Mass. It is the oldest building in California, built in 1777, and is known as *Father Serra's Church*. The church has an ornate altar, made over 300 years ago in Spain. The statue of Fr. Serra and a native youth near the mission entrance and the Moorish-style fountain in the garden plaza were added in the 1920s.

Buildings around the quadrangle have been restored over the years to show what mission life was really like. A museum displays artifacts of Native Americans, Spaniards, and Mexicans. Other buildings are reproductions of the originals that show soap and candle making workshops, vats for tanning hides, and metal-working furnaces. The gardens and pools throughout the grounds make the ruins of the Great Stone Church look beautiful to all visitors. The bells in the nearby campanario, erected in 1813, are still used to ring the mission's calls.

One of the best-known features of San Juan Capistrano is the return of the swallows to build their mud nests in the arches of the ruins. Each year, for as long as people can remember, the swallows have returned around March 19th, St. Joseph's Day. The swallows stay at San Juan Capistrano until about October 19th, St. John's Day. ❖

This photo shows the inside of the courtyard in the late 1800s.

Mission San Juan Capistrano
Corner of Camino Capistrano
and Ortega Highway
P.O. Box 697 or 313
San Juan Capistrano, CA 92693
Phone: 949.248.2048
www.missionsjc.com

Name ______________________

Date ______________________

Review Questions

Write the correct answer in the space provided.

1. The ____________ California mission was San Juan Capistrano, founded first in the year ____________, then again on November 1, ______________. It is also known as the ____.

2. At this mission is the oldest building in California, known as ______________ ____.

3. An expert stonemason from Mexico directed the building of a ____________ ____________________, which took ____________ years to complete. Six years after it was finished, an ______________________ caused it to collapse, trapping and killing ____.

4. A very profitable industry at this mission was selling ______________ that were shipped to New England for use in making ______________.

5. In 1895, ______________________________________ founded The Landmark Club, which preserved the mission as a historical landmark.

6. Explain why this mission had to be founded twice.

____

____

____

7. Explain why the workmanship of parts of the church was worse than others.

____

____

____

8. Explain why the mission's church is important today.

____

____

____

Note: You can find more information about Mission San Juan Capistrano in literature such as *Two Years Before the Mast* by Richard Henry Dana and *Song of the Swallows* by Leo Politi.

☆☆ **Bonus Activity**

Use another resource and write a report on one of the people mentioned in this section, candle making, swallows Italy, Turkey (Turks of 1300s), the history and/or process of making shoes, or native people to the area. Draw maps and pictures for your report.

Mission #8

Santa Clara de Asís

Founded January 12, 1777

Print the names of the missions on the correct lines. (You may need to look back at a previously finished section/map.)

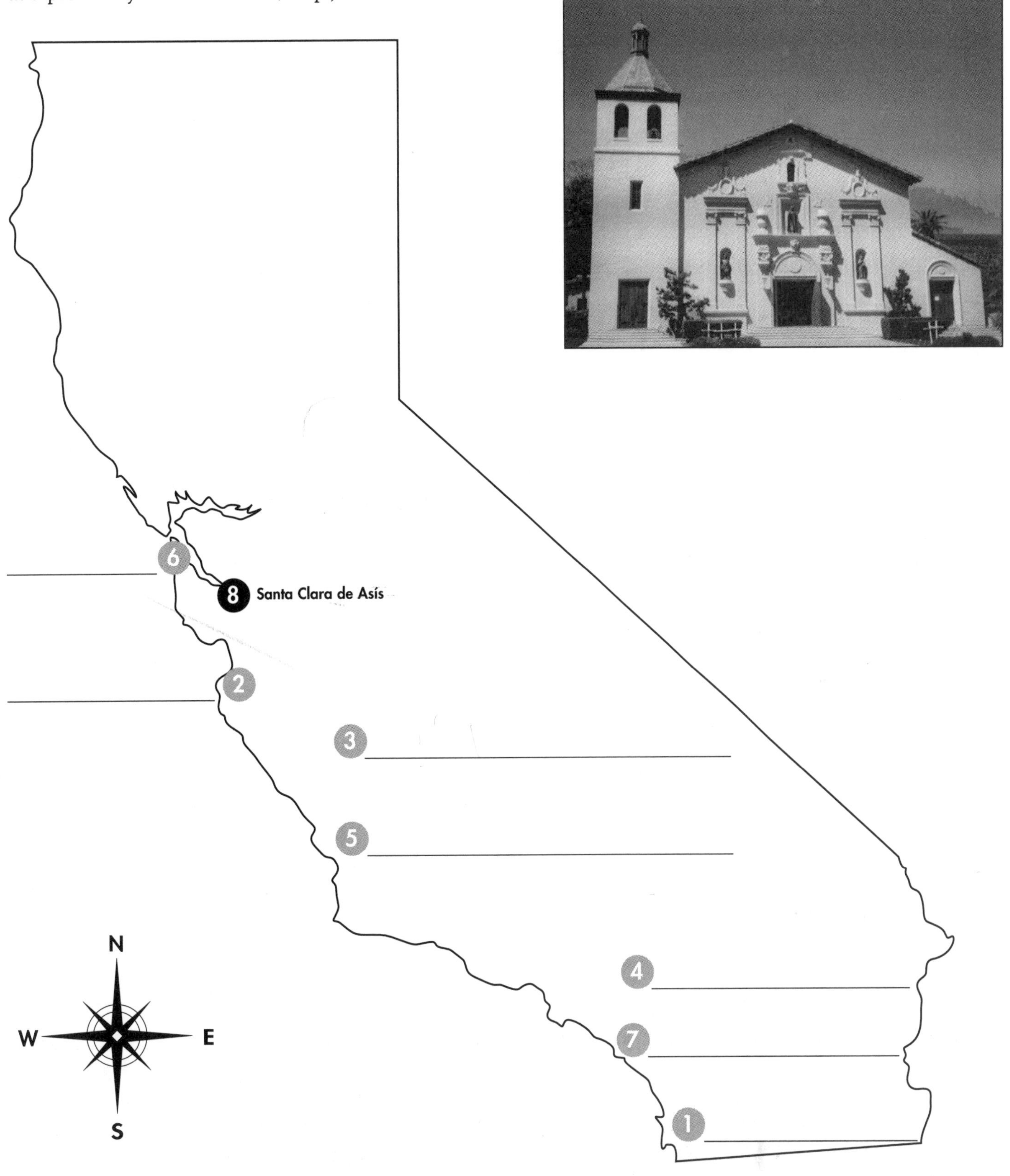

New Words to Learn:

Find the words in the glossary or a dictionary and write the meanings on the line.

1. **artisan**(s): ____________________
2. **dispatch**(ed): ____________________
3. **emigrant**(s): ____________________
4. **institution:** ____________________
5. **jurisdiction:** ____________________
6. **massacre:** ____________________
7. **neophyte:** ____________________
8. **nun**(s): ____________________
9. **plague**(d): ____________________
10. **renown**(ed): ____________________

① ____________________

Mission #8 — Founded January 12, 1777

Layout of the Mission Grounds

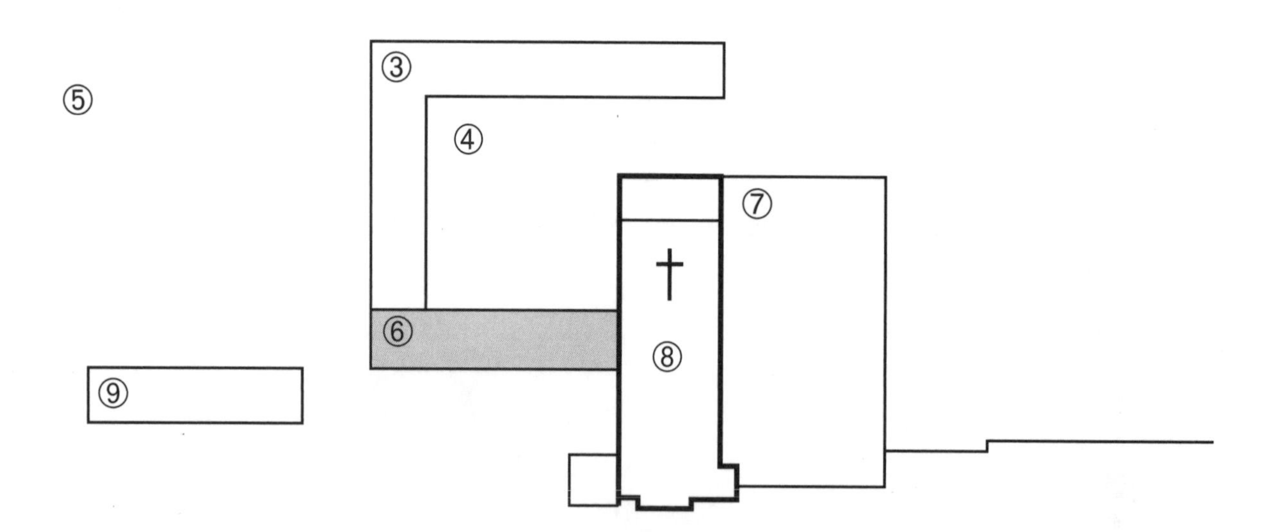

This diagram shows part of the mission grounds about 1830.

Santa Clara de Asís

Name ______________________________

Date ______________________________

This was the first mission named for a female. Clara was born of noble parents in Assisi, Italy in 1194. She founded her own order of **nuns**, the Poor Clares, which was based on the Order of St. Francis, or the Franciscans.

The 8th of 21 Spanish/Catholic Missions

Design of the Mission

Church: (approximate outside measurements) 100 feet long, 44 feet wide, and 25 feet high.
The fifth and most important church was built in 1825 of adobe bricks with a tile roof.

Style:
A simple architectural style was ornamented with paintings, both inside and outside. A professional artist, Agustín Dávila, was brought from Mexico to design and supervise the paintings. The redwood slabs that formed the ceiling show hosts of angels and saints. There are designs on each side of the entrance that look like pillars and statues. The colors are bright reds, yellows, and blues that were made from local minerals and mixed with juice from the maguey cactus. Dávila only supervised the work of the native **artisans** who did the actual painting.

Walls: The walls are wider at the bottom and narrow to only two feet at the top.

Campanario:
The bell tower is a square tower built to the north (left) of the entrance. Two of the three bells were gifts from the King of Spain in 1799.

Mission Compound:
The buildings which formed the quadrangle were the living quarters for Spanish soldiers and Franciscan priests, a guardhouse, workshops, and kitchens. The native workers of Mission Santa Clara were excellent weavers. Their quality of workmanship was **renowned** throughout the missions along El Camino Real. They also made candles and produced good wine and brandy. Mission Santa Clara's greatest accomplishment was in the number of converts; more than 1,200 native workers lived at the mission.

Mission Grounds:
The mission was blessed with rich soil and an ideal climate for agriculture. Its fields and orchards produced grain, peaches, pears, figs, and grapes. Its nearby ranches had 5,000 head of cattle and 1,200 sheep, which added to the mission's prosperity. In an attempt to improve the relationships between the growing Pueblo of San José and the mission, the mission built a grand avenue connecting the two. This attractive avenue was named *The Alameda*, and was lined with a triple row of willow trees.

Do these things using the map provided. (Use the map on page 76.)

1. Write **Mission Santa Clara de Asís** ①, **cattle brand** ②, **workshops** ③, **patio** ④, **vineyards** ⑤, **padres' living quarters** ⑥, **cemetery** ⑦, **church** ⑧, and **soldiers' barracks** ⑨ by the correct number.
2. Do your best job if you color the map.

Santa Clara de Asís

Also known as "Mission Santa Clara"

Name ______________________

Date ______________________

The 8th of 21 Spanish/Catholic Missions

Early History

In the summer of 1776, the viceroy of Mexico sent a letter to Fr. Serra explaining his wishes to establish two more missions. One was to be named after St. Francis and the other after St. Clare. An area south of San Francisco Bay, on the banks of the Guadalupe River, had been selected as the site for Mission Santa Clara. Fr. Palou, was willing to set up his mission at Dolores despite the objections of the military commander — Captain Rivera. However, he decided against the founding of this mission until he had the opportunity to talk with the Captain. His decision to delay the founding of the mission was also because Fr. Serra was in Mexico.

Mission San Francisco (Dolores) was three months old before Fr. Palou met with the military commander, Captain Rivera. He came up the coast and gave his approval, even though late, on everything Fr. Palou had accomplished on his own. The captain's new attitude indicated that he had been "scolded"' by the viceroy of Mexico regarding the establishing of the missions. Rivera seemed happy with Mission Dolores and sent Lieutenant Moraga and Father de Peña to establish the Mission of Santa Clara.

At the time Capt. Rivera gave his belated approval of Mission Santa Clara, he was in the process of being transferred. This was due to Fr. Serra's opposition to the captain and his negative attitude. Fr. Serra had gone to the viceroy of Mexico in Mexico City and voiced his disapproval of the Captain. Orders were given removing Capt. Rivera from military command of Alta California. In this position he had been under the **jurisdiction** of Governor Felipe de Neve in Lower California. The new orders from the Viceroy moved the capital of California and de Neve to Monterey and Rivera was transferred to Loreto. Loreto was the former capital of the coastal provinces. In his new post, Rivera had little authority and de Neve's first order to Rivera was to result in Rivera's death.

The captain was instructed to take a company of soldiers to the northwest provinces of Mexico and bring as many families as possible to settle in California. Most of the people he found were living in poverty. Only a few went with him in hopes of finding a new beginning in the new land. When Rivera arrived at the Colorado River, he sent the **emigrants** on to the coast, escorted by part of his soldiers. He planned to continue on and find additional colonists with the rest of his men. However, after the separation of the two parties, he and all of his men were killed by the Yuma Indians in a surprise uprising.

The mission over 100 years ago.

Santa Clara de Asís

Name ____________________

Date ____________________

The 8th of 21 Spanish/Catholic Missions

Two other mission settlements were also attacked and destroyed by the Yuma. These were not part of the El Camino Real chain, but Father Garces was killed in the attack. (Fr. Garces' journals were great resources recording the history of the California mission chain.) After the destroying of these soldiers and settlements, the authorities in Mexico closed the overland route from Mexico to California. From this time onward, the Spanish colony of California had to depend on the sea routes. The abandonment of the Colorado River crossing by Mexico left the way open to the east. The trail to Mexico was reopened by the United States in 1849.

Mission Santa Clara de Asís was founded as the eighth mission in the growing chain of Franciscan settlements on January 12, 1777. In less than six months Lieutenant Moraga brought settlers up from San Gabriel. He established a new pueblo close to the mission. (Moraga's pueblo today is the prosperous city of San José.) The padres did not like the idea of the pueblo because they knew it would distract their **neophytes**. They also knew it would cause disputes over land boundaries. It was not until 1801 that the boundaries between the mission and the pueblo would be officially fixed.

In 1784, the mission was moved to a new site on higher ground, after a series of disastrous floods. The new buildings were built with the aid of skilled workers. They were unusually elaborate and beautiful. The new mission served the Franciscan fathers until 1818, when it was destroyed by an earthquake.

In May, 1805, a rumor was spread by some converted Indians that the Indians who had not been converted were planning a **massacre** of the missionaries. Word of the story was sent to the presidios at Monterey and San Francisco and troops were immediately **dispatched** to Santa Clara. However, nothing ever came of the rumor.

One night in 1814, Father José Viader was attacked by a huge Indian named Marcelo and two of his companions. Fr. Viader was strong and athletic and beat the three attackers to the ground and then forgave them. Marcelo became one of the father's most **devoted** friends and followers because of Viader's gestures.

A third set of buildings was built on a site a few miles away. These were finished in 1825 and this church was used for many years (and gave form to the replica built in 1929 that we see today). Eventually, it would be replaced by two more wooden churches, both of which were destroyed by fire. In 1851, long after secularization, the need for English speaking fathers for the new Americans caused the mission to be turned over to the Jesuits for a school. Four years later it became Santa Clara College, and later the present university. Although it was used as an educational **institution** since 1851 by the Jesuits, it was not recognized as a college until 1855. These four years of not being recognized caused it to miss the honor of being California's first institution of higher learning.

As a mission, it prospered and became one of the most successful in the entire chain of missions along the El Camino Real. After 1784, only Mission San Gabriel enjoyed more wealth and prosperity. Mission Santa Clara was blessed with ideal climate and rich, fertile soil for growing crops. It was especially well known throughout the mission chain for the high quality and beauty of its weaving.

In the 1830s, after secularization, Mission Santa Clara's wealth, importance, and influence began to decline rapidly. It no longer functioned as a mission under the authority of Mexico. ❖

Santa Clara de Asís

Name ______________________

Date ______________________

Crossword Puzzle

The 8th of 21 Spanish/Catholic Missions

Note: You will have to read page 81 in order to answer all of the questions in this puzzle.

Across

2. Orders from the viceroy of Mexico moved governor Felipe de Neve and the capital of California to ________ .
4. The ________ of Mexico closed the overland route from Mexico.
6. The ________ of Fr. Garces were great resources telling about the California missions.
7. Fr. Serra voiced his ________ of Captain Rivera to the viceroy.
10. ________ was the capital of the coastal provinces before Monterey.
11. People who leave their homes to settle in a different country.
13. Native workers at Mission Santa Clara were excellent ________ .
14. The avenue between San José and the mission was ________ .
17. The mission was turned over to the ________ to be a school.
18. The mission's greatest accomplishment was the number of ________ who lived there.

Down

1. It was not until 1801 that the ________ between the mission and pueblo were official.
3. Only Mission San Gabriel enjoyed more wealth and ________ .
5. Captain Rivera and all of his men were killed by the ________ Indian nation.
8. It was evident by his new attitude that Captain Rivera was ________ by the viceroy of Mexico about the establishment of the missions in California.
9. Agustín Dávila (an artist from Mexico) only supervised the work of the native ________ who did the actually painting of the church interior.
12. Only Mission San Gabriel enjoyed more ________ and prosperity.
15. The decision to postpone the founding of Mission Santa Clara was partly because Fr. Serra was in ________ .
16. Natural ________ plagued Mission Santa Clara as well as all of the missions along El Camino Real.

Santa Clara de Asís

Name ____________________________

Date ____________________________

The 8th of 21 Spanish/Catholic Missions

The Mission Today

As part of the University of Santa Clara, the church was remodeled several times. Each time some of the original design was lost forever. The adobe walls were replaced by wooden ones; the second campanario of the mission was built on the opposite side of the building from the first one; the roof was widened.

Natural disasters **plagued** this particular mission as they did the other missions along El Camino Real. In 1926 a fire destroyed the church and all of the changes were erased. Students attending the university tried to save as much of the furnishings as possible from the fire. One of the bells was melted in the heat and a second bell was cracked by the heat. However, one bell was spared from consumption by the fire and was hung from a nearby tree. At 8:30 P.M. the night of the fire it rang as loudly as it had every night since 1799. Several years later, King Alfonso XIII of Spain donated a new bell to the mission. The two damaged bells were recast. When the bell tower was rebuilt it had four bells hanging in niches.

In 1929 the church was reconstructed in what is called "a modern interpretation in stucco and concrete" of the 1825 church. More than 12,000 roof tiles were salvaged from the earlier missions and used on the new church, which is larger than the original. Replicas of the ceiling paintings were created. The exterior ornamentation was replaced by stone carvings instead of the original paintings. Over the front entrance is a statue of St. Clare, with St. John and St. Francis on either side; all are carved in pearwood. The interior of the church has been restored in a Victorian style, which retains hardly any of the mission's original atmosphere. However, there are some of the original statues inside the church.

A piece of the cross that was part of the first dedication in 1777 stands in a protective casing in a cross of concrete across from the front of the church entrance. The adobe walls that weren't destroyed in the 1926 fire have been restored. The original church cemetery has been turned into the Mission Rose Garden. Many of the plants used throughout the university grounds today were originally part of the grounds of Mission Santa Clara de Asís. ❖

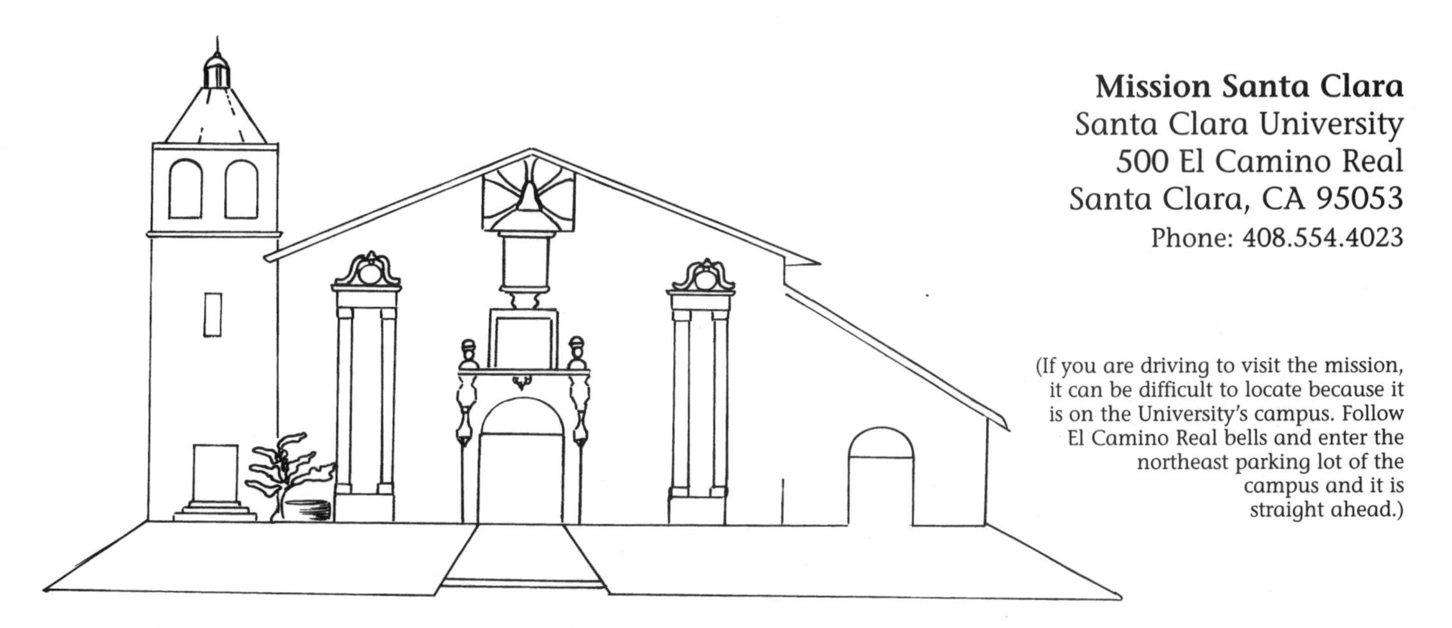

Mission Santa Clara
Santa Clara University
500 El Camino Real
Santa Clara, CA 95053
Phone: 408.554.4023

(If you are driving to visit the mission, it can be difficult to locate because it is on the University's campus. Follow El Camino Real bells and enter the northeast parking lot of the campus and it is straight ahead.)

Santa Clara de Asís

Name ______________________

Date ______________________

REVIEW QUESTIONS

Write the correct answer in the space provided.

1. The eighth California mission was founded on ______________ and named ______________. It was named for Saint ______________, the first female honored by the name of a mission.

2. Lieutenant ______________ founded the nearby pueblo, which is today's prosperous city of ______________.

3. This mission was noted for its production of ______________, ______________, and ______________, and especially for the quality of its ______________. It was also very successful in converting the ______________ to the ______________ faith.

4. This is the only California mission that is part of a college, known as ______________, run by ______________ priests.

5. Retell the story of Fr. Viader and Marcelo, and what resulted from the priest's response to Marcelo's attack.

6. Tell what St. Clara accomplished to become honored as a Catholic saint.

7. Explain why the overland routes from Mexico to California were closed.

Note: The Santa Clara Valley was known for centuries for its abundant agriculture. Now the farms are mostly one, and the area even has a new name *Silicon Valley*.

☆☆ Bonus Activity

Use another resource and write a report on one of the people mentioned in this section, St. Clara, how the Catholic church makes saints, Jesuit Order, the history or process of stucco and/or concrete, or the *Silicon Valley*. Draw maps and pictures for your report.

Mission #9

San Buenaventura

Founded March 31, 1782

Print the names of the missions on the correct lines. (You may need to look back at a previously finished section/map.)

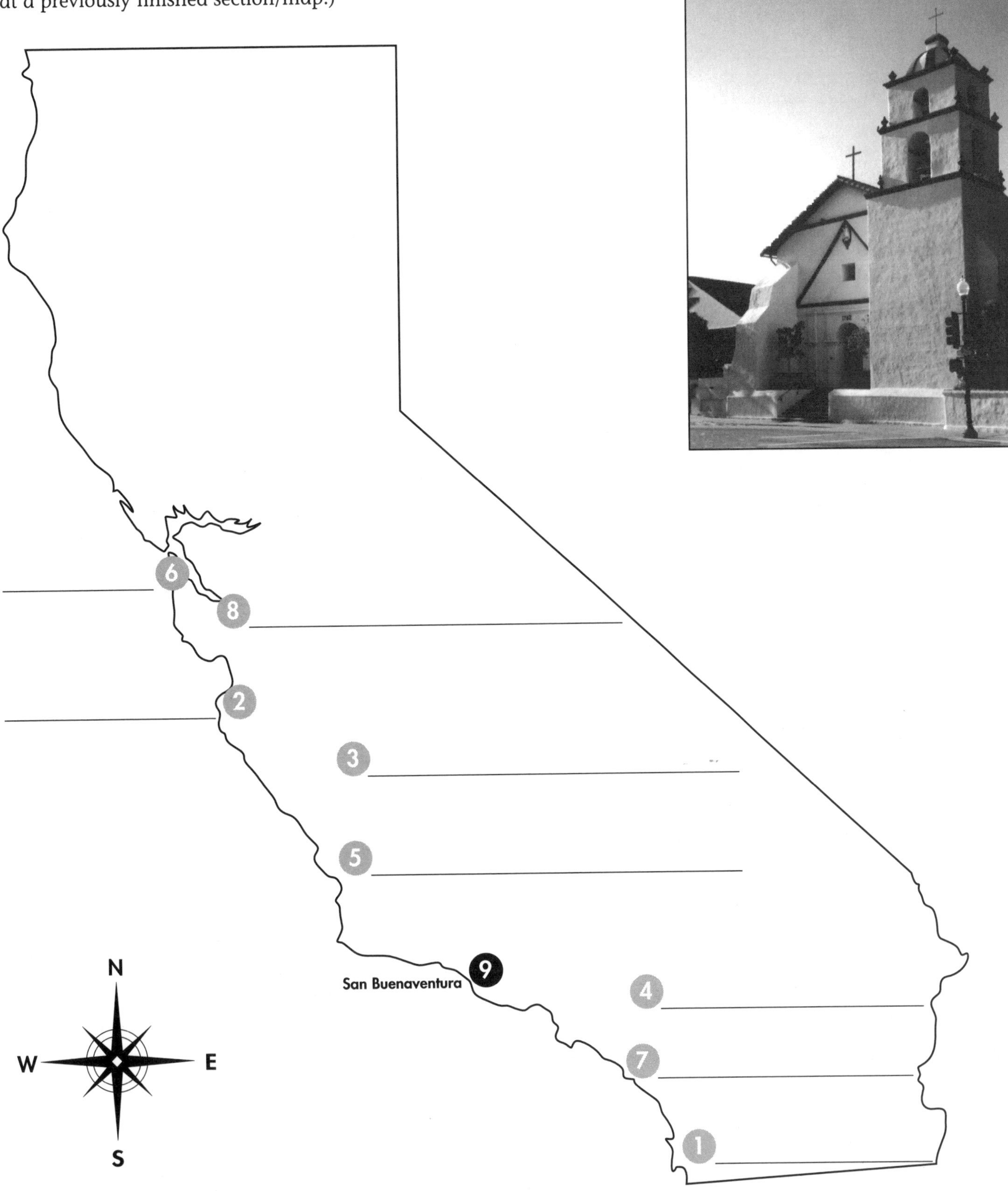

New Words to Learn:

Find the words in the glossary or a dictionary and write the meanings on the line.

1. **colleague**(s): ____________________
2. **conical:** ____________________
3. **defy** (defiance): ____________________
4. **deplete**(ing): ____________________
5. **discretion:** ____________________
6. **flank**(ed): ____________________
7. **industrious:** ____________________
8. **rendezvous:** ____________________

① ____________________

Mission #9 — Founded March 31, 1782

Layout of the Mission Grounds

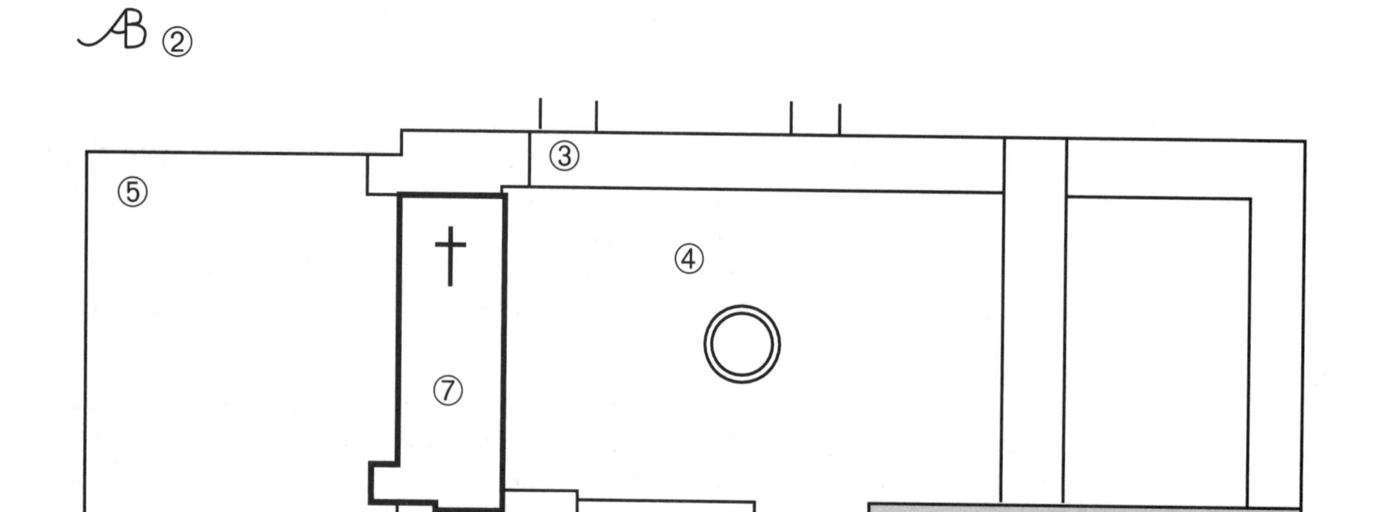

This was the mission quadrangle in the 1820s.

San Buenaventura

Name ______________________

Named for St. Bonaventura, born in Italy in 1221. According to legend, the name Bonaventura was given him when he healed a four year old boy and exclaimed, "Oj Buena Ventura!" (which means Good Fortune).

Date ______________________

The 9th of 21 Spanish/Catholic Missions

Design of the Mission

Church: (approximate outside measurements) 155 feet long, 40 feet wide, and 26 feet high. The mission church is made of adobe bricks and stone. The roof and floors are tile.

Design:

Mission San Buenaventura has the traditional architectural style of many of the other missions along El Camino Real. It is distinguished by a unique triangular design on the **facade**. This may be a religious symbol representing the Holy Trinity. Another interesting architectural feature is the side door situated under a Moorish-style arch and **flanked** by flat ornamental stone columns. There are two curved lines above the door, representing the two rivers that pass on either side of the mission. A heavy stone buttress was built to the left of the entrance to give additional support to the building.

Walls: The walls are six and one half feet thick.

Campanario:

There is a single, tall tower. The tower is quite unusual as it is not symmetrical. The two upper sections are not centered on the lower section. The campanario has five bells; the top bell was made in France in 1956. (This one has an automatic ringing system.) The four bells in the lower section are hand-operated and old (two were cast in 1781, one in 1825, and the fourth one is undated.) The tower is topped by a small dome and cross.

Mission Compound:

The quadrangle was never large, but contained the traditional living quarters for padres and soldiers, **dormitories**, native artisan workshops, and a beautiful garden. The converted Chumash (natives to the region) who worked on the mission preferred to live in their own homes rather than move onto the mission's grounds. Some of the Chumash families built their **conical** huts from willow trees growing near the mission compound.

Mission Grounds:

Mission San Buenaventura was surrounded by beautiful orchards, vineyards, and fields of grain. It was known throughout the mission chain for the abundance of fruits and vegetables it produced, including tropical fruits of bananas, coconuts, figs, and sugarcane. Pears were the mission's specialty crop. Fields extended all the way to the Pacific Ocean. Sailing ships made special efforts to stop at the mission in order to replenish their supplies.

Water System:

Buenaventura was sometimes called *the place of canals*. A reservoir and aqueduct system brought water to the fields, orchards, and mission. One clay pipe was seven miles long. Because the water came from the mouth of a stone horse-head, the reservoir was called *caballo* (Spanish for horse).

Do these things using the map provided. (Use the map on page 84.)

1. Write **Mission San Buenaventura** ①, **cattle brand** ②, **workshops** ③, **patio** ④, **cemetery** ⑤, **padres' living quarters** ⑥, and **church** ⑦ by the correct number.
2. Do your best job if you color the map.

San Buenaventura

Also known as "The Mission by the Sea"

Name ____________________

Date ____________________

The 9th of 21 Spanish/Catholic Missions

Early History

Fr. Serra founded Mission San Buenaventura on Easter Sunday, March 31, 1782. The site had been discovered and claimed for Spain by the great navigator, Juan Rodríguez Cabrillo. This discovery occurred almost 50 years to the day after Christopher Columbus and his three ships landed in the Western Hemisphere.

Even before the very first expedition started for Alta California, the Franciscan missionaries felt that a third mission would be needed half way between San Diego and Monterey. It was their intention to establish this third mission at San Buenaventura. Due to unforeseen circumstances, it was not until 1782 that the opportunity for the actual founding of this mission occurred. In early March of that year, a meeting at Mission San Gabriel took place, including Fr. Serra, three of his **colleagues**, Governor Felipe de Neve, and Lt. José Ortega (whom Fr. Serra wanted to be appointed Governor of California instead of Felipe de Neve).

This meeting between Fr. Serra and Governor de Neve was extremely important to the missionaries. The Governor had been in the territory for almost five years, and for the first time since his arrival, he had agreed to discuss the establishment of a new mission. Fr. Serra was pleased that six new Franciscan padres were being sent from the Franciscan College in Mexico City, but he had to solve some problems before they arrived.

From the viewpoint of the royal authorities in Mexico City, new missions in the California style were too expensive to establish and maintain. The first missions had been supplied mostly with goods taken from the Jesuit missions in Lower California. Now each new mission had to be supplied with materials purchased and shipped from Mexico City. Wars in Europe were **depleting** Spain's treasury and any available funds from Mexico were being sent to Spain, Mexico's mother country. Except for its location, California meant little to the king of Spain because there was nothing in the way of material profit. He felt the money being spent on colonization of California was unnecessary.

This photo show the mission about 100 years ago.

San Buenaventura

Name ____________________

Date ____________________

The 9th of 21 Spanish/Catholic Missions

The Franciscans' position was that all the money was being used from the *Pious Fund*, a fund that was collected privately by the previous missionaries, the Jesuits, to be used only for maintaining the missions of California. However, Spain's Crown had no sympathy for the Franciscan position. In 1493, Pope Alexander VI had issued a decree called the *Patronado* which gave the king of Spain free hand over certain appointments in spreading the Catholic Church in the New World. Because of the Pope's decree, the king argued that the Pious Fund was spent at his **discretion**. And at the present, the king did not want to spend any additional money in California.

The king's position on not wanting to spend money in California led him to support the "civil" point of view. This point of view was that if California could be colonized by distributing land to the new settlers, it meant a less expensive way of protecting the area from other countries colonizing the region. The governors of California always held the position that a few white settlers were more beneficial to the Crown than any number of unpredictable Indians.

The Yuma uprising (read Mission Santa Clara for details) also added to the distrust the Spaniards had for the Indians. Viceroy Bucareli of Mexico adhered to a code of authority which supported the Crown in the use of money and the colonization of California by white settlers. From this code, Governor de Neve formulated new regulations which ordered all future missions be established in the Arizona style. This meant that no mission industries could be founded on Indian labor and only one father was allowed per mission.

The meeting at San Gabriel must have been tense for both Fr. Serra and Governor de Neve. Fr. Serra knew de Neve was instrumental in creating the new regulations while he and the other Franciscans were doing everything they could not to enforce them. The men agreed on the establishment of two new missions; one site was designated as Santa Bárbara and the other site was San Buenaventura. De Neve planned to go with the settlers to Santa Bárbara and set up a presidio nearby. One day after de Neve's party departed for Santa Bárbara, a courier arrived with orders for de Neve and his soldiers to **rendezvous** with Pedro Fages who was coming from Sonora to fight against the Yuma Indians.

In de Neve's absence, Fr. Serra chose to ignore him and proceed to build Mission San Buenaventura according to the original plan — California style, not Arizona style. When de Neve returned several weeks later, everything was running smoothly and the friendly Indians of the area had helped in many areas around the mission, even though none of them had yet been converted to Catholicism. Governor de Neve never said anything about Fr. Serra's **defiance** of the new code. However, the incident resulted in a delay in establishing the next mission at Santa Bárbara.

From the beginning, Mission San Buenaventura grew very quickly. The Indians of the area were exceptionally talented and energetic. The Spaniards called them the *Channel Indians* because the area lies along the Santa Bárbara Channel between the coast of California and the Channel Islands. By 1809, Buenaventura had a great stone and brick church. A reservoir and aqueduct system carried water to the mission's grain fields over a distance of seven miles — all the way to the Pacific Ocean. The mission's prosperity was reported by the English sea captain, George Vancouver, after he visited in 1793. He reported the mission had an abundance of agricultural products. The mission was also fortunate enough to have Father José Senan as its leader as well as to have such **industrious** and cooperative Indians helping.

San Buenaventura

Name ______________________

Date ______________________

The 9th of 21 Spanish/Catholic Missions

The stone face of the church was damaged after the earthquake of 1812. It took almost three years to completely restore the church. The large buttress at the front was added during this time of repair. For six years the mission experienced peace and prosperity. It wasn't until 1818 that the French pirate, Bouchard, brought brutality and violence to the area. The inhabitants of the mission abandoned the settlement for a month because of Bouchard and his men.

In May, 1819, a party of 22 Mojave Indians came to the mission to fraternize with the mission neophytes. The soldiers guarding the mission attempted to stop the Mojaves, which led to a fight and resulted in the death of ten Mojaves and two soldiers. The other twelve Mojaves escaped. After this incident, the Mojaves became bitter enemies of the Spanish.

Secularization of Mission San Buenaventura, which officially took place in June of 1836, was easier and went more smoothly than that which occurred at the other missions. The main reason was the honesty and efficiency of Rafael Gonzales, the head administrator. By the summer of 1845, the mission lands and properties had been completely broken up and sold. It was not until 1862 that the church and a small part of its possessions were returned. ❖

Word Search Puzzle

Find the words listed below in the Word Search Puzzle.

1. ALEXANDER
2. ALTAR
3. ARCHITECTURAL
4. BRUTAL
5. CABALLO
6. CHUMASH
7. CIVIL
8. HEMISPHERE
9. NAVIGATOR
10. ORNAMENTAL
11. PACIFIC
12. PIRATE
13. PRESIDIO
14. PULPIT
15. VENTURA
16. WILLOW
17. YUMA

E	B	A	D	Q	S	T	R	L	B	R	O	T	W	A	P	O
K	O	R	L	N	A	Z	H	G	C	I	Q	I	R	R	C	R
I	V	L	U	T	Q	N	J	F	H	N	L	U	E	T	I	N
Q	P	G	L	T	A	J	B	O	H	L	T	S	H	Q	V	A
Q	I	D	A	A	A	R	T	J	O	N	I	E	D	A	I	M
R	G	N	N	R	B	L	U	W	E	D	M	I	H	G	L	E
O	Z	D	T	S	C	A	T	V	I	I	V	K	I	T	N	N
T	N	E	B	X	N	H	C	O	S	E	Q	E	G	P	W	T
A	T	L	Y	D	K	S	I	P	P	Z	K	M	V	E	D	A
G	H	S	U	A	E	H	H	T	H	U	Y	X	H	V	X	L
I	U	F	P	T	S	E	N	Y	E	C	L	I	L	T	G	J
V	W	P	A	A	R	K	O	B	G	C	I	P	V	X	U	F
A	M	R	M	E	I	B	H	B	G	N	T	F	I	O	C	J
N	I	U	C	G	S	B	J	G	H	R	Y	U	I	T	K	H
P	H	N	C	B	V	E	U	B	E	X	K	K	R	C	W	P
C	Y	U	M	A	E	X	W	M	Y	X	T	B	G	A	A	A
A	L	E	X	A	N	D	E	R	V	B	F	K	V	E	L	P

San Buenaventura

Name ______________________

Date ______________________

The 9th of 21 Spanish/Catholic Missions

The Mission Today

In 1893 Fr. Rubio, the head priest, made extensive changes to the mission. He tore down all of the outer buildings, put in dark stained glass in the church windows after he enlarged them, covered the original Indian designs on the walls with "modern" ones, removed the canopied wooden pulpit, covered the beamed ceiling and the tile floors with wood, white-washed the walls, and removed the Mexican altar.

It took almost 60 years before the mission would look anything like its original form. Restoration began in 1957 and has returned Mission San Buenaventura as much as possible to its 1812 condition and look. The windows were restored to their original size. The wood was removed from the ceiling and floors, revealing the beams and tiles. In 1976 a new pulpit was constructed from pieces of the old one.

Because of Fr. Rubio's ignorance in trying to modernize the mission, none of the original buildings remain except the church on the mission compound. The fields and orchards are now busy streets, modern homes, shopping malls, and other types of buildings we enjoy and use today. An elementary school now covers the mission's cemetery. The city of Ventura has built a beautifully tiled plaza with a fountain across the street from the church's entrance, which has preserved the view from the mission to the ocean.

The museum at the mission displays the work of the Chumash people, who were excellent craftsmen at boatbuilding and wood carving. They also made woven baskets of such high quality that they could hold water.

Some of the more interesting things to see at the mission are the statue of St. Bonaventura in the center niche behind the altar, the old olive press in the garden, and the two wooden bells. These are the only two bells of this type known to be in California. They are lined with metal and were used during special ceremonies. ❖

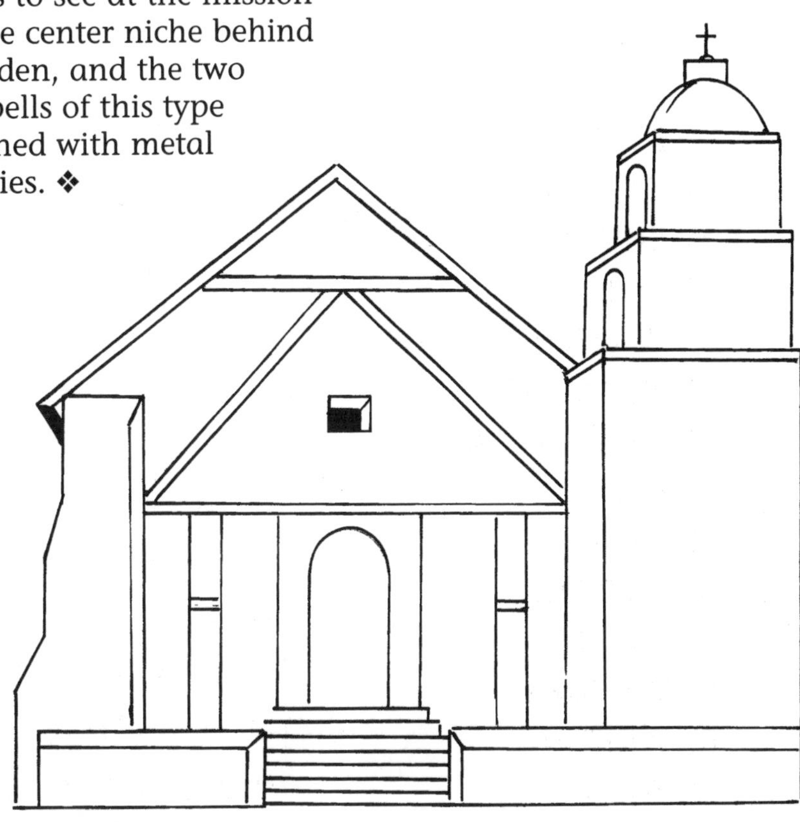

Mission San Buenaventura
211 East Main Street
Ventura, CA 93001
Phone: 805.643.4318

Name ______________________

Date ______________________

Review Questions

Write the correct answer in the space provided.

1. The ninth California mission was named for ______________________, whose name means "good fortune". It was founded by ______________________ in ______________, five years after the eighth mission had started.

2. The natives of the area were of the ______________________ tribe; the Spaniards sometimes called them the ______________________. They were excellent craftsmen at ______________________, and ______________ and were also able to make waterproof ______________.

3. Agricultural products from this area included many fruits and vegetables, especially ______________________.

4. Buenaventura was sometimes called ______________________.

5. The English sea captain, ______________________ reported about the mission's ______________________ after he visited in 1793.

6. Most of this mission was destroyed in 1893, not by natural disasters, but by misguided remodeling efforts. Describe the restoration begun in 1957.

____

____

____

____

____

7. Explain the conflict between the secular government and the church officials which led to the delay in expansion of the mission chain.

____

____

____

____

____

Note: You can learn more about the Native people of the Channel Islands by reading Scott O'dell's book *Island of the Blue Dolphins*.

☆☆ **Bonus Activity**

Use another resource and write a report on one of the people mentioned in this section, the *Patronado* decree of Pope Alexander VI, Arizona style missions, Chumash or Yuma people, weaving (baskets) history and/or as art. Draw maps and pictures for your report.

Mission #10

Santa Bárbara

Founded December 4, 1786

Print the names of the missions on the correct lines. (You may need to look back at a previously finished section/map.)

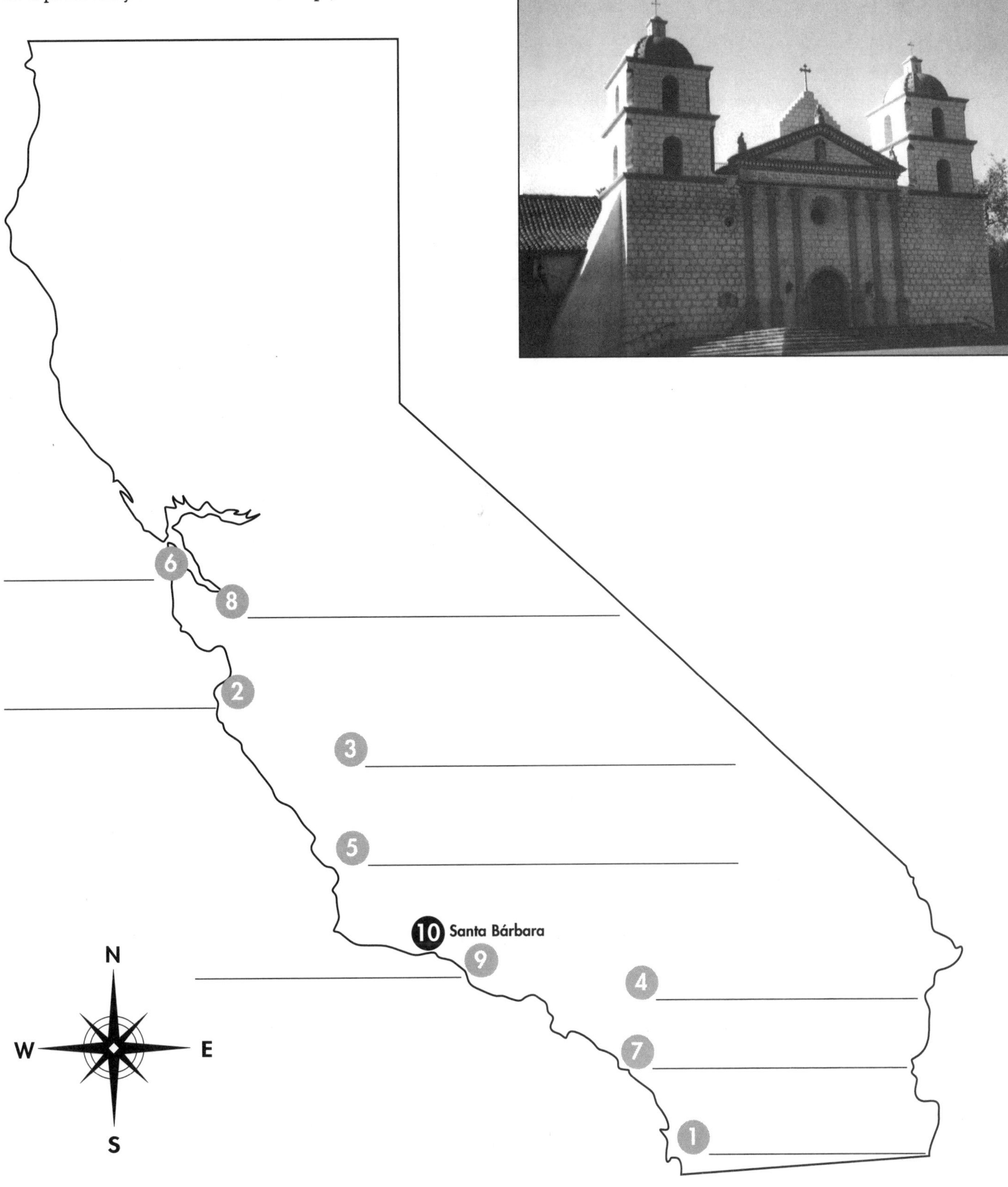

New Words to Learn:

Find the words in the glossary or a dictionary and write the meanings on the line.

1. **armory:** ______
2. **antagonism:** ______
3. **candelabra:** ______
4. **creole:** ______
5. **garland**(s): ______
6. **harbor**(ed): ______
7. **ingenious:** ______
8. **manuscript**(s): ______
9. **monastery:** ______
10. **motif:** ______
11. **pagan:** ______
12. **pardon:** ______
13. **retaliate**(tion): ______

① ______

Mission #10 — Founded December 4, 1786

Layout of the Mission Grounds

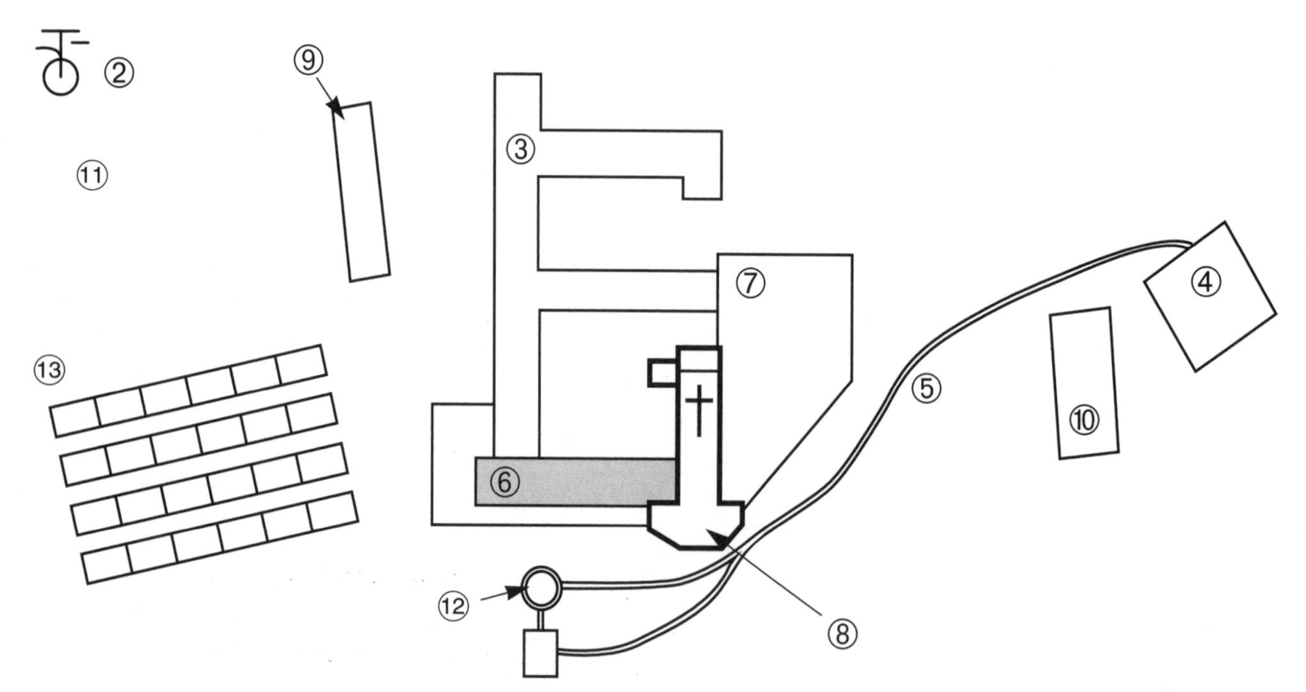

A portion of the Mission grounds in the early 1830s.

Santa Bárbara

Name ____________________

Date ____________________

Named for Saint Bárbara who, according to legend, was the daughter of a **pagan** Roman ruler. When Bárbara became a Christian, her father was so angry that he imprisoned her and finally cut off her head with his sword.

The 10th of 21 Spanish/Catholic Missions

Design of the Mission

Church: (approximate outside measurements) 179 feet long, 38 feet wide, and 30 feet high.

The church is built out of yellow native sandstone, which is held together with lime mortar made of seashells from the nearby beaches. Like most of the missions, it has a tile roof.

Design:

The architectural style is a classic Greco-Roman design, copied from a book in the mission's library. The book's original author was Vitruvius Polion, a Roman architect, who wrote it in 27 B.C. The interior walls are painted with designs of **garlands** and angels.

Walls: The walls are six feet thick with nine-foot square stone buttresses.

Statues: The statues on top of the church represent Faith, Hope, and Charity (Love). The statue of St. Bárbara was added to the church in 1927.

Campanario:

Santa Bárbara has the distinction of being the only mission with two matching bell towers, each 87 feet tall with a 20 foot square base. Interestingly, one tower was built in 1820 and the second was not added for 11 more years. A small passageway in one tower allows access to the bells. There were eight bells in 1833, which were later increased to 11 bells.

Mission Compound:

The church forms one corner of the quadrangle with the patio in the middle. Storage rooms, the kitchen, offices, dormitories, and living quarters for the priests face the patio. There were about 250 small adobe dwellings that were built in rows near the mission compound for the native workers. These were built of adobe, plastered, and whitewashed and like the church had tile roofs.

Mission Grounds:

Outside of the main compound of the mission were larger workshops, a cemetery, fields and orchards, fields for livestock, and a reservoir for water.

Water System:

The water system (some of which is still usable) at Mission Santa Bárbara was the most advanced and complete of any of the missions along El Camino Real. The site was chosen by Fr. Serra because of its closeness to a good water supply. Two dams and stone basins were built on Pedregoso Creek. Aqueducts brought the water down to the mission. Some water went through a filtration system and was used for drinking. Some went into a fountain in front of the mission, where mission women washed clothes.

Do these things using the map provided. (Use the map on page 92.)

1. Write **Mission Santa Bárbara** ①, **cattle brand** ②, **workshops** ③, **reservoir** ④, **aqueduct** ⑤, **padres' living quarters** ⑥, **cemetery** ⑦, **church** ⑧, **granary** ⑨, **pottery** ⑩, **orchards** ⑪, **fountain** ⑫, and **houses for native workers** ⑬, by the correct number.
2. Do your best job if you color the map.

Santa Bárbara

Also known as "Queen of the Mission"

Name ______________________

Date ______________________

The 10th of 21 Spanish/Catholic Missions

Early History

Long before the arrival of the Franciscan missionaries, Santa Bárbara, as well as San Diego and Monterey were listed on Spanish maps of California. It was named by the Spanish explorer, Sebastian Vizcaíño, about 60 years after it was discovered by another Spanish explorer named Juan Rodríguez Cabrillo in 1542. From the first march of the Don Gaspar de Portolá expedition from San Diego (read San Diego de Asís section) Santa Bárbara had been considered as an excellent location for a mission.

It took 13 years before an opportunity opened up for the padres to establish a mission at Santa Bárbara. By then, Governor Felipe de Neve was their adversary who openly preferred white colonists to the local people (Indian nation). Nevertheless, he agreed at a meeting in Mission San Gabriel to allow missions to be established in San Buenaventura and Santa Bárbara. He had also planned to build a presidio in Santa Bárbara. Fr. Junípero Serra, Governor de Neve, and the others at the meeting agreed that all three would be established in one expedition. This would keep costs at a minimum, as the king of Spain was not thrilled about spending money on establishing missions in California. The padres and their military escorts started out from Mission San Gabriel in the spring of 1782. Governor de Neve could not accompany the expedition or participate in the founding of Mission San Buenaventura because he received orders to go the the Yuma Indian uprising to the southwest.

Some time later, de Neve finally caught up with the expedition and they continued on to Santa Bárbara. He immediately established the presidio. Fr. Serra delighted in preparing the military chapel. After the chapel was completed and the governor had not ordered the founding of the mission, Fr. Serra asked de Neve when he intended to get the mission started. The governor informed him that Mission Santa Bárbara could wait until the Franciscan adhered to the new Reglamento (regulations) which had been ignored at San Buenaventura. The new regulations stated that all future missions would be built Arizona style, which was de Neve's preference versus California style, which was Fr. Serra's preference. (Read Section #9 about Mission San Buenaventura to note the differences in the two styles of missions.) Both men realized that the other would not give in on his position. Fr. Serra also realized that de Neve had won the argument at Santa Bárbara, and since he could do nothing else, he returned to his own mission at Carmel.

It was five years before Fr. Serra received word that a mission would finally be established at Santa Bárbara. De Neve was gone and former governor Pedro Fages had taken his place. Several years before, Fr. Serra had made a long journey to Mexico City in order to have Fages removed as governor. What a shock it must have been for the aging padre to learn that his former enemy had returned. He did not live long after Fages' appointment, as he died on August 28, 1784. Fr. Fermín Lasuén took over Fr. Serra's position, responsibilities, and burdens as president of the missions.

The period of time Fr. Lasuén was president of the missions has often been called the *Golden Age of California Missions*. Even though the prosperity extended beyond the 18 years he was in charge, his constructive energy and executive ability set the pattern for the growth and prosperity the missions would enjoy.

Santa Bárbara

Name ______________________

Date ______________________

The 10th of 21 Spanish/Catholic Missions

Santa Bárbara became an active mission on December 4, 1786. It was the first mission Fr. Lasuén established, and it enjoyed good fortune from its beginning. Its first permanent church was a grand structure, built of adobe with a red tile roof, and opened for Mass in 1789. Because the mission enjoyed such rapid growth, within five years, another structure had to be built to accommodate the mission's population. The second structure was destroyed by an earthquake in 1812 and construction on the existing stone church was begun shortly afterward. This structure remained solid for 105 years. The earthquake of 1925 did so much damage that restoration took two years to complete.

The very advanced Chumash tribe lived in the area of Santa Bárbara, and liked the mission system of living. Shortly after the beginning of the nineteenth century, the mission had more than 1,700 neophytes living in about 250 adobe houses. Like the natives at Mission San Buenaventura, they were a more adaptable and energetic tribe than any other the padres had previously dealt with. Because of the hard work of the Chumash people, the mission soon became self-sustaining. They built a large, stone reservoir so advanced that it is still being used by the city of Santa Bárbara.

In 1818, a padre at Mission Santa Bárbara received advanced knowledge that the French pirate, Bouchard was sailing to the area from South America. This padre armed 150 of the Chumash neophytes in expectation of a fight. The armed Indians and Spanish soldiers at the presidio were able to show the pirate that they meant to fight for their protection. Bouchard, who was normally brutal and reckless, was impressed by the display of force and left the harbor without testing the settlement's forces in a fight. This was, however, one of the first and definitely the last instance of cooperation between the Indians and the soldiers.

In 1822 news arrived that Mexico was fighting for its independence against Spain in a revolution. From then on the conflict between the Franciscan fathers and the soldiers continued to increase. One of the reasons is that for over 200 years, those who had been born in the Americas (North, Central, and South) had **harbored antagonism** toward the Spanish-born people. This resulted from the fact that Spanish kings always sent the leaders in authority from Spain instead of promoting **creole** officers. The Royal Family felt that Spaniards would be more loyal to the throne than officers born outside of the mother country. The Spanish-American people, no matter how influential or wealthy, were always kept out of the profitable positions of governing and administration.

Mission Santa Bárbara in the 1880s.

Santa Bárbara

Name ______________________

Date ______________________

The 10th of 21 Spanish/Catholic Missions

After the Mexican revolution, creole resentment of the Spanish born was displayed by the first official pronouncement to reach California from its capital, Mexico City. The law ordered all Spaniards under the age of 60 to immediately leave the province. Although the order (Spanish exclusion policy) was never carried out, it added to the problems of the Franciscan padres: all were born in Spain. Their authority over the native Indians was in question and the soldiers were told to assume the work of policy making for the natives.

In the spring of 1824, an Indian uprising protesting the cruelty and violence of the soldiers occurred at three missions, with Santa Bárbara being one of them. Here the Indians broke into the **armory** and were successful in defeating the mission guard. In the fight, two soldiers were wounded and the Spanish **retaliation** was so brutally severe that all of the Indians not captured fled from the area. It took the president of the Missions over six months to obtain a general **pardon** for all of the native Indians. Not until this pardon was obtained did any of neophytes return to the mission.

By now, the "golden days" enjoyed by settlers and workers at Mission Santa Bárbara were quickly coming to an end. The effects of secularization had begun to take hold at the mission. However, two men were determined to save it from the complete destruction that overtook most of the other missions. In 1833, the Spanish exclusion policy was followed by the removal of all Spanish-born padres and replaced by American-born Franciscans. The new Governor, José Figueroa, brought ten Zacatecan friars with him and placed them in charge of all of the missions north of San Antonio, Texas. Shortly after this the president of the missions, Fr. Narciso Durán, moved his headquarters from Mission Carmel to Mission Santa Bárbara. It is here that the padre conducted the last struggle to save the mission system. In 1842, the first Bishop of the Californias, Francisco Garcia Diego, also moved his headquarters to Mission Santa Bárbara. The presence of both the bishop and president of the missions was the only thing that saved Mission Santa Bárbara from the destructive fate of the other missions, but only until 1846, when both men died within a month of each other.

After the death of the bishop and the father *presidente*, the new governor, Pio Pico, came to the mission to make a final sale of the Franciscan mission chain. As fate would have it, he was too late, for California became a territory of the United States before the buyer could occupy his newly purchased property. Santa Bárbara, *The Queen of the Missions*, thus became the only mission along El Camino Real to remain in constant occupation by the Franciscan Order from the day it was founded to today. And because of this continuous occupation, one of California's true historical treasures has remained much the same as it was in past days. ❖

Quotefalls Puzzle

Solve this puzzle. Directions on pg. 64.

I	H			Q	U						S			C	O		S	C	O	S			R			C			
T	O	D		O	Y	L	Y	H	M		F	E	I	N	C		M	T	A	N	I	L	N	S		R	C	U	
N	E	E		B	N	E	T	T	E	I	F	S	A	H	E	N	A	I	A	N	T	O	Y	L	E	C	A	M	P
T	H	E	R	E	A	L	E	N	O	O	B	R	T	O	N	I	S	L	S	N	G	O	E	D	O	W	A	S	I
			■						■			■				■									■				■
			■					■								■						■			■				
		■					■			■			■											■					
			■			■				■											■						■	■	■

Santa Bárbara

Name ______________________

Date ______________________

The 10th of 21 Spanish/Catholic Missions

The Mission Today

Since the Mission Santa Bárbara has been continually occupied, it closely resembles its original appearance — truly one of the most impressive and beautiful missions along El Camino Real. It escaped vandalism because the buildings have remained in continuous use. The rooms where the mission's museum is located have not changed for over 160 years. The museum at Mission Santa Bárbara is the best organized and most documented of any of the other missions. Each room of the museum has a central theme. The music room, for example, has a collection of musical instruments, **manuscripts** with hand-lettered notes that the Chumash (natives to the area) used to learn songs, and other items relating to music. Another room includes exhibits of the Chumash people relating to their life before any settlers/missionaries arrived. They were a very advanced tribe, excellent craftsmen, and they especially excelled at building, painting, and music.

The tile flooring and ceiling decorations are both original. Two large paintings in the church are over 200 years old. The light on the altar is said to have been burning continuously since it was lit by Fr. Lasuén in 1789.

In the rear of the church is the choir loft where the neophytes sang. Its interior has unusual decorative effects which give the appearance of marble. **Ingenious** "S" shaped chains suspend beautiful **candelabra** from the ceiling. A startling "flash of lightning" design that resembles an Aztec Indian **motif** can be seen at the point where the chains are attached to the ceiling.

The church was damaged by a series of earthquakes, with the most destructive one coming in 1925. It destroyed one of the towers and the second floor of the **monastery** was seriously damaged. The facade (front) of the church and towers were rebuilt to the original design and the restoration was completed in 1927. Cracks developed some years later and the present facade was completely rebuilt with reinforced concrete in 1950.

From 1896 to 1968, the mission was used as a school for training Franciscan priests. It is now used to conduct church services and special ceremonies such as weddings for the people of Santa Bárbara. Each August a *Fiesta of Old Spanish Days* is held by the city. The fiesta always begins at the mission, commemorating its founding with music and feasting. ❖

Old Mission (Santa Bárbara)
2201 Laguna Street
Santa Barbara, CA 93105
Phone: 805.682.4713

Name ______________________

Date ______________________

Review Questions

Write the correct answer in the space provided.

1. The tenth mission in California was founded on ______________ and named ______________ . It was founded by the ______________ ______________ order of the Catholic church.

2. This was the first mission founded by ______________ , who became the president of the mission when ______________ died.

3. The unique features of this mission include twin ______________ and hanging ______________ from "S" shaped chains. Its stone ______________ was so well built advanced that it is still being used by the city of Santa Barbara.

4. Fr. Lasuén's 18 years as president of the missions are known as the ______________ of California Missions.

5. Explain what happens at the Mission Santa Bárbara every August.

6. Explain how historical events, such as California becoming a U.S. territory contributed to the preservation of Mission Santa Bárbara.

7. Explain what the Spanish exclusion policy was and its affect on the mission and the people connected to the mission.

☆☆ Bonus Activity

Pretend you are living at Mission Santa Bárbara in the 1790s and write a dialogue between two women washing clothes in the fountain, or two men building the stone reservoir, church, or other parts of the mission compound. (Use other resources to get information if you need to.) Draw maps and pictures for your report.

Mission #11

La Purísima Concepción

Founded December 8, 1787

Print the names of the missions on the correct lines. (You may need to look back at a previously finished section/map.)

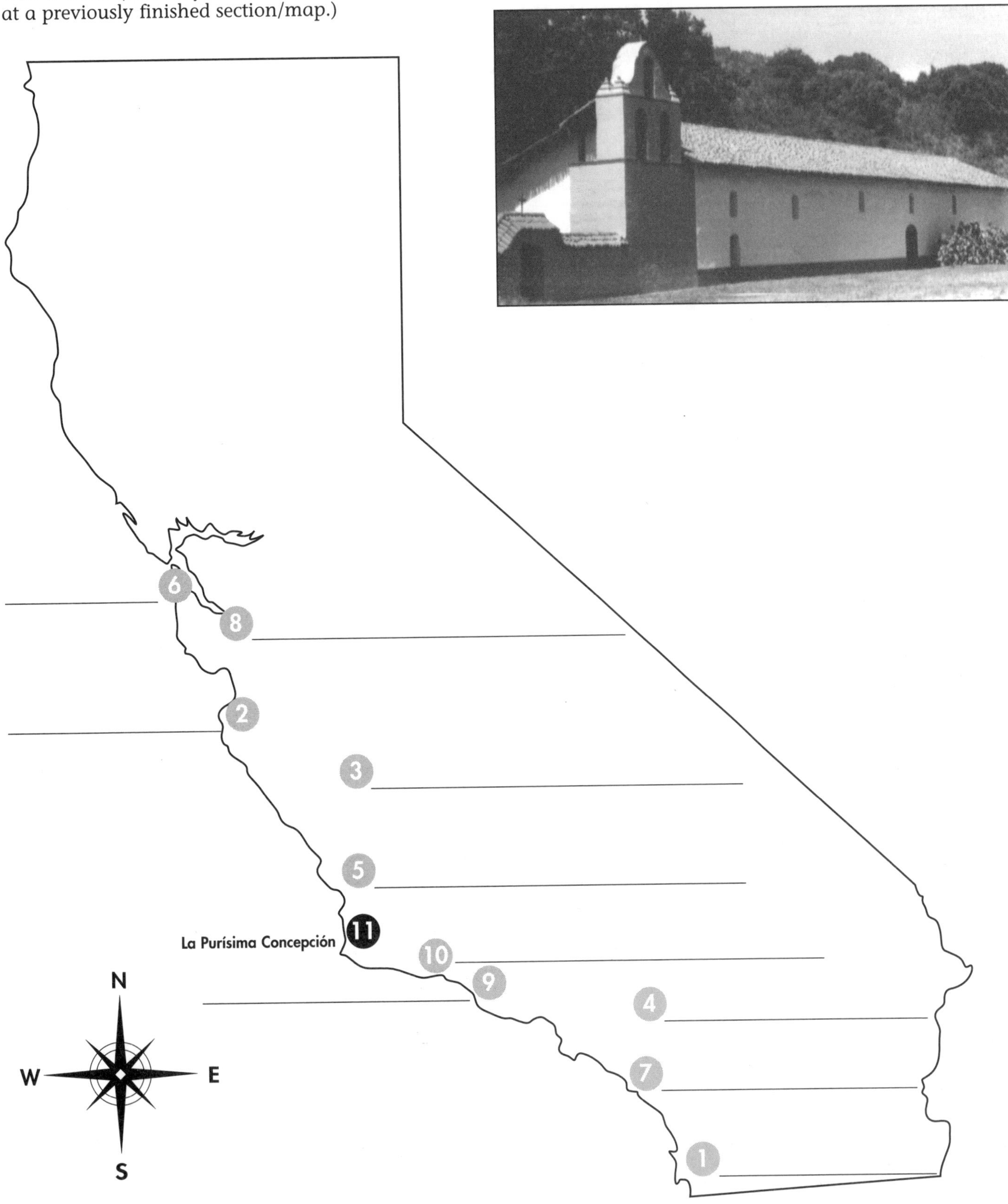

New Words to Learn:

Find the words in the glossary or a dictionary and write the meanings on the line.

1. **barricade:** ______________________________
2. **cistern:** ______________________________
3. **fault:** ______________________________
4. **flora:** ______________________________
5. **immaculate:** ______________________________
6. **irony** (ironically): ______________________________
7. **prominent:** ______________________________
8. **replicate**(ing): ______________________________
9. **seize:** ______________________________
10. **strata** (stratum): ______________________________

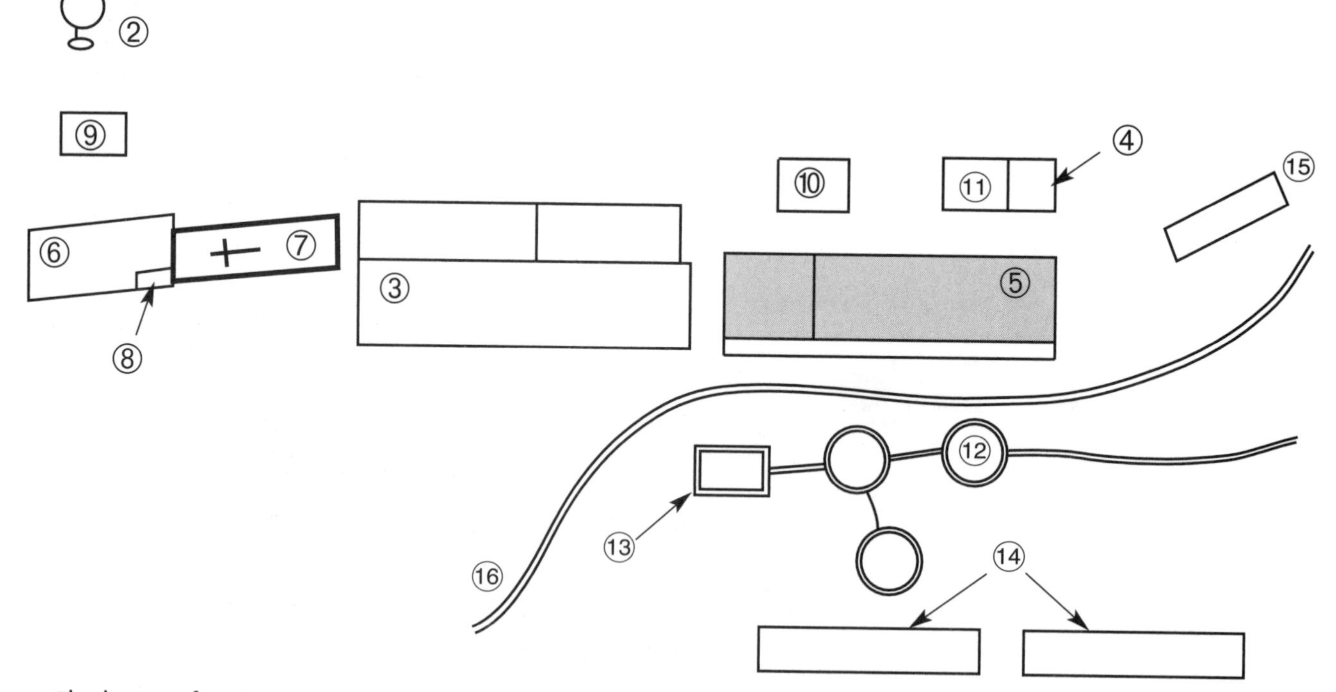

The layout of La Purísima Concepción is unique to the California mission system.

La Purísima Concepción

Name ______________________________

Date ______________________________

The 11th of 21 Spanish/Catholic Missions

Named for "The Most Pure (**Immaculate**) Conception of Mary Most Holy." This is one of two missions dedicated to Mary, Mother of Jesus. Christians believe she conceived Jesus as a virgin, through God's Holy Spirit, making Jesus the son of God.

Design of the Mission

Church: (approximate outside measurements) 174 feet long, 34 feet wide, and 16.5 feet high. The church has a tile roof and tile floors.

Design:
The architectural style of La Purísima is plain. The church was built for practicality, not beauty. Unlike most of the other missions that used arches to support the roof, square posts were used here. The interior was constructed of rough-plastered surfaces, with exposed beams that are lashed together with rawhide. The walls are painted with rich, colorful native designs. The entrance is on the side wall, not the typical front wall.

Walls: The walls are four and one half feet thick.

Campanario:
No drawing exists of the original bell tower for La Purísima, so during the reconstruction of the mission, the one from Mission Santa Inés was copied and constructed. Three bells, one on top and two below, hang in niches. The original bronze bells were cast in Lima, Peru in 1817 and 1818. The campanario extends out from one end of the church and forms part of one of the cemetery walls.

Mission Compound:
It is interesting that Mission La Purísima was not built in the traditional quadrangle as most of the other missions. There is a series of long buildings arranged in a line. Some people think the designers of the mission did this arrangement in order to provide a faster exit in case of an earthquake. Buildings at the mission include a small hospital, living quarters with kitchens and a guest room, warehouses for hides and tallow, and workshops for the workers — blacksmiths, carpenters, potters, leather workers, and weavers. The quality of the woven wool blankets was excellent. The residence building is 300 feet long and has a walkway with 20 columns.

Mission Grounds:
About 100 Chumash (the tribe native to the area) built adobe houses nearby, because they preferred not to live on the mission grounds like many of the native people near other missions did. The buildings were surrounded by large vats for making soap and tallow, a 10-acre vineyard, gardens, and a fruit orchard. Only two other missions produced more agricultural crops than La Purísima. The mission owned more than 20,000 head of livestock.

Do these things using the map provided. (Use the map on page 100.)

1. Write **Mission La Purísima Concepción** ①, **cattle brand** ②, **workshops** ③, **kitchen** ④, **padres' living quarters** ⑤, **cemetery** ⑥, **church** ⑦, **bell wall** ⑧, **tallow vats** ⑨, **pottery** ⑩, **grist mill** ⑪, **fountain** ⑫, **cistern** ⑬, **workers' quarters** ⑭,**blacksmith** ⑮, and **El Camino Real** ⑯ by the correct number.
2. Do your best job if you color the map.

La Purísima Concepción

Name ______________________

Date ______________________

The full name of the mission is
Mission La Concepción Purísima de María Santísima or
"The Immaculate Conception of Mary the Most Pure."

The 11th of 21 Spanish/Catholic Missions

Early History

The original location of La Purísima Concepción is where the town of Lompoc, California is located today. Fr. Lasuén founded the eleventh mission along El Camino Real on December 8, 1787. The Chumash Indians living near the mission site were friendly and receptive to the mission system being introduced to them by the Franciscan settlers. About 100 of the neophytes were living nearby and working on the mission soon after it began.

Construction of the first chapel and cluster of buildings was completed in 1788. They were built of wooden poles and plastered with mud. Within ten years the chapel was outgrown and construction on a new church was started using adobe for the walls and tile for the roof. The new church building was completed in 1802. The friars realized that if the mission were to be truly prosperous it would need to develop an elaborate irrigation system. They built a water system that brought water from the nearby springs in the hills through three miles of open aqueducts (clay pipes), dams, and reservoirs. The water flowed from the hills, to fountains, to laundry pools (lavanderías), and then on to the fields for irrigation. By 1800, the mission had more than 20,000 head of livestock. The mission was favored with fertile soil, and became the third most productive mission in agricultural products.

In 1812, the notable prosperity of Mission La Purísima was undone by a fateful earthquake. This earthquake caused considerable damage to many of the missions and completely leveled La Purísima to the ground. The buildings were located near the major **fault** line and the earth continued to slip for more than a week. Everything except the sturdiest equipment was lost or destroyed. The Franciscans and Chumash chose to rebuild the mission in a different location. Four months after the earthquake, the mission was re-established where it stands today — four miles to the north and east of Lompoc, in the valley of Los Berros.

The hero of the earthquake disaster was Father Mariano Payeras. (He was the last of the Spanish friars who were from Spain's island of Mallorca which had given the settlement of California so many great men — Frs. Serra, Palou, and Crespi and Captain Juan Perez of the ship *San Antonio*.) Fr. Payeras was born in 1769, the year Fr. Serra founded Mission San Diego. He had come to La Purísima in 1803 and there he died some 20 years later.

Note the square pillars that support the roof at Mission La Purísima. The use of arches were the most common design of the missions.

La Purísima Concepción

Name ______________________

Date ______________________

The 11th of 21 Spanish/Catholic Missions

Fr. Payeras served four years as president of the missions. Like some of the earlier Franciscan friars, he liked to travel through the unexplored areas, visiting native people and discovering possible locations for future missions. Even though Spain's and Mexico's authorities disapproved, he was always friendly to foreign visitors. After Napoleon conquered Spain, he signed the first trade agreement between the California missions and the English. The Englishman who signed the trade agreement was William Hartnell, who would eventually become one of California's first **prominent** citizens after its independence. **Ironically**, he would also be a leader in the secularization of the missions in 1833.

At the new site, Mission La Purísima regained its earlier prosperity avoiding further difficulty until 1824, a year after Fr. Payeras' death. At this time, a native uprising at Mission Santa Inés led the Indians at La Purísima to **seize** the mission.

The Indians drove off the small military guard, erected a wooden fort and cut holes in the walls where they mounted a pair of small cannons. Firmly entrenched in the **barricade,** the Chumash held the mission for over a month. It took a Spanish military force of more than 100 trained soldiers from Monterey to regain possession. Even then, for the Indians to surrender, a padre had to convince them that they had no hope of defeating the soldiers.

The Indian uprising took the lives of six Spaniards, four of whom were travelers who happened to be at the mission when the incident occurred. Seventeen of the Indians were killed during the fighting, while four of their captured leaders were put to death for their part in the killings.

After the uprising had been suppressed, mission life returned to normal. However, ten years after the uprising the mission was under the authority of a secular administrator. The period of Mission La Purísima's greatest prosperity had passed. For a time, the Franciscans were allowed to remain on the grounds and occupy their living quarters even though no Indians remained. The church and other buildings were left to decay and be reduced to rubble. The once prosperous rancho was abandoned and offered for sale after it had been returned to the Catholic Church. ❖

La Purísima Concepción

Name ____________________

Date ____________________

Crossword Puzzle

The 11th of 21 Spanish/Catholic Missions

Note: You will have to read page 105 in order to answer all of the questions in this puzzle.

Across

2. All volunteers at the mission today assume roles of mission ________ during the 1820s.

5. The ________ Conception of Mary, the mother of Jesus.

8. Spanish for *laundry pools.* ________

14. William Hartnell was a leader in the ________ of the missions.

17. The mission had to have an elaborate irrigation system in order to be ________ .

18. Fr. Payeras was always ________ to foreign visitors.

19. The ________ took more than one hundred thousand bricks to reconstruct.

20. The ________ of 1812 completely leveled La Purísima to the ground.

Down

1. Unlike most of the other missions, ________ posts support the roof instead of arches.

3. Anybody who is born in a region or country is a ________ of that region or country.
Examples: The Chumash who were born near La Purísima were ________ to the area (California).
If you were born in California, you are a ________ Californian.
Any person born in America, regardless of their ethnic heritage, is a ________ American, but some people mistakenly think and teach that only people of American Indian heritage are ________ Americans.

4. The Chumash people were entrenched in a ________ and held the mission for over a month during an uprising.

6. Father Mariano Payeras was the ________ during the earthquake of 1812.

7. The ________ forms part of one of the cemetery walls.

9. The church at la Purísima was built for ________ , not beauty.

10. Fr. Payeras served as ________ of the missions for four years.

11. William Hartnell became a prominent California citizen after it won its ________ .

12. Mission La Purísima was not built in the traditional ________ design as most of the other missions.

13. A fracture in rock **strata** where movement takes place. ________

15. Christians believe that the Immaculate ________ of Mary (a virgin and mother of Jesus) by God's Holy Spirit make him the Son of God.

16. The ________ preferred not to live on the mission grounds like many of the other native people near other missions did.

La Purísima Concepción

Name ____________________

Date ____________________

The 11th of 21 Spanish/Catholic Missions

The Mission Today

In 1934, 500 acres of the former mission property were acquired by Santa Barbara County and with the cooperation of the state and the United States National Park Service, a program for restoring Mission La Purísima Concepción was begun. A Civil Conservation Corps camp was located on the mission grounds, where more than 200 workers and craftsmen worked for over seven years in the restoration process. On July 7th, the first adobe brick was laid and the restoration process was started. A great deal of research took place to reconstruct the mission as closely as possible to the original. The monastery took more than 110,000 adobe bricks, 32,000 roof tiles, and 10,000 floor tiles to accurately reconstruct.

Instead of destroying the few existing ruins, the workers incorporated them into the new buildings. As a result, people today can compare the later columns with the original ones and only by very careful inspection tell the difference. After the structures were completed and met every rigid reconstruction standard, the young craftsmen turned to the creation of furniture, with every piece being an exact replica of pieces in other mission museums. The monastery, church, and endless rows of rooms for soldiers and Indians were all restored to their original condition. La Purísima provides visitors with the opportunity to experience the size and scope of a large mission establishment.

After **replicating** the furnishings of the compound, workers of the Conservation Corps concentrated on recreating the mission gardens. They began by rebuilding the elaborate water system which collects water from springs above the mission and carries the water more than a mile through the gardens and on to the fields below. The water first flows into a fountain. From there it flows into a circular pool where the slanting stone banks form the laundry where the Indian women did the mission wash. After passing through a settling pool, the water continues to the grain fields. Every plant, tree, and shrub in the garden was known to the padres and the native people of the area. Today, this garden is considered the finest collection of early California **flora** in existence.

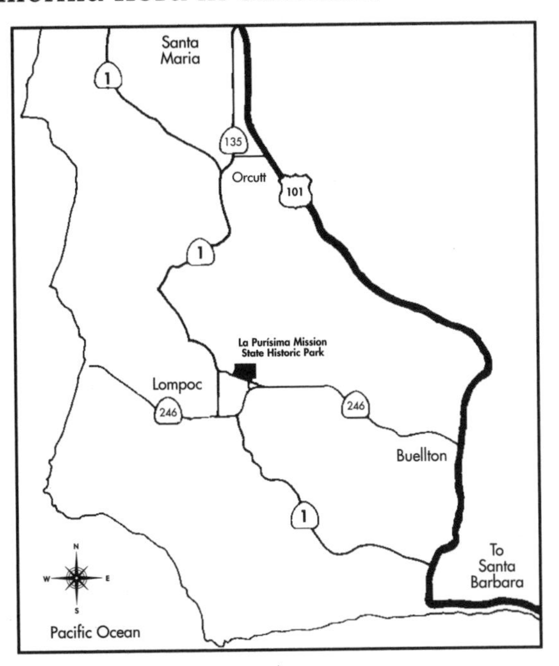

At a dedication ceremony on December 7, 1941, the property became *La Purísima Mission State Historical Park*. It is currently operated by the Division of Beaches and Parks, with an area of 967 acres. All volunteers assume the roles of mission inhabitants in the early 1820s. In historic dress, they conduct tours, spin and weave wool, produce iron **implements** in the iron shop from the mission era, and much more.

Of all the missions, Mission La Purísima Concepción gives visitors the feeling of being at a mission along El Camino Real during the golden years of the Franciscan missions. ❖

Mission La Purísima Concepción
RFD #102; (Gift Shop 2295 Purísima Rd.)
Lompoc, CA 93436
Phone: 805.733.7782

La Purísima Concepción

Name ____________________

Date ____________________

REVIEW QUESTIONS

Write the correct answer in the space provided.

1. The eleventh California mission, ____________________, was established by ____________________ on ____________________.

2. __________ Spaniards and __________ Indians died due to the uprising at the mission in which the __________ Indians held Mission La Purísima for over a ____________________.

3. The __________ in __________ caused this mission to be destroyed and re-established where it stands today, northeast of __________.

4. The __________ mile long water system of this mission utilized __________, __________, and __________ to help move water to the mission.

5. Some people think that the designers of the mission went away from the traditional __________ design in order to provide a faster __________ in case there was an ____________________.

6. What are some things the friars might have done to aid in the recovery of the mission from the natives?

____

____

____

____

7. Do you think Fr. Payeras may have been able to settle the uprising with less bloodshed? __________ Explain why you think your answer is correct.

____

____

____

____

____

☆☆ Bonus Activity

Use another resource (the internet would help here) and write a report on the name of the fault La Purísima Conceptíon was originally constructed over, the number of faults in all of California, how many times these faults have been active since the mission era, earthquakes in general, the history of earthquakes, the earthquake in San Francisco during the world series (between the San Francisco Giants and Oakland Athletics), or the reconstruction that has taken place since the quake. Draw maps and pictures for your report.

Mission #12

Santa Cruz

Founded September 25, 1791

Print the names of the missions on the correct lines. (You may need to look back at a previously finished section/map.)

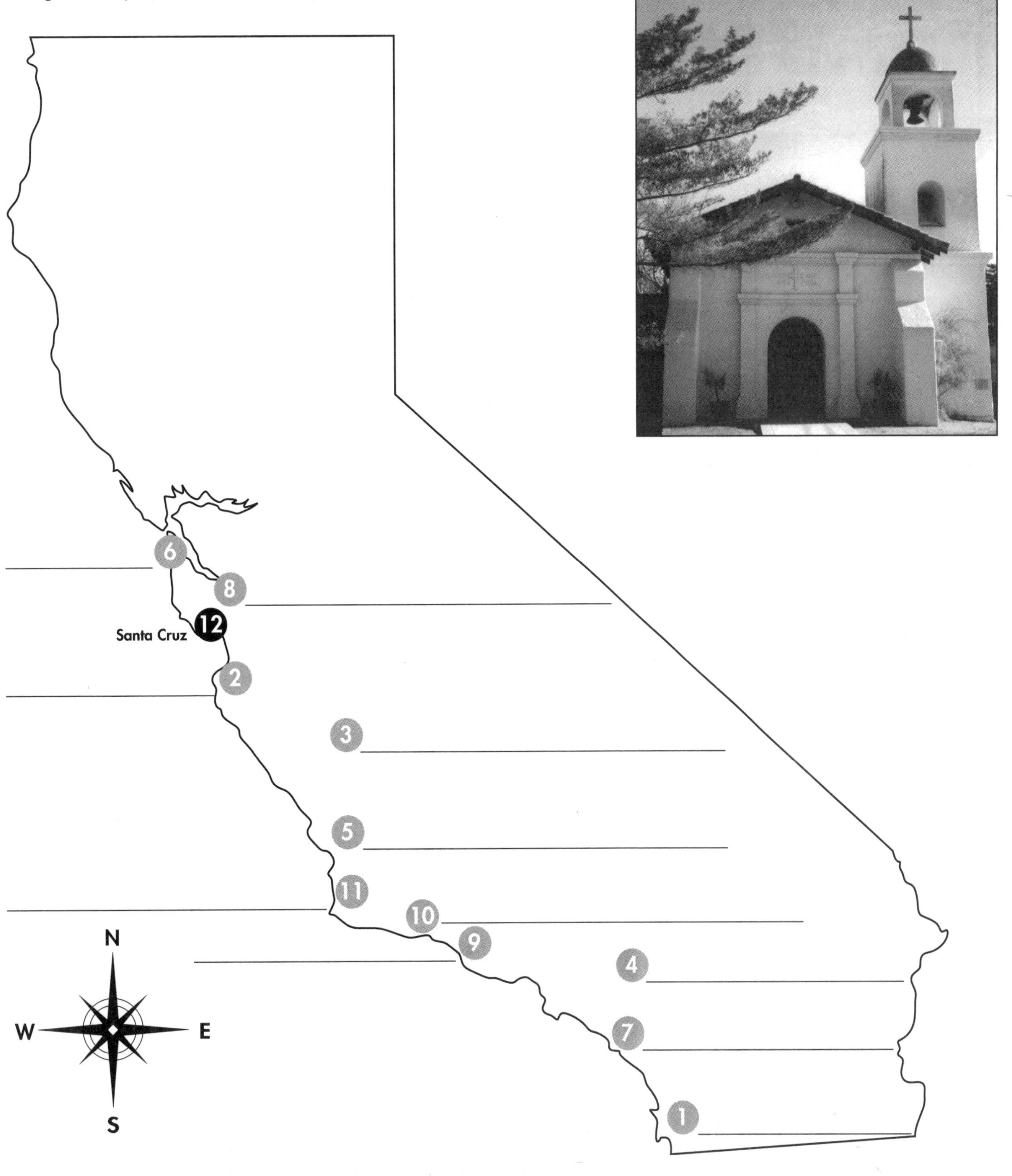

New Words to Learn:

Find the words in the glossary or a dictionary and write the meanings on the line.

1. **awe**(d): ______________________
2. **backslide**(rs): ______________________
3. **degrade**(ing): ______________________
4. **encroach**(ing): ______________________
5. **haven:** ______________________
6. **logic**(ally): ______________________
7. **proportion:** ______________________
8. **regime:** ______________________
9. **successor:** ______________________
10. **trademark:** ______________________

① ______________________

Mission #12 — Founded September 25, 1791

Layout of the Mission Grounds

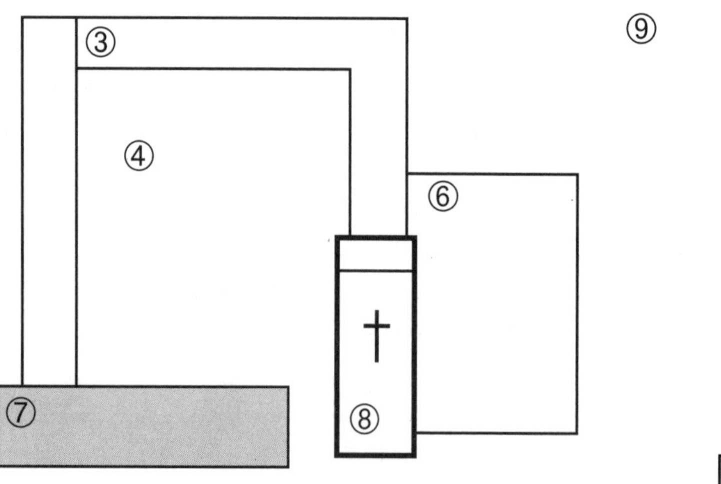

This diagram shows how Mission Santa Cruz may have been laid out in the 1830s.

Santa Cruz

Named for the Holy Cross (Saint Cross). The Cross on which Jesus Christ died is the most holy symbol of Christianity.

Name ____________________

Date ____________________

The 12th of 21 Spanish/Catholic Missions

Design of the Mission

Church: (Original approximate outside measurements) 112 feet long, 30 feet wide, and 26 feet high.
The church was destroyed in the 1800s. It was built on a three-foot foundation, with walls of adobe and a stone facade. It had a tile roof.

Design:
Very little is known about what the original church looked like. There is a painting of it hanging in the museum showing the church, however, it was done after the mission was destroyed. There most likely were stone buttresses on each side of the entrance. Redwood was probably used for the ceiling beams, as it is plentiful in the region. There is one drawing of the interior that was made the day after the building collapsed in an earthquake.

Walls: The walls are reported to have been five feet thick.

Campanario:
The painting shows a square-based bell tower with a dome on the top to the left of the entrance (as you exit). Some historical records from 1835 mention that there were ten bells, but none of them are at the mission today.

Mission Compound:
The buildings forming a quadrangle around the central patio were used for workshops, living quarters, and a two-story granary. The mission had very few native workers, which meant that only a few crafts were developed, like weaving, and only on a small scale.

Mission Grounds:
Supposedly, the ironworks to operate a mill for grinding corn and wheat were donated to the mission by the English explorer, Captain George Vancouver. It is reported that he stopped by in 1794 to purchase produce on his journey to what is now the northwestern states of Oregon and Washington. Even though crops and livestock did well, the mission was never prosperous. The site had good, fertile soil and plenty of fresh water, but its development was hindered by conflicts with the nearby pueblo. These conflicts resulted in Mission Santa Cruz losing portions of its land and much of its goods.

Do these things using the map provided. (Use the map on page 108.)

1. Write **Mission Santa Cruz** ①, **cattle brand** ②, **workshops** ③, **patio** ④, **barracks** ⑤, **cemetery** ⑥, **padres' living quarters** ⑦, **church** ⑧, **granary** ⑨, and **orchard** ⑩ by the correct number.
2. Do your best job if you color the map.

Santa Cruz is Spanish for "Sacred Cross"

Name ___________________________

Date ___________________________

The 12th of 21 Spanish/Catholic Missions

Early History

The mission site was chosen by Fr. Lasuén. It is a beautiful setting where the San Lorenzo River runs into Monterey Bay. Mission Santa Cruz was founded on September 25, 1791, however, Fr. Lasuén was unable to attend the actual dedication. The event was attended by the friars from Santa Clara and the commandante of the presidio at San Francisco. (The relations between the Franciscan friars and the military had improved a great deal, as is evident by the commandante's presence.)

The new viceroy of Mexico was sympathetic to the Franciscan missionaries and their efforts. The best news for the Franciscans, however, was that Governor Fages of California still a province of Mexico — had left for Mexico City in April of 1791. His replacement, José Antonio Roméu, was extremely ill when he arrived in California and was expected to live less than a year. He did not interfere and allowed the padres to use their own judgement on matters concerning the missions. His **successor**, José Joaquín de Arrillaga, was of a similar mindset about the Franciscans making the decisions regarding the missions. This allowed the Franciscans and military to live without conflict in the early years of the mission. The new governor arrived in October of 1794. His name was Diego Borica, and his arrival would end the years of peace at the mission.

Other missions sent gifts to the new mission at Santa Cruz. There were 87 converted Indians within three months' time. The first permanent church was completed in 1794, and located overlooking the San Lorenzo River.

(It is interesting to note here that most of the mission buildings were built long and narrow. This design could even be considered a **trademark** of the missions. They had to build the buildings in this shape because they did not have any engineers helping them — only the help of the native people to the region. The width of the mission buildings was determined by how long the wood beams which supported the flat roof were. The adobe walls could not stand much weight or side pressure, such as stone or other materials. The Carmel Mission departed from the typical mission design — flat and narrow — because it had the help of a master mason, Manuel Ruíz, from Mexico City.)

The other buildings that were part of Mission Santa Cruz compound were soon completed and enclosed a patio area. In 1796, a grain mill was built outside of the quadrangle buildings. The padres were excited about continuing to expand the mission. Unfortunately, their dreams were never to come true. They came to look at the first few years as the mission's most prosperous, and pointed to the new governor, Diego Borica, as the cause of their misfortune. Governor Borica founded California's third pueblo just across the river from the mission in 1797, which proved to be the cause of much strife and division among the natives, military, and Franciscan missionaries.

After the founding of Mission Dolores, in San Francisco, El Camino Real was developed for travelers to get from one mission to the other. When Fr. Francisco Palou first crossed the San Lorenzo River in 1774, he was **awed** by the land and its resources. There was plenty of fresh water, green vegetation, and large trees that could be used for timber. He knew that the area could easily support a large and prosperous community.

Santa Cruz

Name ________________________

Date ________________________

The 12th of 21 Spanish/Catholic Missions

The new pueblo (civilian community), named Branciforte (after the Viceroy of Mexico), that Governor Borica started in 1797 was to be the model city. It was a perfect city laid out on paper. The community was arranged similar to an ancient Roman frontier colony with all of the houses arranged in neat squares. The farming area was one huge field that was divided into smaller plots, and each individual plot was assigned to a settler.

Branciforte was California's first true real estate development. Governor Borica promoted the city with empty promises. He asked Mexico's viceroy to send him healthy, hard-working colonists, promising them neat, white houses, a salary of $116 annually for two years, and $66 annually for the following three years. He also promised that each settler would receive free clothes, farm tools, and furniture. When the settlers arrived, they discovered that the houses had not been built. Governor Borica, on the other hand, discovered that the settlers were not what he had expected. Instead of hard-working, respectable citizens, the Mexican (Spanish) government sent troublemakers and criminals from Mexico City who were given the choice of founding the city or going to jail. After arriving, one of the first things they built was a race track. The new settlers preferred to spend their time gambling rather than pursuing any constructive and profitable industry.

The pueblo of Branciforte was conceived under the Spanish idea of mixing the races — an idea that proved very successful in colonizing other Spanish provinces in Central America. Each alternate house was to be occupied by an "Indian Chief." It was believed that such an arrangement would turn the natives into ideal Spanish citizens much quicker than if left alone. The plan worked well in parts of Mexico, but there were no king-like chiefs in the Branciforte area like there were in the Indian civilizations to the south. The natives that came to Branciforte were not fellow citizens, but rather, they were usually runaway neophytes from across the river at Mission Santa Cruz. They often found pleasure in the white man's alcohol and then were somewhat forced into working for the lazy white men.

Although Branciforte was never prosperous under the Spanish **regime**, it did contribute to the downfall of Mission Santa Cruz. All of the missions were dependent on the work of the natives in the area in order to be prosperous. In 1796, Mission Santa Cruz had more than 500 natives working at the mission. In under two years, due to the **degrading** influence of the pueblo of Branciforte, more than 200 natives left the mission, causing bitterness toward the pueblo, as well as economic hardship.

Fr. Lasuén complained to Governor Borica that the new community was **encroaching** on mission property. The governor **logically** pointed out to the president of the missions that the mission land actually belonged to the neophytes and therefore since there were fewer of them at the mission, then the mission would require less land.

The Franciscans were unable to retaliate against the pueblo they hated so much. However, they applied swift punishment to the native **backsliders** they were able to bring back to the mission. The severe punishments the padres placed upon the natives who returned most likely accelerated the decline of Mission Santa Cruz and hindered the relationship between the natives and white men (especially Franciscans) then and on into the future.

Name ______________________

Date ______________________

The 12th of 21 Spanish/Catholic Missions

In 1818, the news that Bouchard, a French pirate, had attacked Monterey came with orders for the friars to hide or bring all of the mission's valuables and **retreat** to Mission Santa Clara until word came that the danger was over. The settlers at Branciforte volunteered to help move the mission's valuables. These "concerned citizens" did more damage than any pirate ship could have. Anything that the volunteers did not lose, steal, or smash was buried with such neglect that it was damaged beyond use. The padre in charge was so mad that he pleaded for the governor to either move the pueblo to another location or close the mission. The governor didn't do either.

For the next 15 years, until the act of secularization in 1834, Mission Santa Cruz had an exciting existence. The city of Branciforte attracted the roughest of settlers and people passing by the shores of California. It was actually a **haven** for smugglers. Located on the Bay of Monterey, yet conveniently out of sight from the governor at the Monterey Presidio, Mission Santa Cruz developed a trade with hide and tallow smugglers. Even after the restrictions were removed, its economy centered around trading hides. It was put out of business by secularization, just like the other missions.

In 1840 an earthquake destroyed the church. The civilian authorities attempted the required land distribution to its native people, but in 1845 Santa Cruz was a settlement of around 400 people, of which only 100 or so were Indians. In 1846, there was hardly anything left for Governor Pio Pico to sell. In 1857, another earthquake totally destroyed the remaining wall of the mission. Mission Santa Cruz was lost forever to the pages of California history. ❖

KrissKross Puzzle

Directions for Solving KrissKross Puzzles:

Start with either the longest or shortest word from the list of word. Write the word in the correct place. Then fill in the next word that KrissKrosses the first word, counting the number of squares and then matching the number of letters and/or the correct letter where they KrissKross. For less confusion, mark the words off the list as you use them.

- ERA
- PUEBLO
- STRIFE
- PROMOTE
- BARRACKS
- CONFLICT
- ENGINEER
- FRONTIER
- NEOPHYTE
- PERMANENT
- FRANCISCAN
- HISTORICAL
- MISFORTUNE
- SYMPATHETIC
- TROUBLEMAKERS

Name ____________________________

Date ____________________________

The 12th of 21 Spanish/Catholic Missions

The Mission Today

Today the city of Santa Cruz is where the settlement of Branciforte once was. Only the street name of Branciforte is a reminder to the citizens of Santa Cruz that the community existed. On the original site of Mission Santa Cruz is a church, Holy Cross Church, built out of white painted bricks, in a Gothic style with a tall steeple which has a dome on top.

About 200 feet from the Holy Cross Church stands a replica of Mission Santa Cruz that is built in exact **proportion** to the original church. This modern replica was built in 1931 and is half the size of the original. It was built as a memorial and paid for by Gladys Sullivan Doyle. She was interested in California's history and donated it to the Catholic Church. The exterior was built by whatever was known about the original church, but that was very little. The chapel has a painting in it of Our Lady of Guadalupe. This painting could have been in the original chapel, as its origin dates back to 1797. The replica is used for private ceremonies such as weddings. A small museum next to the chapel contains a few statues, paintings, and candlesticks from the original Mission Santa Cruz. The garden displays the original baptismal font that is carved out of sandstone from around the area.

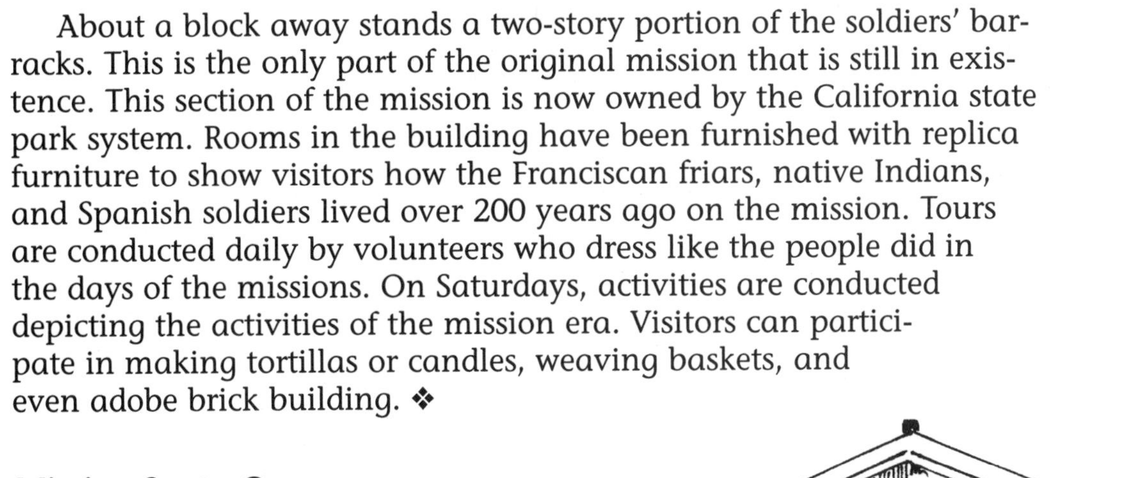

About a block away stands a two-story portion of the soldiers' barracks. This is the only part of the original mission that is still in existence. This section of the mission is now owned by the California state park system. Rooms in the building have been furnished with replica furniture to show visitors how the Franciscan friars, native Indians, and Spanish soldiers lived over 200 years ago on the mission. Tours are conducted daily by volunteers who dress like the people did in the days of the missions. On Saturdays, activities are conducted depicting the activities of the mission era. Visitors can participate in making tortillas or candles, weaving baskets, and even adobe brick building. ❖

Mission Santa Cruz
126 High Street
Santa Cruz, CA 95060
Phone: 831.426.5686

Name ______________________

Date ______________________

Review Questions

Write the correct answer in the space provided.

1. ______________________, was founded on ______________________ in ____________ , __________ years ago. This was the 12th California mission.

2. The city of __________________ became a haven for ______________ and attracted the ________________________ people on passing ships.

3. In __________ this missions church was destroyed by an ______________ . The mission was not completely destroyed until it was hit by an ____________ ______________________________________ again in ______________ .

4. The arrival of Gov. Diego Borica marked the end of ______________ between the __________________________ and Franciscans at this mission.

5. Explain what you would do if you were:
a.) Governor Borica when the *unexpected* settlers arrived.

____

____

____

____

b.) The settlers arriving to find no houses.

____

____

____

____

c.) The friar in charge of the mission.

____

____

____

____

____

☆☆ Bonus Activity

Pretend you are in charge establishing a pueblo or mission (not necessarily Catholic). First, find a good location on a map, then draw a picture of what your town or mission grounds will look like when they are finished. Second, describe what types of people you would want as your first settlers and the incentives you would offer them to come with you. Finally, create an advertisement trying to get these people to come with you.

Mission #13

Nuestra Señora de la Soledad

Founded October 9, 1791

Print the names of the missions on the correct lines. (You may need to look back at a previously finished section/map.)

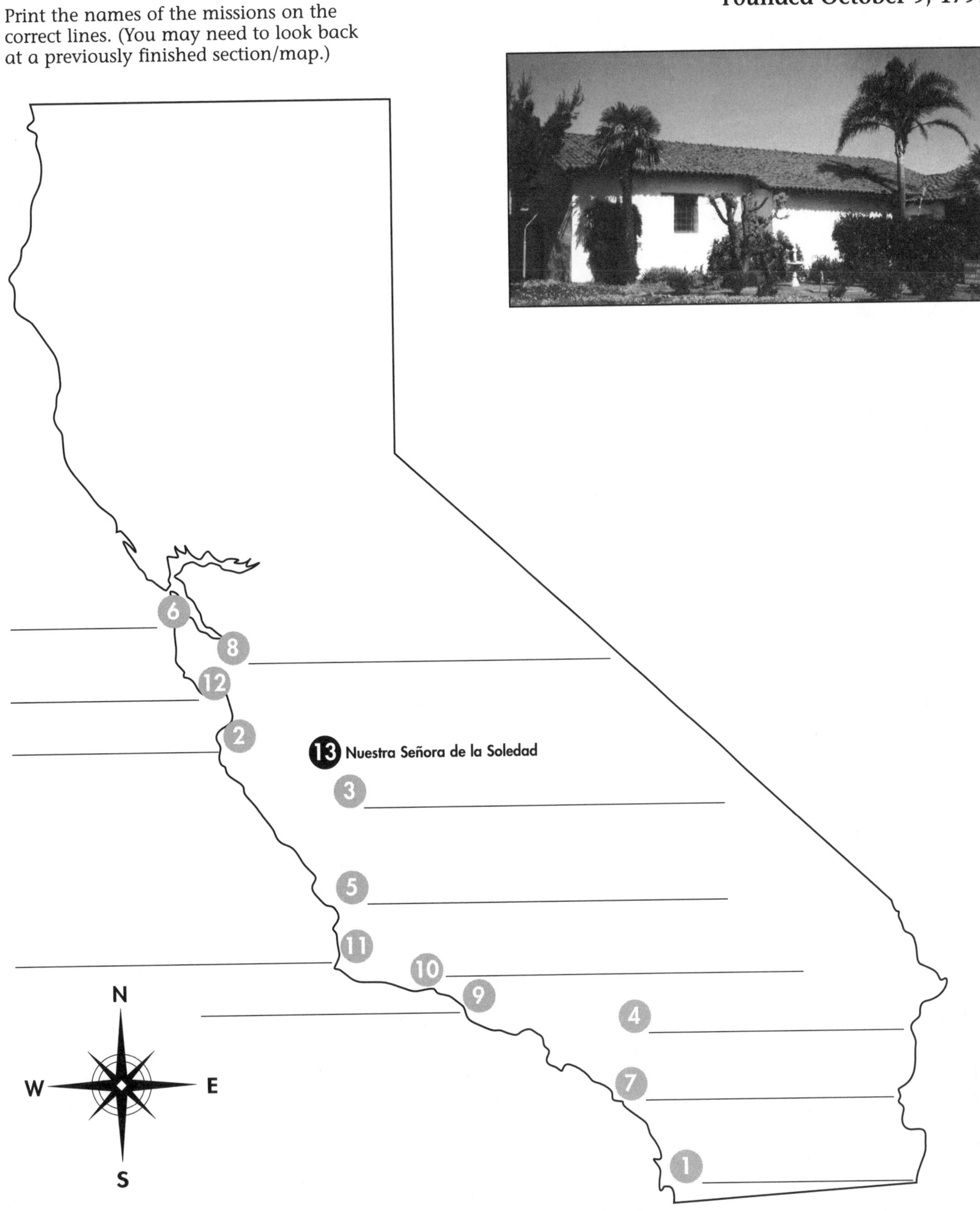

New Words to Learn:

Find the words in the glossary or a dictionary and write the meanings on the line.

1. (un)**conventional:** ____________________
2. **emaciate**(d): ____________________
3. **epidemic:** ____________________
4. **meager:** ____________________
5. **mourn**(ing): ____________________
6. **outlandish:** ____________________
7. **peer**(s): ____________________
8. **prank**(s): ____________________
9. **rheumatism:** ____________________
10. **solitude:** ____________________

① ____________________

Mission #13 — Founded October 9, 1791

Layout of the Mission Grounds

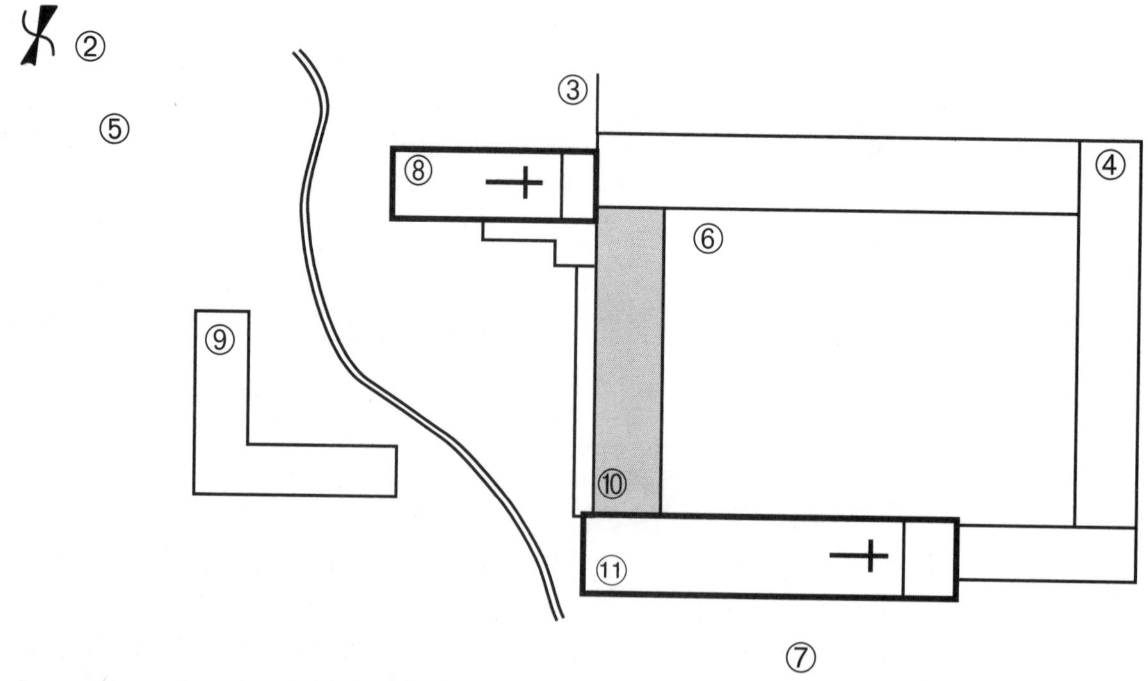

This layout of the mission compound shows the restored chapel and site of the original church.

Nuestra Señora de la Soledad

Name ______________________

Date ______________________

Named for the Mother of Jesus (Our Most Sorrowful Lady of **Solitude**).

The 13th of 21 Spanish/Catholic Missions

Design of the Mission

Church: (approximate outside measurements) 68 feet long, 25 feet wide, and 14 feet high.

Not much is known about the original church. The current chapel was converted from part of a storehouse, after the original church was destroyed. This small chapel is constructed of adobe and has a tile roof.

Design:

The building is plain and white. The walls of the chapel display paintings of the 14 stations of the cross. Behind the altar is a statue of Mary, Mother of Jesus, dressed in black robes, which are **mourning** robes worn by a Spanish widow.

Campanario:

This mission is one of the few along El Camino Real that has no bell tower. There is a single bell that hangs from a wooden beam next to the chapel's entrance. This bell was made in Mexico in the 1790s.

Mission Compound:

The construction often met with setbacks because the buildings were repeatedly destroyed by floods. At one time, however, there was a small quadrangle of buildings that adjoined the original church. The compound had separate living quarters for padres and workers, as well as storerooms and workshops for craftsmen such as weavers, tanners, masons, carpenters, and blacksmiths.

Mission Grounds:

When the mission was first founded, the site was barren and dry. An irrigation system was built and in a short period of time, a fertile valley surrounded the mission. The mission possessed about 6,000 head of cattle and 6,400 sheep at the height of its prosperity. The fields grew an abundance of corn, wheat, beans, horse peas, and Spanish peas. About 20 acres of vineyard produced grapes for making wine and brandy. Water came from the Salinas and Arroyo Seco Rivers using cement aqueducts that were built by the natives who worked on the mission. Adobe huts were built outside the quadrangle buildings. The Soledad Mission was never very large or prosperous, partly because it had an undesirable climate — hot, dry, and windy summers, while freezing and wet in the winter. Priests, and especially the natives, at the Mission Soledad experienced a great deal of sickness, especially **rheumatism**. With the exception of Father Florencio Ibáñez who stayed 15 years, most of the padres at Soledad did not stay long (a total of 30 padres in a span of 44 years). All of the missions were considered places of refuge for anybody who needed it. With Soledad being so isolated it was often visited for this reason.

Do these things using the map provided. (Use the map on page 116.)

1. Write **Mission Nuestra Señora de la Soledad** ①, **cattle brand** ②, **bell** ③, **workshops** ④, **orchards** ⑤, **patio** ⑥, **cemetery** ⑦, **chapel** ⑧, **workers' quarters** ⑨, **padres' living quarters** ⑩, **original church** ⑪, **storerooms** ⑫, and **El Camino Real** ⑬ by the correct number.
2. Do your best job if you color the map.

Nuestra Señora de la Soledad

Name ____________________

Date ____________________

The 13th of 21 Spanish/Catholic Missions

Also known as "Soledad Mission"

Early History

The site selected for the 13th Franciscan mission was discovered by the Governor of California, Don Gaspar de Portolá, who gave it the name of Soledad. Portolá discovered the area during his first land expedition in 1770, when he and his men left Mission San Diego by land to meet with Fr. Junípero Serra who left by ship (the *San Antonio*) to find the harbor at Monterey. While Portolá and his men camped in the area, one of the Indians approached the party and responded to Portolá's questions by repeating one word over and over again. The native's word, which sounded similar to the Spanish word for solitude, "soledad," seemed like a perfect description of the region. Portolá marked the map of the expedition as Soledad. When the mission was founded on October 9, 1791, it was quite appropriate for the Francis-cans to name it in honor of Mary, the Mother of Jesus, *Our Lady of Solitude*. The founding of Nuestra Señora de la Soledad coincided with the "Golden Age" of California's missions.

The green rolling hills and fertile land surrounding the mission encouraged the Franciscans that the mission would be an immediate success. They had high hopes of producing great quantities of agricultural goods. Yet from the founding of the mission, the name it had received by an Indian and Portolá was a prediction of the ultimate future of the 13th mission along El Camino Real.

Hardship seemed to hunt Soledad Mission out in order to have a place to operate. Before Soledad Mission was ever founded, the royal family in Spain sent gifts to the mission to help equip it with the goods needed to get started. The items, however, never arrived at the mission. Fr. Lasuén was forced to ask other missions along *The King's Highway* (El Camino Real) to donate the items Soledad needed. The brushwood shelter that was first dedicated as the mission in 1791 took six years to be replaced by an adobe structure. Even after the permanent buildings were finally completed, they seemed to disintegrate under the extreme changes in the climate. One instance illustrates this perfectly: the church that was supposedly completely repaired in 1824 collapsed in 1832 as a consequence of the harsh winter weather. For the winter months every padre and native worker on the mission was exposed to severe cold and dampness, and the few, small fireplaces had no chance of bringing comfort and warmth to the mission's inhabitants. The padres who were assigned to the mission were often sick with rheumatism from the dampness and had to ask to be transferred to locations with less extreme climate changes.

A hand-carved wooden chair from the mission era.

The exception to the friars who left the mission after so little time in service was Fr. Florencio Ibáñez who devoted over 15 years to the growth of the mission and the neophytes living there. Fr. Ibáñez is the only Franciscan buried at the site. The grave next to his is that of the well-respected Spaniard, Governor José Arrillaga. Arrillaga, after being ill for some time, moved to Soledad in order to be with his dear friend, Fr. Ibáñez. Arrillaga's illness eventually killed him and he was buried by his Franciscan friend on July 24, 1814. In a short four years Fr. Ibáñez was buried next to him.

Nuestra Señora de la Soledad

Name ______________________

Date ______________________

The 13th of 21 Spanish/Catholic Missions

The native population near Mission Soledad was not very large. The padres labored diligently over the years to convert them to the Catholic faith. After 15 years of hard work toward the conversion of the natives, the mission had a **meager** population of 700 neophytes. After 1805, the population at the mission declined very rapidly. One of the misfortunes that led to the declining population was that in 1802 a serious **epidemic** swept through the mission. The plague killed many of the converts, and fear of the plague drove off many more of the Indians who determined the mysterious sickness was a direct result of their acceptance of the new religion.

Mission Soledad and its history has no singular achievement among any of California's missions, yet it still managed to win a place in history because of the appearance of three of the mission's friars. The story of Fr. Mariano Rubi and Fr. Bartólome Gili begins in the College of San Fernando (in Mexico City) where all California Franciscan attended. The two friars arrived at the college in 1788 and began to pull **pranks** that made their **peers** uncomfortable. The college records indicate that the two were accused of everything from robbing the storeroom of the community's chocolate to rolling bowling balls through the dormitory at midnight. They often slept during the day when they were supposed to be doing their studies and working and then at night would climb the walls and spend the night in town.

Nobody knows for sure why the leaders of the college tolerated the two. Perhaps the Franciscans were too embarrassed to let the public know about their **unconventional** friars; or that Fr. Palou, who was head of the college at the time was too old and ill to know or care about their behavior. Anyway, the two prankster padres were wanting to get transferred, and were finally sent to California (you guessed it — to Mission Soledad). Fr. Rubi arrived in 1790 and Fr. Gili replaced Rubi's companion padre in 1791.

Once again together, the two soon made a reputation for **outlandish** behavior. They continually complained and devoted themselves to returning to Mexico. The two friars sent word again and again to the missions' president that the discomforts of Soledad were beyond the call of duty, the worst being that there was a constant shortage of altar wine.

It took Fr. Lasuén very little time to agree that they would be much better off in a different place, but the viceroy who just approved their move to California did not want them to return to Mexico. The padres claimed to be ill, and after examination by a doctor, Fr. Rubi was found to have definite illness. He was allowed to return to Mexico in 1793. It took another year for Fr. Lasuén to receive an okay for Fr. Gili's transfer, but he happily saw him off on a boat. The captain of the ship refused to allow the Franciscan ashore when they reached Loreto, Mexico and carried him away to the Philippines with the rest of the crew. Nobody knows where he went from there.

In 1824 the Salinas River flooded the mission, destroying much of it. In 1828 the river flooded again leaving even less of it standing. The last of the Franciscan padres at Mission Soledad was the inspirational Father. Vincente Francisco de Sarría, who served both as president and administrator of the missions. Also in 1828, unrest in Mexico and growing hostilities of the Californians, were reasons no new friars were being sent to missions in California. When Fr. Sarría realized that it was not possible to find another padre for Soledad, he took on the responsibility himself.

Nuestra Señora de la Soledad

Name ____________________

Date ____________________

The 13th of 21 Spanish/Catholic Missions

As always, the fortunes of Soledad grew worse. Fr. Sarría, alone at the mission, carried on his work among the Indians until May, 1835, a year after secularization. His worn and **emaciated** body was discovered at the foot of the altar. With his death came the death of the Soledad Mission. A few days after his body was found, the last one of his native followers carried his body to Mission San Antonio de Padua, leaving the structures to the mercy of the climate. The secularization decrees set forth in 1834 removed Soledad's name as an active mission, and all of the mission's records and materials were transferred to Mission San Antonio de Padua. In 1846, the site of Soledad was sold by Governor Pio Poco for $800. By the time the mission was returned to the Catholic Church by the United States government, the buildings were in such disrepair that it was never reoccupied. Over the years, the weather took its toll on the adobe structures and **eroded** them to short stubs. ❖

KrissKross Puzzle

Directions for Solving KrissKross Puzzles:

Start with either the longest or shortest word from the list of words. Write the word in the correct place. Then fill in the next word that KrissKrosses the first word, counting the number of squares and then matching the number of letters and/or the correct letter where they KrissKross. For less confusion, mark the words off the list as you use them.

- RUBI
- WIDOW
- FLOODS
- LORETO
- REFUGE
- SARRÍA
- CLIMATE
- SALINAS
- EPIDEMIC
- SOLITUDE
- BRUSHWOOD
- PRANKSTER
- CALIFORNIA
- FRANCISCAN
- QUADRANGLE
- HOSTILITIES
- PHILIPPINES
- UNCONVENTIONAL

Nuestra Señora de la Soledad

Name ______________________

Date ______________________

The 13th of 21 Spanish/Catholic Missions

The Mission Today

Mission Soledad was abandoned and at the mercy of the weather for almost 100 years. By the 1950s the only walls that were still standing were from one corner of the chapel. Restoration of the mission began under the supervision and care of one organization, the Native Daughters of the Golden West.

In 1954 adobe bricks were made from the dust of the original ones and used to reconstruct the small chapel. As the mission's original possessions were located, they have been returned to Mission Soledad. The original bell that was cast in Mexico in the 1790s is once again hanging on a wooden beam to the left of the chapel entrance. The paintings of the stations of the cross and some religious garments were somehow preserved over the years at other missions while Soledad was abandoned and inhabited.

In 1963 the residence wing of the original quadrangle was rebuilt. Ruins of other buildings that once were part of the mission compound can be seen beyond the rebuilt residence wing. Excavation efforts as part of the restoration efforts have uncovered the tile floor of the original church, along with the graves of Fr. Ibáñez and Governor Arrillaga, the Spanish governor of Alta California.

Even though Soledad Mission is a part of the Catholic parish at Soledad, no priest has served at the mission on a full time basis since 1835. Mass at the mission is only held four times a year.

The mission is isolated and a little out of the way. People visiting the mission can appreciate the beautiful garden and small museum. As funds become available, more restoration efforts are being conducted by local people. Each October a Mission Fiesta takes place to raise money for the restoration of Mission Soledad to continue. ❖

Old Mission (Soledad)
c/o Our Lady of Soledad Parish
P.O. Box 506
36641 Fort Romie Road
Soledad, CA 93960
Phone: 831.678.2586

Nuestra Señora de la Soledad
REVIEW QUESTIONS

Name ____________________

Date ____________________

Write the correct answer in the space provided.

1. The Mission Señora de la Soledad, was the ______________ mission the was established along ____________________________.

2. The mission site was first discovered by ____________________ in ____________ (______________ years ago).

3. Because Soledad was so ______________ it was often visited by padres.

4. Hardship seemed to ______________ Mission Soledad out. Before the mission was ever founded, ______________ sent from the royal family in ______________ never arrived at the mission.

5. The padres who were assigned to the mission were often ______________ with rheumatism and asked to ______________ to other locations.

6. Explain why Mission Soledad was never as prosperous as other missions.

____

____

____

____

7. Explain how/why Padres Rubi and Gili were transferred to Mission Soledad.

____

____

____

____

8. Why was it almost impossible for the mission to be preserved over the years?

____

____

____

____

☆☆ **Bonus Activity**

Use another resource and write a report on one of the people mentioned in this section, the College of San Fernando (in Mexico City), weather in California, the Philippine Islands, transportation in the 1700s, the history and/or process of wood carving, Mexico, Spain, Mary (the Mother of Jesus), Jesus, or the history and/or beliefs of Judaism, Catholicism, or Christianity. Draw maps and pictures for your report.

Mission #14

San José

Founded June 11, 1797

Print the names of the missions on the correct lines. (You may need to look back at a previously finished section/map.)

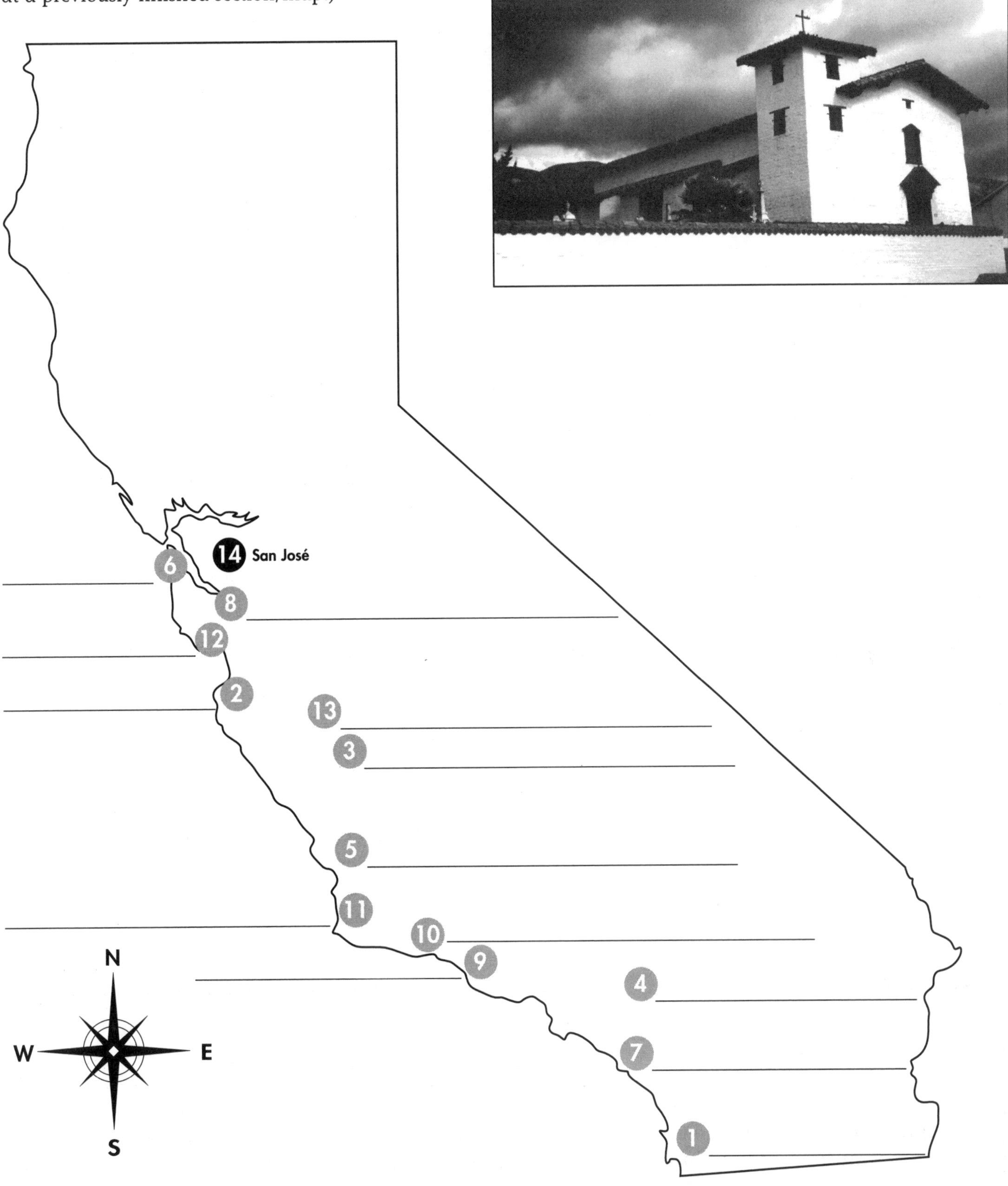

New Words to Learn:

Find the words in the glossary or a dictionary and write the meanings on the line. (Not many new words in this section!!!)

1. **foray**(s):____
2. **plunder**(ed):____
3. **viol**(s):____

① ____

Mission #14 — Founded June 11, 1797

Layout of the Mission Grounds

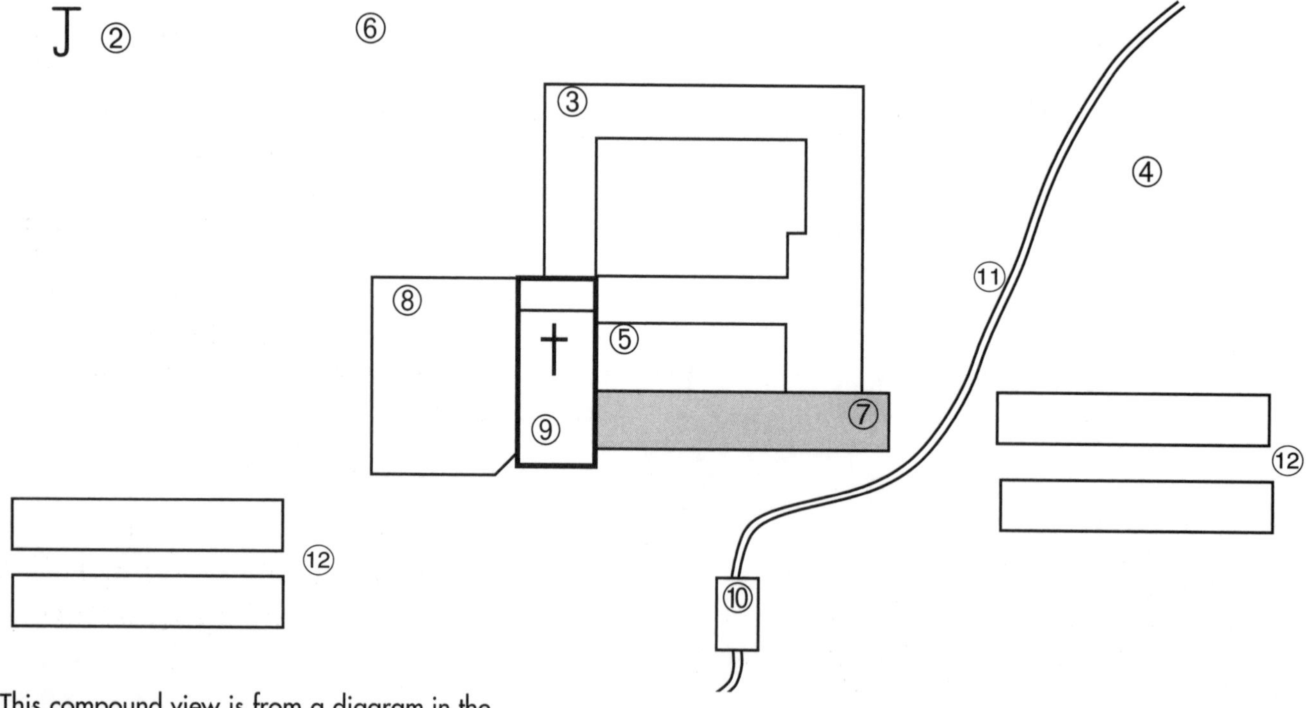

This compound view is from a diagram in the mission's museum. The diagram is dated 1820.

San José

Named for the husband of Mary, the virgin Mother of Jesus. Joseph was the foster father of Jesus.

Name ______________________

Date ______________________

The 14th of 21 Spanish/Catholic Missions

Design of the Mission

Church: (approximate outside measurements) 124 feet long, 30 feet wide, and 30 feet high. The church is made of adobe and redwood. There is tile on both the roof and floor.

Design:
Like many of the missions in California, San José's architecture is plain. The exterior is undecorated and whitewashed. The side walls are supported by large buttresses. The church is slightly raised from the sidewalk. There are brick steps, laid in a semi-circle, that lead up to the entrance. The Mexican artist, Agustín Dávila painted both the interior and the wooden base of the copper baptismal. The altar area has carved, wooden furnishings, 23-karat gold leaf trim, and a very old statue depicting St. Joseph.

Walls: The walls vary in thickness from four to five feet thick.

Campanario:
The bell tower is a low square that adjoins the church. The four original bells hang in the tower.

Mission Compound:
The traditional mission quadrangle of buildings covered about five acres. The buildings which housed padres, storerooms, and workshops opened into a patio area. Fathers Durán and Fortuni taught the mission's workers the crafts of carpentry, sewing, weaving, leather tanning, and making shoes and rope. Mission San José had the great fortune of having hot springs nearby. They channeled warm water through aqueducts into a lavandería (laundry basin) in front of the church.

Mission Grounds:
Mission Santa Clara blessed Mission San José at its founding by giving it 600 head of cattle and a flock of sheep. These herds of livestock multiplied; and the mission had rich fertile soil which helped produce great vineyards for grapes, as well as fruit and olive orchards. The mission had a tannery, flour mill, and soap factory. Adobe houses were built for the workers to live in. This was the most successful of all of the northern missions in terms of the number of native workers it employed and the amount of agricultural products the mission and its workers produced. In 1832 the mission owned more than 24,000 head of livestock and about 20,000 acres of land. During the mission's early years, soldiers from the nearby San Francisco Presidio used it as their base to conduct raids when they attacked and **plundered** the local Indian tribes. In 1827 trapper Jedediah Smith stayed at the mission, and records show that Kit Carson visited the mission in 1830.

Do these things using the map provided. (Use the map on page 124.)

1. Write **Mission San José** ①, **cattle brand** ②, **workshops** ③, **orchard** ④, **patio** ⑤, **vineyard** ⑥, **padres' living quarters** ⑦, **cemetery** ⑧, **church** ⑨, **lavandería** ⑩, **warm water aqueduct** ⑪, and **native living quarters** ⑫ by the correct number.
2. Do your best job if you color the map.

San José

The full name is "Mission del Gloriosísimo Patriarca Señor San José"

Name ______________________________

Date ______________________________

The 14th of 21 Spanish/Catholic Missions

Early History

By 1796, the southernmost mission at San Diego and the northernmost mission at San Francisco were linked by the well traveled *El Camino Real.* Along the highway were areas where natives hostile to white settlers lived. Because of the possibility of being attacked by the Indians, it was necessary for the military to provide protection for most of the travelers who journeyed along *The King's Highway.* It was the Franciscans' hope that they could establish a mission at the end of each day's journey along the highway. With the arrival of California's new governor from Mexico, Diego Borica, the mission president, Fr. Lasuén, realized the time was perfect for establishing a new mission. He and Governor Borica agreed that a total of five new missions were needed.

In August of 1796, Governor Borica sent a request to Mexico's Viceroy Branciforte (see Mission Santa Cruz for information about the pueblo with his name) asking permission for the Franciscans to carry out the plan for the five new missions. Borica logically argued that the project would require no more soldiers than were already in California, and that they could save about $15,000 a year because military protection would not be needed once the Franciscan friars converted the Indians to Christianity. The viceroy saw validity in the argument and gave permission for the plans to go forward.

On June 11, 1797, Fr. Lasuén, Sergeant Pedro Amador, and five soldiers dedicated Mission San José at a location 15 miles to the north of the pueblo which had the same name. (The pueblo of San José had been founded 20 years earlier by Lieutenant Moraga. This is why the mission is in the current city of Fremont, not San José.) The mission was purposely founded a great distance from the pueblo in order to relieve the friars and natives from the problems other missions had when built too close to other colonial settlements. (See the section on Mission Santa Cruz for more details.)

The padres envisioned this site as a base to control the native Californians in the San Joaquin and Sacramento Valleys. Military expeditions were sent out to subdue the troublesome tribes in the valleys, and Mission San José was midway on the main route to the valleys. The mission served as a headquarters for Indian fighters. **Forays** against the native people took place often, with the first occurring soon after Mission San José opened. The mission padres were well aware of the fact that a hostile tribe was harboring a number of runaway neophytes from Mission San Francisco (Mission Dolores). Sergeant Amador took a military expedition against the natives. He returned with 80 runaways and nine additional "**pagans**" who had been captured after a short battle. More trouble came in 1805 when a different group of hostile Indians attacked white travelers, killing four people. This triggered a savage reaction from the Spanish, who in turn killed 11 Indians and captured 30 more.

In 1826, Estanislao — an Indian Chieftain and favorite of Father Durán led an uprising in the San Joaquin Valley. Twice he successfully defended his fortress in the woods along what is now the Stanilaus River.

San José

Name ______________________________

Date ______________________________

The 14th of 21 Spanish/Catholic Missions

In May of 1826, a third expedition led by Lieutenant Vallejo and Lieutenant José Sanchez marched against the chieftain and his band of more than 1,000 men. The army chased and fought the natives for over three days, until the Spanish soldiers had complete victory. All of the surviving Indians, except Estanislao, were brutally hung without trials or apparent good reason, by the Spanish soldiers. The chieftain was brought back to Mission San José as a captured enemy. Father Durán was outraged by the commandante's violent treatment of the natives. He received no sympathy from Vallejo for his protests, but managed to obtain the release of his former neophyte, Estanislao. He died ten years later of smallpox. (Some historians believe that the river near the site of the fight and the county through which it runs bear the name "Stanislaus" in memory of the native chieftain.)

The missionaries serving at Mission San José had early problems with the local natives. They were either hostile toward whites or totally indifferent to the mission system and its religion. By the end of the first year, only 33 neophytes were at the mission. These converts were too young to do much of the construction work the mission needed. However, the situation changed and San José eventually became the most successful mission in northern California. It ranked third behind missions Santa Clara and San Gabriel in the number of converted natives, with 6,673. It was third in total head of livestock it owned, and was second, only behind San Gabriel, in total agricultural production. By 1800 the mission had a total of 286 natives living on the compound. After this, the situation improved until 1831, when the Indian population reached a high of 1,877. The neophyte population dropped rapidly after 1831. In nine short years only 580 natives remained on the mission.

Much of the success of Mission San José was due to the extraordinary efforts and gifts of Fr. Narciso Durán. He supervised the mission for 27 years. He arrived in California from Mexico in 1806 and was assigned to Mission San José the same year, along with Father Buenaventura Fortuni. For over 20 years, until Fr. Fortuni was transferred to Sonoma, they worked long and hard to make the mission prosperous and successful. Just before Fr. Fortuni left for Sonoma, Fr. Durán was elected president of the missions. He held this office from 1825 through 1827 and again from 1831 to 1838.

Fr. Durán seemed to excel at everything he undertook. Under his supervision the mission constructed an irrigation system. He wrote and taught music. His native American orchestra became quite famous and learned how to play European instruments including the flute, violin, trumpet, and drums. His administrative abilities were comparable to those of Fr. Lasuén. Even though the mission system was doomed when he took office as president, under his leadership the existence of the missions prolonged for many years.

Mission San José as it appeared in the late 1880s.

San José

Name ______________________

Date ______________________

The 14th of 21 Spanish/Catholic Missions

Because Mexico was at war with Spain, no new missionaries from Spain and the Franciscan College of San Fernando in Mexico City were allowed to come to California. The college suffered a decline because of the anti-Spanish feeling that developed in the new republic of Mexico. The Mexican government asked the Zacatecan College to supply the additional Franciscan missionaries that were needed. In 1833, California's Governor Figueroa brought in a number of Zacatecan padres who had been born in Mexico, not Spain. The new padres were placed in charge of the northern missions. Fr. Durán moved his headquarters to Mission Santa Bárbara, leaving Mission San José under the supervision of the Zacatecans.

Mission San José was secularized three years later. Its property was turned over to the administrator, Jesús Vallejo, the brother of Mariano. At this time the transferred livestock and other property was valued at $155,000. In just over two years, the value of the mission's property was near zero. The Englishman named Hartnell who was the inspector general of the missions after the Secularization Act reported that much of the mission's property could be found on a ranch that was owned by the Vallejo brothers. Nothing was ever done about the matter, and in 1846 Governor Pio Pico sold what remained to his brother, Andres, and former Governor Alvarado. This sale was eventually annulled and the property (about 28 acres) was returned to the Catholic Church by the Congress of the United States. ❖

Scrambled Sentences

Write the unscrambled sentence on the line below the scrambled sentence. (Use capital letters and punctuation.)

1. a wooden protection was over the built remains for from new erosion roof

____

2. a californians the padres control envisioned san mission josé as base to the native

____

3. mission nearby josé of fortune san had the having hot springs great

____

4. returned sale of the the the the mission annulled was and property to church by catholic

____

5. durán efforts much of success mission was gifts due to and the the the of of father

____

6. and the smith stayed carson at the trapper records show jedediah visited mission it kit

____

7. northern successful san became the most josé in mission california

____

Name ______________________________

Date ______________________________

The 14th of 21 Spanish/Catholic Missions

The Mission Today

The mission suffered the usual effects after secularization, but remained a parish church for some years. For a number of years the normal deterioration and erosion took its toll on the mission. On October 12, 1868 the earthquake on the Hayward Fault brought the final blow to the mission. The earthquake was considered the strongest in California's history. After the earthquake only a small part of the west wing (padres' living quarters) of the quadrangle that once covered five acres remained standing. A white, wooden frame church with a tall steeple was erected on the site after the original adobe structure was destroyed by the earthquake. In 1916 a new wooden roof was built over the portion of the remains to protect the adobe from further erosion and deterioration.

It was not until 1982 that a major effort was made to restore the mission. After 3 years of work, a replica of the mission chapel from about 1835 was completed on the original foundation. Authentic materials and tools matching those used during the mission era were used, though the new adobe was reinforced to make it stronger and more durable. Archeologists discovered some of the original floor tiles which were used in the replica. Richard Menn of Carmel was able to recreate Agustín Dávila's paintings by following the designs from the baptismal font.

The mission's museum displays several artifacts from the mission era including items showing the craftsmanship of the Ohlone people (natives to the area) and lifestyle on the mission.

Mission San José was very well-known for its musical accomplishments (orchestra and choir). People came from other missions to hear concerts, and the orchestra was often requested to play at weddings, ceremonies, and fiestas. In 1832 the orchestra had 20 violins, four bass **viols**, one contrabass, one drum, one hand organ, and 26 band uniforms. In 1819 Fr. Durán requested a pipe organ be sent to the mission. It took 170 years for the request to be granted when a 19th century Mexican style pipe organ was installed in 1989. ❖

Mission San José
P.O. Box 3276
43300 Mission Blvd.
San Jose, CA 94538
Phone: 510.657.1797

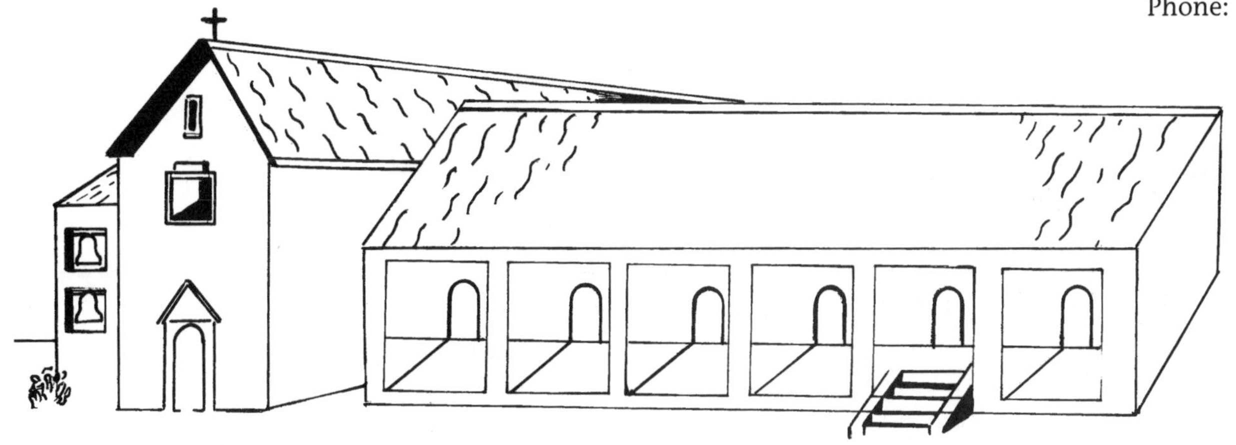

This shows the first church and monastery at Mission San José.

Name ______________________

Date ______________________

Review Questions

Write the correct answer in the space provided.

1. Mission San José was the ________________ mission that was established along *the King's Highway*. It has become the most ________________ mission in northern ________________ .

2. Mission San José was founded ________________ years ago.

3. Mission San José ranked ____________ in the number of ____________ native people (neophytes), behind missions Santa Clara and ____________ .

4. The earthquake on the ____________________ destroyed the mission. The ________________ of 1868 was considered the ____________ in the history of ________________ .

5. Explain why Mission San José was successful.

6. Explain why the military used the Mission San José.

7. Name some of Fr. Durán's accomplishments while at the mission.

8. Tell what Mission San José was noted for.

☆☆ Bonus Activity

Use another resource and write a report on one of the people mentioned in this section, the Zacatecan College, Hayward Fault, hot springs, redwood trees, the history or making of a viol, contrabass, hand organ, or pipe organ, or a native tribe in the San Joaquin or Sacramento Valleys. Draw maps and pictures for your report.

Mission #15

San Juan Bautista

Founded June 24, 1797

Print the names of the missions on the correct lines. (You may need to look back at a previously finished section/map.)

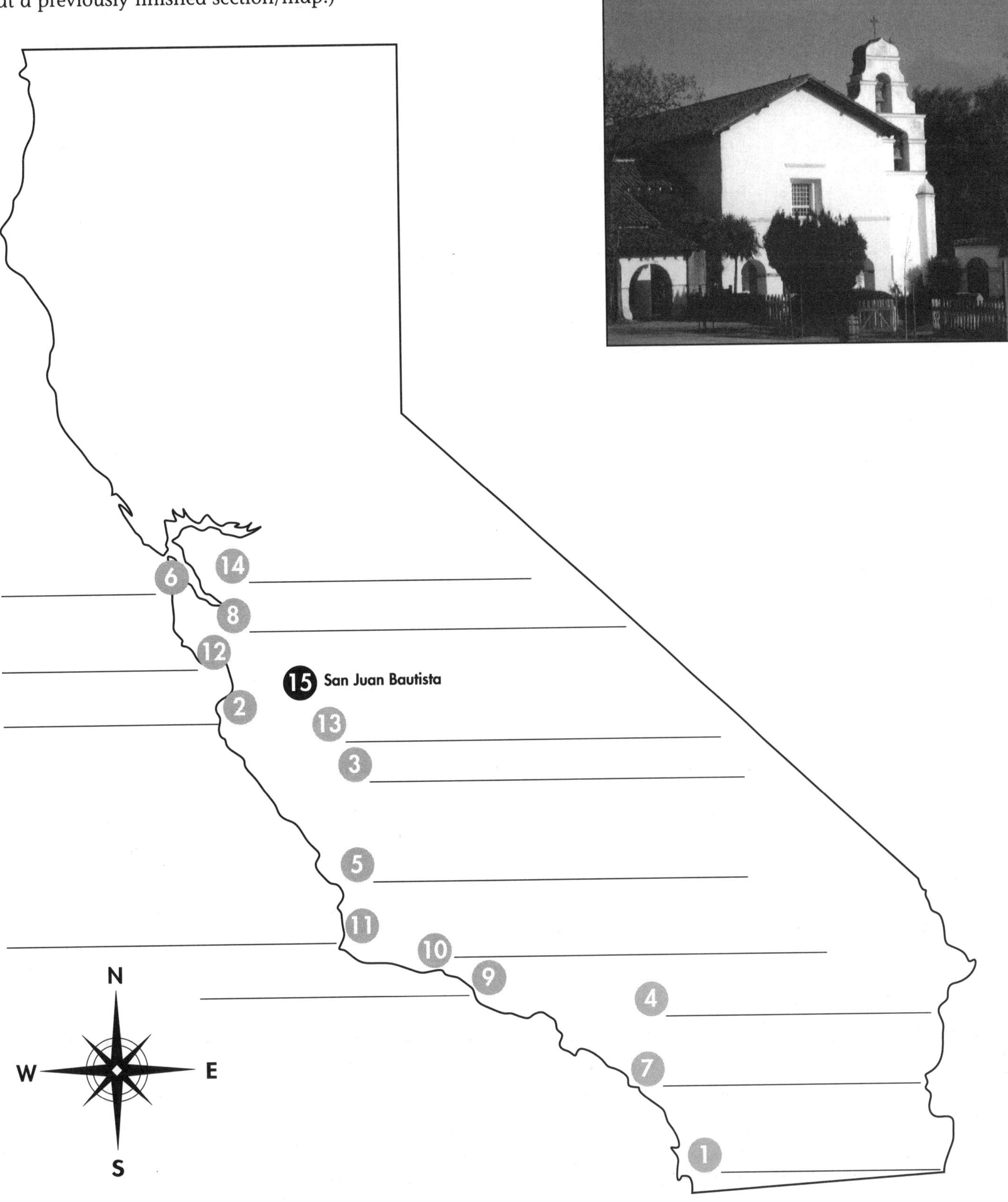

New Words to Learn:

Find the words in the glossary or a dictionary and write the meanings on the line.

1. **cornerstone:** ______________________________
2. **dialect**(s)**:** ______________________________
3. **embellish:** ______________________________
4. **forerunner:** ______________________________
5. **liquidate**(d)**:** ______________________________
6. **rendition:** ______________________________
7. **zeal:** ______________________________

① ______________________________

Mission # 15 — Founded June 24, 1797

Layout of the Mission Grounds

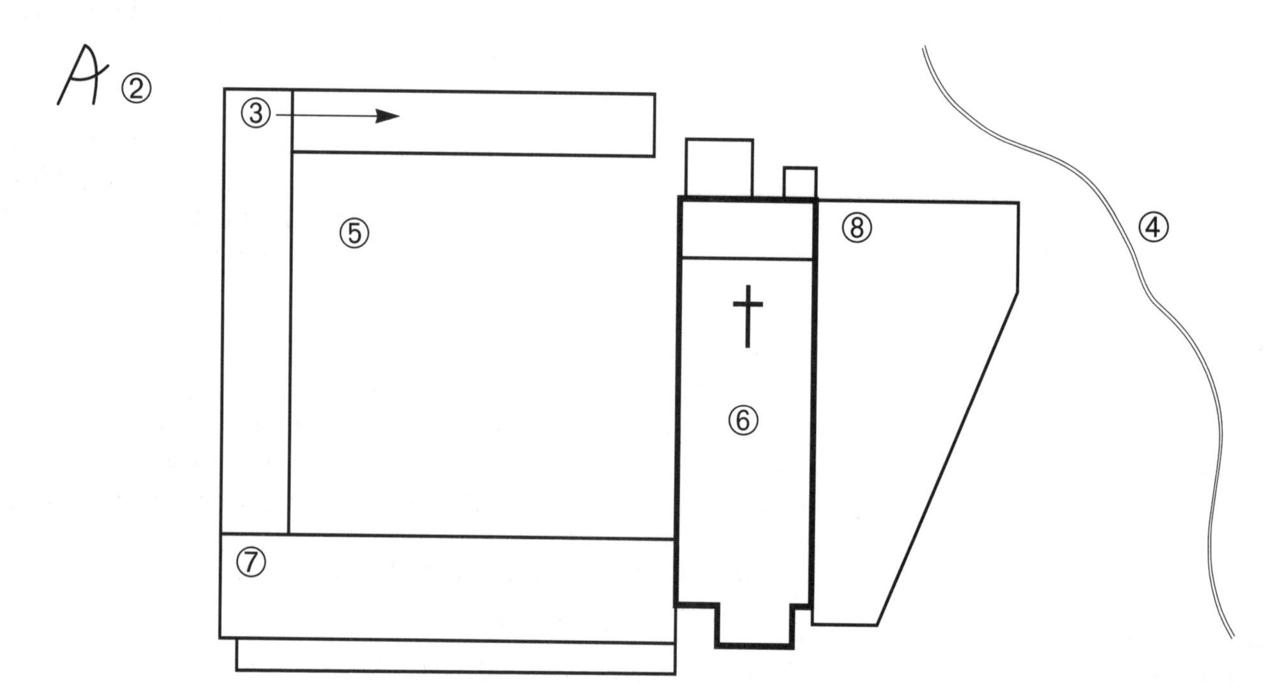

This is a diagram showing an early view of Mission San Juan Bautista's compound.

San Juan Bautista

Named for Saint John the Baptist. John the Baptist was the **forerunner** of Jesus and the person who baptized Jesus.

Name ______________________

Date ______________________

The 15th of 21 Spanish/Catholic Missions

Design of the Mission

Church: (approximate outside measurements) 184 feet long, 72 feet wide, and 40 feet high.

The church at San Juan Bautista is larger than any other California mission church. It is made of adobe and has a tile roof and tile floor.

Design:

The style of this church is grand and large. The entrance is plain. It has three arches in front — one large arch in the middle with smaller ones to each side. These arches create a covered patio-type entrance. There is a window directly above the center arch. This church has three aisles instead of the traditional single aisle. The interior walls are painted with native-style designs in addition to the bright colors painted by a sailor from Boston, Massachusetts who lived at the mission. Some walls are painted to resemble marble. There is bright red drapery covering the wall behind the altar. The wall has niches that hold statues, including an impressive life-size **rendition** of John the Baptist.

Walls: The walls are three feet thick with cement supports.

Campanario:

The original church had no bell tower. The bells hung from a wooden crossbar in the yard. A wooden steeple in a New England design was added in 1867 by Fr. Rubio and damaged in a wind storm in 1915; a shorter, stucco tower was built in 1929 and then taken down in 1949. In 1976 a bell tower in the traditional mission style (similar to the one at Mission San Diego) was built where stone foundations were found to indicate one may have been originally planned. Most of the nine original bells were lost or destroyed over the years. The present campanario holds three bells, with two being original. The third bell was a gift from Fr. Lasuén's (founding father) home village in Spain.

Mission Compound:

The living quarters were in a wing 230 feet long and have 19 arches in front of the structure. Interestingly, the first and 13th arches are square instead of rounded, maybe to allow wider and taller objects to pass through. There is a large kitchen that has a fireplace built along one entire wall. The quadrangle buildings housed workshops for weaving, candle making, carpentry, and leather work.

Mission Grounds:

Mission San Juan Bautista was a wealthy mission with 36 acres of pear and apple orchards, and several herds of livestock. The agriculture that was started by the early padres still continues today. When the ships docked at the harbor in Monterey, the mission would trade hides and tallow for their merchandise (mostly machinery and tools).

Do these things using the map provided. (Use the map on page 132.)

1. Write **Mission San Juan Bautista** ①, **cattle brand** ②, **workshops** ③, **El Camino Real** ④, **patio** ⑤, **church** ⑥, **padres' living quarters** ⑦, and **cemetery** ⑧ by the correct number.
2. Do your best job if you color the map.

San Juan Bautista

Also known as "The Mission of Music"

Name ______________________

Date ______________________

The 15th of 21 Spanish/Catholic Missions

Early History

It took only 13 days after the dedication of Mission San José for Fr. Lasuén to perform the dedication ceremony at San Juan Bautista — June 24, 1797.

In a short six months the newest mission in the growing Franciscan chain had an adobe church, a monastery, a granary, a guardhouse, and even several adobe houses for the mission's native workers/converts. By as early as 1800 there were more than 500 Indians living on the mission grounds. In October of the same year, an earthquake damaged the structures quite a bit. The padres in charge of the mission decided it was a perfect time — while doing the needed repairs — to enlarge the church as well as add new facilities that were needed. As the native neophyte population continued to increase, so did the plans of the padres. In 1803 plans were drawn to add another church. When construction began, the mission held an elaborate ceremony and invited people from all over the province of California. During the dedication of the new structure, a written account of the event was sealed in a bottle and placed in the **cornerstone** of the foundation.

In 1808, a new padre named Father Arroyo de la Cuesta arrived at Mission San Juan Bautista. He had a great deal of ambition, education, imagination, and **zeal**. He convinced the builders that instead of the traditional long and narrow **nave**, a wide church with three naves would be a tremendous asset to San Juan Bautista. In 1812, at its completion, the church was the largest in the entire California province and the only structure of its kind ever built by the Franciscan friars in California.

Ironically, during the construction of the church, the neophyte population for whom it was being built declined steadily. In 1805, the native population living on the mission was about 1,100. By the time the church was completed in 1812, the neophyte population was less than 550. The huge structure dwarfed the people attending the church meetings, so Fr. de la Cuesta had the two rows of arches that separated the three naves of the church walled in. After these alterations, the interior looked similar to most of the other mission churches. The two new outer naves formed large, separate rooms.

When it came to decorating and furnishing the church, Padre de la Cuesta sought out articles of the finest workmanship available. In 1820 he hired Thomas Doak, an American carpenter with a true gift for decorating, to **embellish** the plain interior walls. Thomas Doak was not only a gifted craftsman, he was also the first American *citizen* to settle in California. In 1816 he deserted the ship he was sailing on and came ashore at Monterey. He then became a Spanish citizen and found permanent residence at Mission San Juan Bautista. He later married the daughter of José Castro.

In 1790 the Spanish throne began to show interest in expanding the settlement to the east of El Camino Real (*The King's Highway*). The three Franciscan settlements, Soledad, San José, and San Juan Bautista were direct results of their interest in expanding to the east. Unfriendly natives were no longer avoided by the Spanish military leaders and soldiers. Vallejo, Amador, Moraga, and Peralta were frequent visitors to Missions San José and San Juan Bautista. Even so, starting more missions to the east of El Camino Real was an alternative to fighting which the Franciscans still wished to accomplish.

San Juan Bautista

Name ______________________

Date ______________________

The 15th of 21 Spanish/Catholic Missions

One such effort to establish mission settlements to the east of El Camino Real took place in the 1830s. A stonemason from Boston Massachusetts, Caleb Merrill, came to Mission San Diego. His talents and workmanship were so well liked by the Franciscans that he was soon working at Mission Headquarters at Mission Carmel. After a short time there, a missionary expedition was sent from San Juan Bautista to find a site twenty miles south of present-day Fresno. Merrill was with the expedition and was placed in charge of supervising the construction of the mission. The expedition made several hundred adobe bricks after arriving at the site, but were forced to abandon their efforts by the natives living in the area, the Tulare people. The expedition returned to San Juan Bautista and left behind the pile of adobe bricks that could still be seen in the 1860s.

In 1812, Father Estévan Tápis retired from being president of the missions and joined Fr. de la Cuesta at Mission San Juan Bautista. (Fr. Tápis had been president of the missions since the death of Fr. Lasuén in 1803.) Like Fr. Durán of Mission San José, Fr. Tápis was very talented and gifted in music. He did a great deal to develop choral singing among the neophytes at Mission San Juan Bautista. He introduced the use of colored notes to represent different vocal parts on sheet music. He died at San Juan Bautista at the age of seventy-one in 1825.

Fr. de la Cuesta was the supervisor of San Juan Bautista until the mission was passed into the leadership of the college of Zacatecan Franciscan. He was more educated, imaginative, and forceful than the majority of his peers. He knew more than a dozen native Californian languages and could say Mass in seven different Native American **dialects**. He wrote two historically important works while at San Juan; one was a collection of native phrases and the other a detailed study of the Mutsumi language, which received scientific recognition in 1860. After Fr. de la Cuesta turned the leadership of Mission San Juan Bautista over to a Zacatecan friar in 1833, he moved to live with his own Franciscans at Mission San Miguel until he died in 1840.

The Zacatecan leadership lasted only two years. In 1835, under the Secularization Act, the mission was placed under a civil administrator and its assets were **liquidated**. A small settlement of non-natives to California began and soon replaced the native village near the mission. There were about 50 inhabitants by the end of 1839. The new pueblo became the small town of San Juan Bautista. Padres have lived at the mission from the day of its founding. On November 19, 1859, President James Buchanan and the U.S. Congress gave the Mission San Juan Bautista back to the Catholic Church. ❖

Mission San Juan Bautista in the late1800s.

San Juan Bautista

Name ________________

Date ________________

Crossword Puzzle

The 15th of 21 Spanish/Catholic Missions

Note: You will have to read page 137 in order to answer all of the questions in this puzzle.

Across

3. Captain George ________ reportedly brought a hand-organ to the mission in 1792.
4. Stonemason, Caleb Merrill's talent and ________ was so good that he transferred to work on Mission Head-quarters, at Carmel.
5. In 1812, Fr. Tápis retired from being ________ of the missions.
8. Fr. Arroyo de la Cuesta had a lot of ________ , education, imagination, and zeal.
11. The expedition sent to establish a mission south of present-day Fresno had to ________ their efforts.
14. Extensive renovation and ________ restored the original three naves.
18. The Spanish ________ showed interest in expanding the San Juan Bautista to the east of El Camino Real.
19. In 1976 extensive ________ began on the mission.
20. Fr. Arroyo de la Cuesta knew more than a dozen ________ .
21. Fr. Arroyo de la Cuesta could give Mass in seven different Native American ________ .

Down

1. The ________ of the mission system lasted only two years.
2. Fr. Arroyo de la Cuesta left a detailed study of the native ________ language.
6. A sailor from ________ painted the interior walls with bright colors.
7. Mission San Juan Bautista was built over the San ________ fault.
9. The ________ that was started by the early padres continues today.
10. ________ have lived at the mission from the day of its founding.
12. People from all over the ________ of California were invited to an elaborate ceremony, held at the mission, when construction began.
13. Under secularization, a civilian administrator oversaw the ________ of the mission's assets.
15. A written account of the dedication was sealed in a bottle and placed in the ________ of the foundation.
16. A wooden ________ was added to the campanario by Father Rubio in 1867.
17. During construction of the church, the ________ population steadily declined.

San Juan Bautista

Name ______________________

Date ______________________

The 15th of 21 Spanish/Catholic Missions

The Mission Today

Mission San Juan Bautista was built over the San Andreas fault line, the earthquake of 1906 did extensive damage to the Mission church but the monastery was not affected. Most likely it suffered so little damage because Fr. de la Cuesta had the interior arches filled in, which added more support to the structure. After 1906 all of the buildings were strengthened with steel and concrete. Because the church has been in continual use since its founding, vandalism and decay have not been a factor. In 1949 the stucco bell tower was removed and the bells were hung from a wooden crossbar in front of the church. During the same period, the interior was restored to its 1820 condition. Fortunately, most of the original paintings done on the walls in 1820 were still bright.

Extensive renovation and reconstruction in 1976 opened up the filled in arches into the side aisles, restoring the three original naves. This once again made Mission San Juan Bautista's church the largest mission church in California. A new campanario was erected where excavators found a stone foundation (suggesting one may have been originally planned). The tower's design is similar to that at Mission San Diego, but is a completely new addition where none had ever existed at San Juan Bautista.

Mission San Juan Bautista is a parish church, that serves the Spanish-speaking people living in the community in a similar setting as that in 1820. The area is surrounded by ranches and farms on rolling hills. The only part of the mission's quadrangle still standing is the large front wing. The plaza facing the mission and the surrounding buildings built in the 1840s has become a State Historical Monument.

The mission's museum shows the influences of the two Franciscan friars who spent the most years there. The museum also houses a hand-organ, which is reported to have been brought to California in 1792 by the English explorer, Captain George Vancouver. One story is told about a group of hostile Indians attacking the mission who were so charmed by the beautiful music coming from the hand-organ that they stopped their attack in order to listen.

Mission San Juan Bautista showing the nineteen arches of the living quarters.

Near the cemetery is one of the few places left where a section of the old El Camino Real can be seen. The authentic setting of Mission San Juan Bautista is truly an experience to be enjoyed and remembered. ❖

Mission San Juan Bautista
P.O. Box 41
2nd and Mariposa Streets
San Juan Bautista, CA 95045
Phone: 408.623.2127

San Juan Bautista

Name ____________________

Date ____________________

Review Questions

Write the correct answer in the space provided.

1. The fifteenth California mission was founded on ____________________ ____________________ years ago, and named ____________________ It was named for ____________________

2. The mission was constructed over the ____________________ fault line

3. Mission San Juan Bautista was a ____________________ mission. The ____________________ that was started by the early padres still continues.

4. This church had ____________________ aisles in stead of the usual single aisle.

5. Do you think Mission San Juan Bautista would be considered a wealthy mission by today's standard of living? ____________________ Explain your answer.

6. Explain Thomas Doak's talents and how he arrived in California.

7. Explain the results of the Spanish throne's desire to expand east of El Camino Real.

☆☆ Bonus Activity

Use another resource and write a report on one of the people mentioned in this section, agriculture history or techniques, native tribal language(s), the development of languages, John the Baptist, baptism (reasons why, practices, etc.), or the use of arches in architecture. Draw maps and pictures for your report.

Mission #16

San Miguel Arcángel

Founded July 25, 1797

Print the names of the missions on the correct lines. (You may need to look back at a previously finished section/map.)

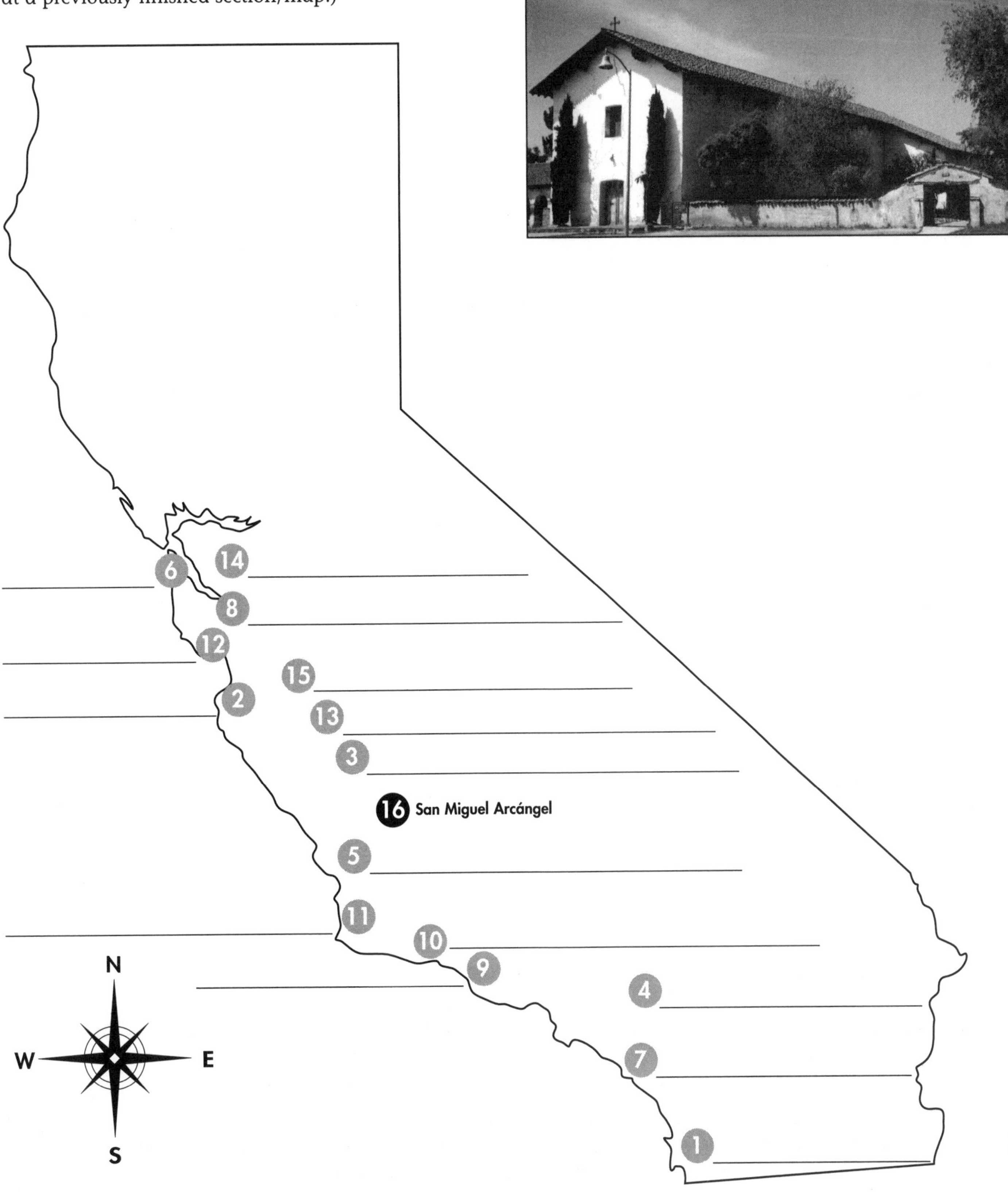

New Words to Learn:

Find the words in the glossary or a dictionary and write the meanings on the line.

1. **ellipse** (elliptical): ____________________
2. **intrusion:** ____________________
3. **monogamy:** ____________________
4. **mural**(s): ____________________
5. **optimism:** ____________________
6. **scaffold:** ____________________
7. **terrain:** ____________________
8. **transparent** (transparency): ____________________
9. (un)**warrant**(ed): ____________________

① ____________________

Mission #16 — Founded July 25, 1797

Layout of the Mission Grounds

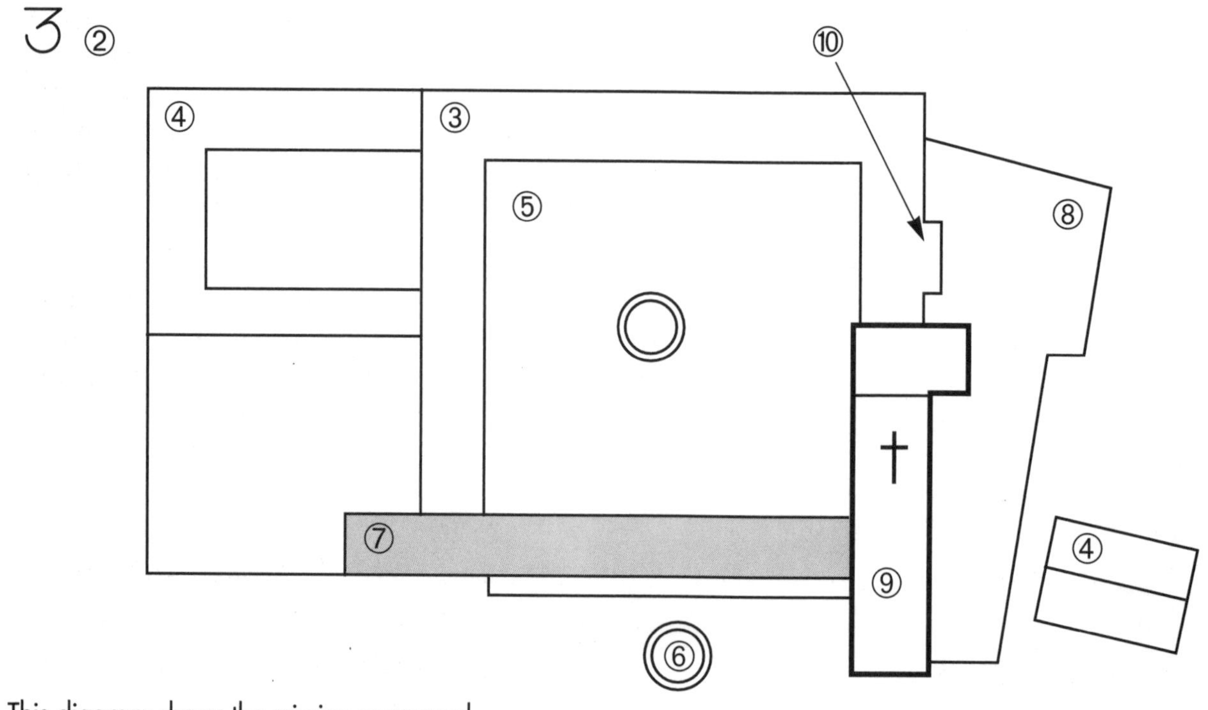

This diagram shows the mission compound in the 1820s.

San Miguel Arcángel

Name ______________________

Date ______________________

Named for the Angel Michael, the leader of God's Army against Satan. Michael is considered the highest ranking of the archangels and the protector of Christians, especially when they are facing death.

The 16th of 21 Spanish/Catholic Missions

Design of the Mission

Church: (approximate outside measurements) 157 feet long, 38 feet wide, and 30 feet high.

The church has adobe walls built on a stone foundation. The roof is made of tile and the floor is made of brick.

Design:

The style of the church is plain on the exterior. The interior is almost glowing with elaborate paintings and **murals**, which were done by natives under the supervision of Estévan Munars from Catalonia, Spain. The stenciled designs of flowers and leaves are done in vibrant colors. Behind the altar above a statue depicting St. Michael is a painting of the "all-seeing eye of God" in gold and white. Floor bricks alternate in rows of squares and rectangles to make an interesting effect. Beams made of pine brought from the Santa Lucia Mountains 40 miles away were used for the roof and ceiling. Only four small windows provide light.

Walls: The walls are six feet thick.

Campanario:

The first bell was hung on a wooden **scaffold** in front of the church. Many years later (1930) a bell tower was built behind the church, attached to part of the quadrangle. This tower holds three bells, with one weighing about 2,000 pounds (the largest bell in any of the missions). It was recast of bells from other missions and rang for the first time on Christmas Day, 1888.

Mission Compound:

A large 200-foot square quadrangle had workshops for the mission craftsmen to work on carpentry, leather, wool (weaving), stone, and iron products. A unique arcade fronts the padres' quarters. It has a series of 12 arches in a row, similar to most of the other missions. What sets this series of arches apart is that they vary in height, width, and shape, yet are arranged symmetrically around the center arches. The first arch at each end is smaller and semicircular, followed by four large arches, then a large **elliptical** arch flanks each side of the center. Nobody has ever determined the reason for such a unique design.

Mission Grounds:

San Miguel's land extended nearly 50 miles from its northern and southern boundaries and over the mountains to the ocean. Several ranchos provided land for the mission's 13,000 head of livestock to graze. There were numerous acres of wheat, barley, and vineyards. Closer to the compound workers made soap and roof tiles, and worked in a gristmill and granaries. Elaborate dams, reservoirs, and viaducts provided water from the Salinas River.

Do these things using the map provided. (Use the map on page 140.)

1. Write **Mission San Miguel Arcángel** ①, **cattle brand** ②, **workshops** ③, **workers' quarters** ④, **patio** ⑤, **fountain** ⑥, **padres' living quarters** ⑦, **cemetery** ⑧, **church** ⑨, and **bell wall** ⑩ by the correct number.
2. Do your best job if you color the map.

San Miguel Arcángel

Name ______________________________

Date ______________________________

The second of three missions named for angels. Michael is the "Captain of God's Army."

The 16th of 21 Spanish/Catholic Missions

Early History

In a period of four months, President Fermín de Lasuén founded four missions. On a site about halfway between Missions San Luís Obispo and San Antonio de Padua the third of the these four missions was Mission San Miguel Arcángel — founded July 25, 1797.

The Franciscans now considered the northern part of the mission chain, from San Luís Obispo to Dolores in San Francisco, to be complete. They hoped for Mission San Miguel to be very prosperous, as it was situated in an area with great climate, flat **terrain**, and fertile soil. Water was plentiful, as it was located near where the Nacimiento and Salinas Rivers met. In addition to the favorable geographical elements, on the day of their arrival they were greeted by a number of natives to the area. These friendly natives helped the Franciscans work and set up the mission. The padres took these friendly, helpful attitudes as a good sign for success in converting the local people to Catholicism and for the future growth of the mission. As it turned out, their **optimism** was correct, and Mission San Miguel soon became a thriving community.

In six years, the mission recorded more than 1,000 native people baptized; and in under ten years reported about 1,000 neophytes living at the mission. The compound consisted of the mission-style quadrangle, along with several other buildings. The workers became skilled blacksmiths, masons, carpenters, soap makers, weavers, and leather workers. Hundreds of other workers tended the livestock, orchards, and vineyards, and even produced charcoal for use in the tile ovens. In addition to these duties, the women performed the tasks of cooking food and doing other daily routines for all who lived on the mission. For several years there were few, if any, conflicts at Mission San Miguel.

In 1806, a huge fire destroyed or did serious damage to most of the mission's buildings. Perhaps worst of all, its storehouses of wool, cloth, leather goods, and more than 6,000 bushels of grain were destroyed or made useless. Other missions came to San Miguel's aid and new adobe buildings with tile roofs were soon built where the original ones had stood. A new and larger church was erected, and by 1816 all that was needed to complete the structure was a roof. The nearest timber for the beams that were to hold the roof tiles was in the mountains about 40 miles from the mission compound. The lumber had to be hauled over rough and trackless terrain. The workers completed this task in 1818, and the final decorations were added three years later under the watchful supervision of the artisan-builder, Estévan Munras, from Catalonia, Spain.

Similar to the other northern missions, San Miguel developed an interest in converting the native people living in the valleys of central California. Father Juan Cabot, who was in charge of Mission San Miguel after 1800, sent several expeditions into the central valley (San Joaquín) with the hopes of starting a mission there. There the expeditions met with the Tulare Indians, who were warlike tribes that strongly resented the **intrusion** of white settlers and soldiers. Fr. Cabot's success of converting these people was just like those of other missions and padres who tried — it never happened. He eventually stopped sending expeditions. After 1820, the hostilities and conflicts between the Franciscans and the civil authorities had escalated so much he eventually scrapped his plans altogether for mission expansion into the central valleys. Instead of gaining more influence, land, and property, the Franciscans eventually lost all of their material wealth to the civilian settlers.

San Miguel Arcángel

Name ______________________________

Date ______________________________

The 16th of 21 Spanish/Catholic Missions

Mission San Miguel's possessions were so vast that the Indians living in the San Joaquín Valley were actually next door neighbors, as they lived on land that bordered the land of the mission. Fr. Cabot wrote a report describing the mission's holdings and boundaries in 1827. It read:

> *"From the mission to the beach the land consists almost entirely of mountain ridges...for this reason it is not occupied until it reaches the coast where the mission has a house of adobe...eight hundred cattle, some tame horses and breeding mares are kept at said rancho, which is San Simeon. In the direction toward the south all land is occupied, for the mission there maintains all its sheep, besides horses for the guards. There it has Rancho de Santa Isabel, where there is a small vineyard. Other ranchos of the mission in that direction are San Antonio, where barley is planted; Rancho del Paso Robles, where wheat is sown; and Rancho de la Asunción."*

Mission San Miguel stood 18 miles from its rancho at San Simeon and its north and south boundaries were almost 50 miles apart, with its southern boundary joining the northern boundary of Mission San Luís Obispo. The fertile fields and ranchos of this vast area were kept in order under the supervision of two Franciscan padres, who were assisted by a few Spanish soldiers. San Miguel, however, was not the largest mission in terms of area; San Luís Rey, for instance, had a rancho almost 40 miles away from its mission compound.

In order to keep this vast program organized and running smoothly, the Franciscans had to depend on the native converts. These natives were not treated as slaves who were locked up at night and then forced to work days. But they were a community of workmen (and women) who worked within a system of authority of their own. Harsh punishment was only administered to the few who threatened the general peace and security of the mission.

An exception, however, was that whenever a married woman's husband was sent to one of the ranchos to work for a period of time, she would be housed in the same dormitory as the unmarried girls were and it was locked for the night. The new converts had difficulties practicing **monogamy,** which was (and still is) a fundamental principle in the Christian faith. Unfortunately, the padres could think of no other way to keep the girls from having sexual relations if they were unsupervised during the night. Today, this might be looked upon as cruel and **unwarranted** treatment, but, without excusing their methods, from the padres' point of view they most likely were only trying to protect the girls. As noted in this book and history, the Franciscans, on the most part, respected and cared for the welfare of the native people. Most instances of brutality and cruelty occurred when Spanish soldiers were involved. The native people were not forced to adopt the Catholic beliefs, and many did not, but lived as they always had.

Mission San Miguel Arcángel about 1886.

San Miguel Arcángel

Name ______________________________

Date ______________________________

The 16th of 21 Spanish/Catholic Missions

Mission San Miguel Arcángel was one of the last missions to be secularized as well as the last mission to be sold. The last Franciscan left the mission in 1841. The property was illegally sold by the dishonest and greedy Governor, Pio Pico, in 1846 to Petronillo Rios and William Reed for the sum of $600. Reed had been to the gold fields and had brought back some gold dust. In December 1848, five deserters from a British Man of War dined with the Reeds. Hearing of his good fortune they came back in the night and murdered Reed, his entire family, servants and guests– eleven in all. After ransacking the mission in a futile search for the gold they fled. A posse tracked them down near Santa Barbara. One was shot, another drowned after jumping into the ocean and the other three were hung. Legend has it that ghosts prowled the ruins at the mission. Following this incident, the long monastery building was rented out and used as a number of stores, one of which was the most popular saloon along El Camino Real. The church had no priest and only an unpaid indian took care of the mission. In 1878 a priest was again assigned to the mission. However it was not until 1928, when the Franciscans were once again given control of the mission, that extensive restoration and preservation began. ❖

The campanario at the south end of the mission compound.

Scrambled Sentences

Write the unscrambled sentence on the line below the scrambled sentence. (Use capital letters and punctuation.)

1. lasuén period in a missions of months de four founded four fermín father

____

2. in san central converting miguel an people interest the native in developed living california

____

3. helped natives friendly franciscans the the work and set mission up

____

4. were were not treated native as who work converts locked up at night and slaves forced to

____

5. adopt the people native were beliefs forced to the and many did catholic not not

____

6. property san dishonest was pio sold governor by the and greedy miguel's illegally pico

____

San Miguel Arcángel

Name ____________________

Date ____________________

The 16th of 21 Spanish/Catholic Missions

The Mission Today

For many years Mission San Miguel Arcángel was unattended and not maintained by any single group or organization. Amazingly, the mission escaped the usual devastation brought about by vandalism and the weather and natural disasters that so many of the other missions experienced. The interior remained in its original condition. Perhaps even more surprising, is that it never fell into the hands of well-intentioned, but terrible restorers.

In 1928, Mission San Miguel was returned to the Franciscan Order of the Catholic Church and once again became used as a parish church. They did extensive repairs and renovations, and have maintained the buildings and grounds ever since. The interior displays the workmanship and artistic designs created in 1820 by the talented artisan and friend of Fr. Cabot, Estévan Munras. They were both from Catalonia, Spain, and Munras offered to decorate the interior without charging for his work. The paintings are in the original bright colors of green, blue, pink, and brown. Mission San Miguel Arcángel is known to have the best-preserved interior of any of the California missions and the only paintings and decorations that have never been touched by anybody but the original artist.

The long monastery where the padres once lived is now a museum, with several rooms furnished as they would have been in the mission era. One interesting exhibit shows how sheepskin or cowhide was used in the windows while the padres were waiting for glass to arrive. The "window" is a wooden frame with the hide stretched over it very thinly and then shaved and greased to increase its **transparency**. These windows were placed in the openings during harsh weather. Other exhibits show historical tools the mission workers had to use to produce their crafts and merchandise, such as a spinning wheel and loom, traditional "beehive" oven, branding irons for livestock, metal forging tools, fish traps, and a tile kiln for firing clay pots.

The large fountain that once served as part of the mission's water system has been rebuilt. It was modeled after the beautiful fountain at Mission Santa Bárbara. Near the fountain are the cactus gardens that have been a part of the mission since its beginning. There is a symmetrical, arched entry to a garden area in front of the museum with a statue of Fr. Serra centered by the walkway. At the south end of the compound there is an impressive brick campanario, built in the traditional style of the missions, that houses five bells in niches. Mission San Miguel Arcángel is definitely a place to view some of the achievements of California's natives and pioneers. ❖

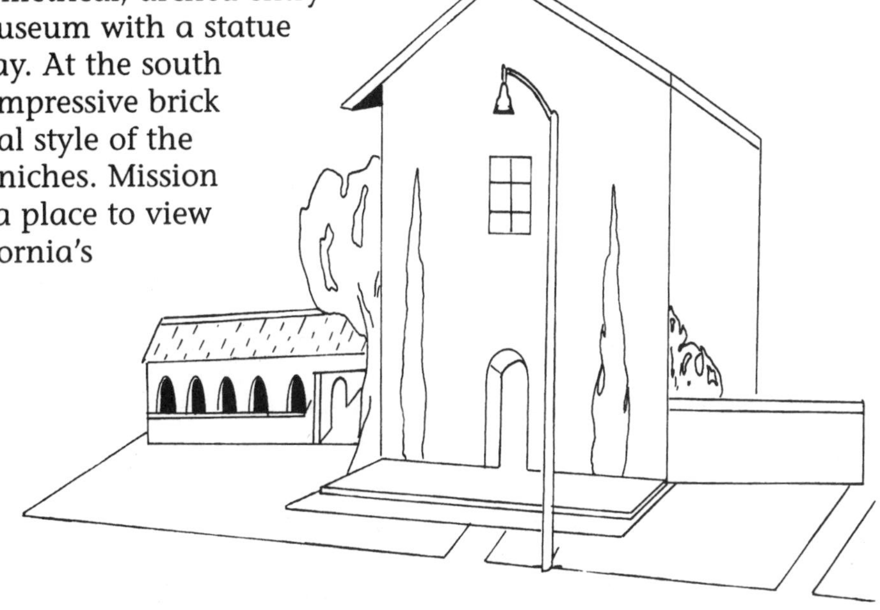

Old Mission
(Mission San Miguel)
P.O. Box 69
775 Mission Street
San Miguel, CA 93451
Phone: 805.467.3256

San Miguel Arcángel

Name ______________________

Date ______________________

Review Questions

Write the correct answer in the space provided.

1. Mission San Miguel Arcángel was founded ______________ years ago, on ______________ and is named after ______________.

2. Mission San Miguel's ______________ were so vast that the Indian nations living in the ______________ were the mission's next door ______________ because they lived on land that bordered mission land.

3. Native workers became skilled ______________, ______________, ______________, ______________, ______________ ,and ______________.

4. The mission's interior in the ______________ of any of the missions. Its painting and ______________ are the only ones of all the missions that have never been touched by anybody but the ______________ artists.

5. Fr. John Cabot sent several ______________ into the central valley (San Joaquín) with hopes of starting a ______________ there.

6. Explain why Fr. Cabot's expansion efforts failed.

____

____

____

7. Explain why some of the native women were locked up at night.

____

____

____

8. Do you think the padres handled the situation with the married women correctly? ______________ What would you have done? Support your answer.

____

____

____

____

☆☆ Bonus Activity

Use another resource and write a report on one of the people mentioned in this section, Michael (God's Arcángel), angels in general, Native people of the San Joaquín Valley (or near the mission), slavery throughout the world (history and practices), or Spanish conquest and treatment of native people in Mexico, Central America, and/or South America. Draw maps and pictures for your report.

Mission #17

San Fernando Rey de España

Founded September 8, 1797

Print the names of the missions on the correct lines. (You may need to look back at a previously finished section/map.)

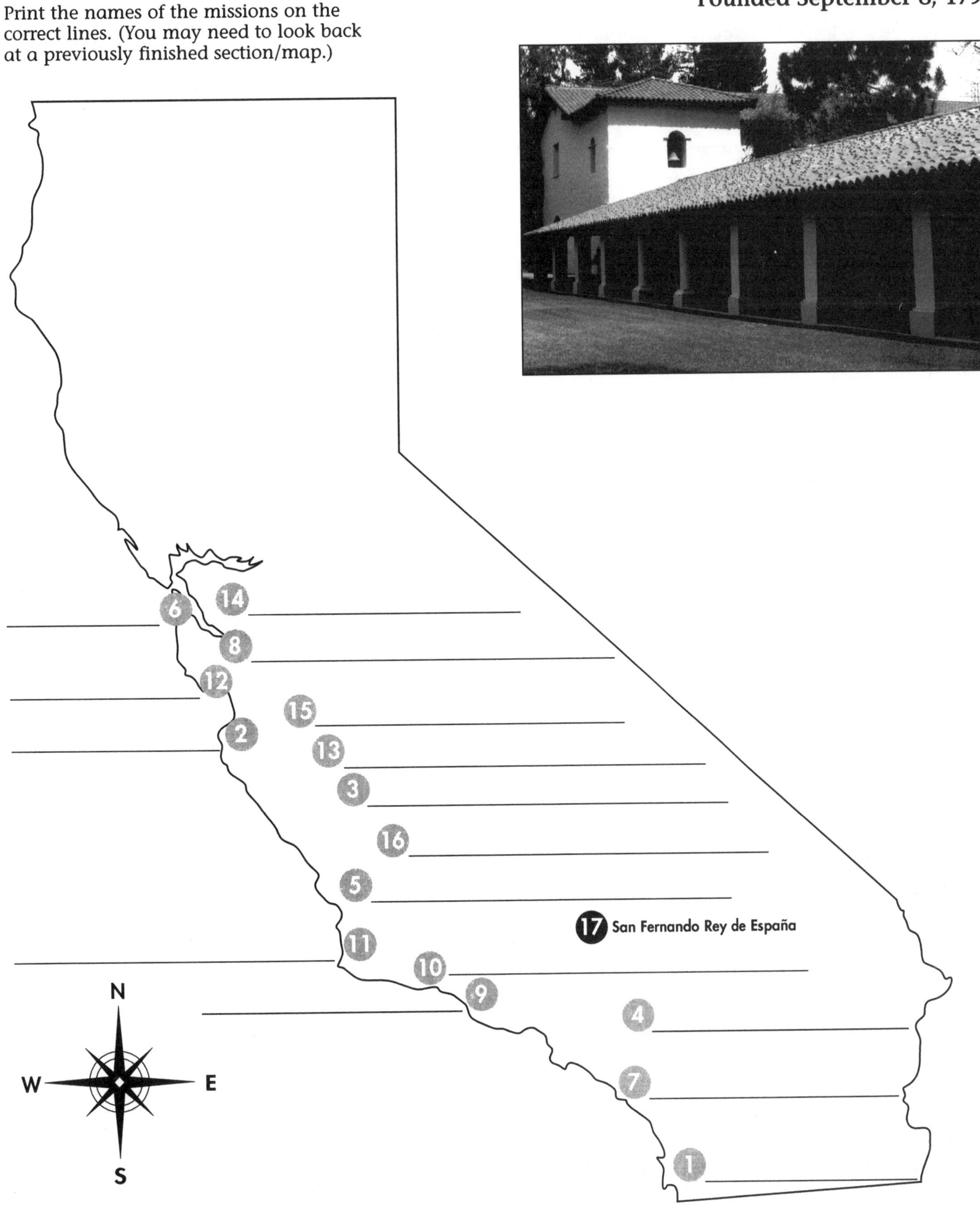

New Words to Learn:

Find the words in the glossary or a dictionary and write the meanings on the line.

1. **adjacent:** ______
2. **allegiance:** ______
3. **dilapidate**(d): ______
4. **hospice:** ______
5. **integrity:** ______
6. **remote:** ______
7. **renounce:** ______
8. **squatter:** ______

① ______

Mission #17 — Founded September 8, 1797

Layout of the Mission Grounds

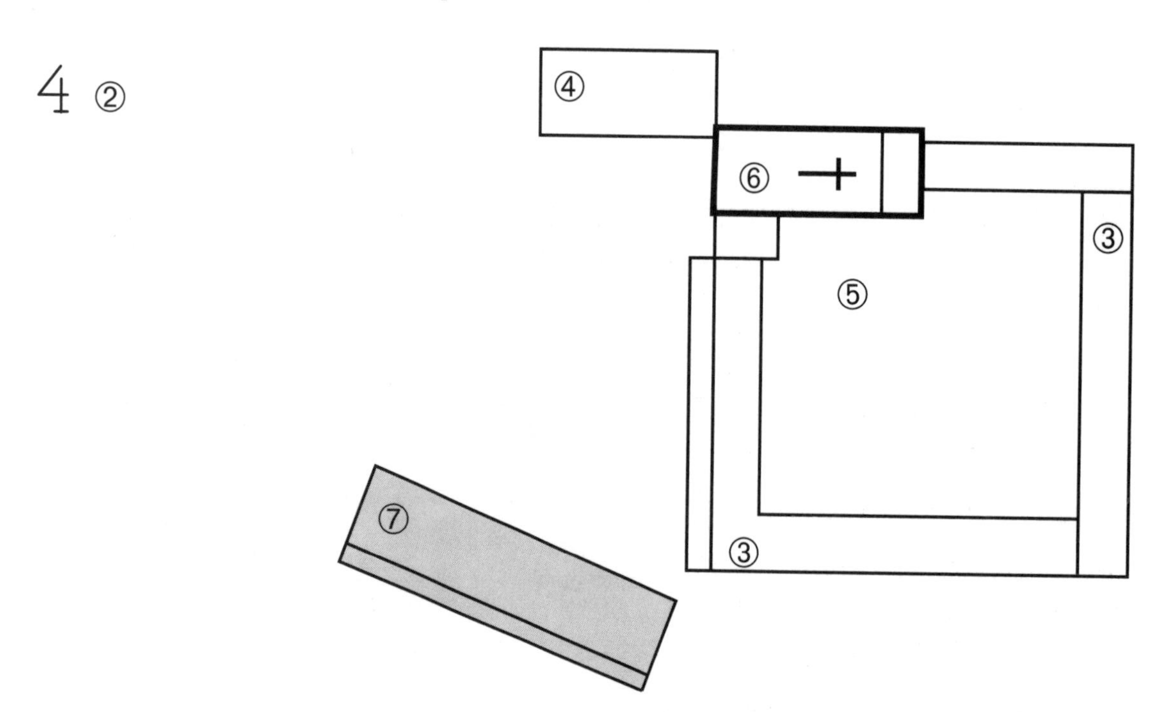

This view shows the mission compound and grounds after 1812.

San Fernando Rey de España

Name ______________________

Date ______________________

Named for King Ferdinand III of Castile, Spain (1216 A.D.)

The 17th of 21 Spanish/Catholic Missions

Design of the Mission

Church: (approximate outside measurements) 164 feet long, 37 feet wide, and 26.5 feet high
The church walls are made of adobe and it has a tile roof.

Design:
The church is plain and not very impressive. The Long Building (also called the *Mission House*) is much larger and has more interesting architectural features. The church's interior has native designs painted in bright colors. The altar has a statue of St. Ferdinand, which is backed by a wall of mirrors.

Walls: The walls are seven feet thick at the base and taper to five feet thick at the top.

Campanario:
The campanario is a plain, two-story square tower that was built between the church and the quadrangle. It holds three bells.

Mission Compound:
There was a large quadrangle of buildings built around a patio. The buildings measured 295 feet by 315 feet and included storage, quarters for the Chumash people living on the mission, a flour mill, and workshops for making candles, soap, wine and brandy, woven goods, saddle making and carpentry. The most impressive part of San Fernando Rey is the Long Building. This was built outside of the quadrangle and served as the padres' quarters and as an inn for travelers. This two-story building is 243 feet long (thus the name) and 50 feet wide. The walls are four feet thick with deep-set arched windows. The tile roof extends over an **adjacent** walkway that has 21 arches in the traditional mission style. The Mission House contains 20 rooms, including a kitchen, large dining room, and reception room that are all decorated with ironwork and tile floors. Before 1971 a bell hung from a small arch on the roof, but it was "removed" by an earthquake.

Mission Grounds:
At one time Mission San Fernando Rey owned 121,500 acres of land, which gave its cattle plenty of space to graze. It had more than 21,000 head of livestock which led to a prosperous business in making and selling hides, tallow, and saddle and shoe making. The nearby pueblo of Los Angeles was the main market for the mission's products, which also included, wine, olives, fruits, nuts, and dates. Gold was discovered on an outer rancho of the mission in the mid-1800s, creating a mini-gold rush, but it only lasted for a few years before seekers lost interest.

Do these things using the map provided. (Use the map on page 148.)

1. Write **Mission San Fernando Rey de España** ①, **cattle brand** ②, **workshops** ③, **soldiers' quarters** ④, **patio** ⑤, **church** ⑥, and **padres' living quarters** ⑦ by the correct number.
2. Do your best job if you color the map.

San Fernando Rey de España

Name ____________________

Date ____________________

The 17th of 21 Spanish/Catholic Missions

Early History

The fourth mission Fr. Fermín Lasuén founded in a period of four months was named San Fernando Rey de España, after King Ferdinand III of Spain, whom the Catholic Church made a saint in 1671 — 400 years after his death. The 17th Franciscan mission was founded on September 8, 1797. This mission was supposed to be for travelers of the long march between Missions San Gabriel and San Buenaventura, but Fr. Lasuén established it at a site somewhat to the south because the middle area was barren and had poor drainage.

The location he chose to build Mission San Fernando Rey had its own problems. The land best suited for the mission compound was already occupied by Francisco Reyes, a Spanish settler and the mayor of the pueblo of Los Angeles. Historians differ in their opinions regarding Reyes' willingness to give the land to the Franciscans. Some believe that he was granted the land from the King of Spain and was forced to give it up. Others believe that he had only "**squatted**" on the land and that he moved without a conflict. Although records do not confirm either account, they do, however, record that Reyes was at the mission's dedication ceremony and that he was godfather of the first child to be baptized at the mission.

As with other inland missions, success at San Fernando Rey was almost immediate. In only two short months after the dedication, the church was completed and the mission had a neophyte population of about 40. The padres and the native workers on the mission continued to prosper and by 1806, the mission was producing and selling or trading hides, tallow, soap, cloth, and other products in large quantities. Unlike some of the more **remote** missions, like Soledad, San Fernando had a ready market for its merchandise, as the pueblo of Los Angeles was nearby and growing with settlers who needed the mission's products. At the height of its prosperity, San Fernando owned approximately 13,000 cattle, 8,000 sheep, and 2,300 horses (which was the third largest herd of all the missions). The wealth of Mission San Fernando was not extraordinary, however, among the California missions.

When Fr. Lasuén chose the site for the mission, he had no idea how the locale would affect its growth. It was situated directly on the highway that led to the fastest growing settlement in California, Los Angeles, and in turn became the most popular stopping place for travelers on El Camino Real. The growing number of travelers visiting the mission was overwhelming. All visitors were welcome at the mission. The need for **hospice** space resulted in the construction of the famous "long house." After thirteen years of adding to the facilities to accommodate the needs of the mission's visitors, the building finally ended up being 243 feet long and 50 feet wide. A special room, called the *governor's chamber*, was set aside for the mission's more distinguished visitors.

Mission San Fernando Rey de España was once neglected and in ruin.

San Fernando Rey de España

Name ______________________

Date ______________________

The 17th of 21 Spanish/Catholic Missions

After 1811, the native population living and working on the mission declined steadily. Because the native people were so vital to the prosperity and success of Mission San Fernando Rey (and all of the other missions), as their population decreased so did the production of the mission's merchandise. Productivity got so low that, frequently, the Franciscan fathers were barely able to supply the military headquarters at Los Angeles the fruits and vegetable goods it had become accustomed to.

More misfortune came to the mission during the huge earthquake of 1812 which did considerable damage to the mission buildings. Rebuilding them was necessary to ensure the safety of the buildings and the people living at the mission. From then on the padres fought a losing fight against the growing number of settlers to the Los Angeles area and their **encroachment** on the mission lands and property.

In 1827, Mexico's Governor Echeandia arrived and asked Father Ibarra, the head of the mission, to **renounce** his **allegiance** to the royal family in Spain. Fr. Ibarra, being a Spaniard, refused. The governor thought about having the padre removed as head of the mission, but he was allowed to stay because it would have been too difficult to get a replacement. In 1835, Fr. Ibarra deserted the mission. This was brought on because he so strongly disapproved of the corrupt actions of the civil authorities under the secularization act. He had so much **integrity** that he left the mission rather than be a part of something so wrong.

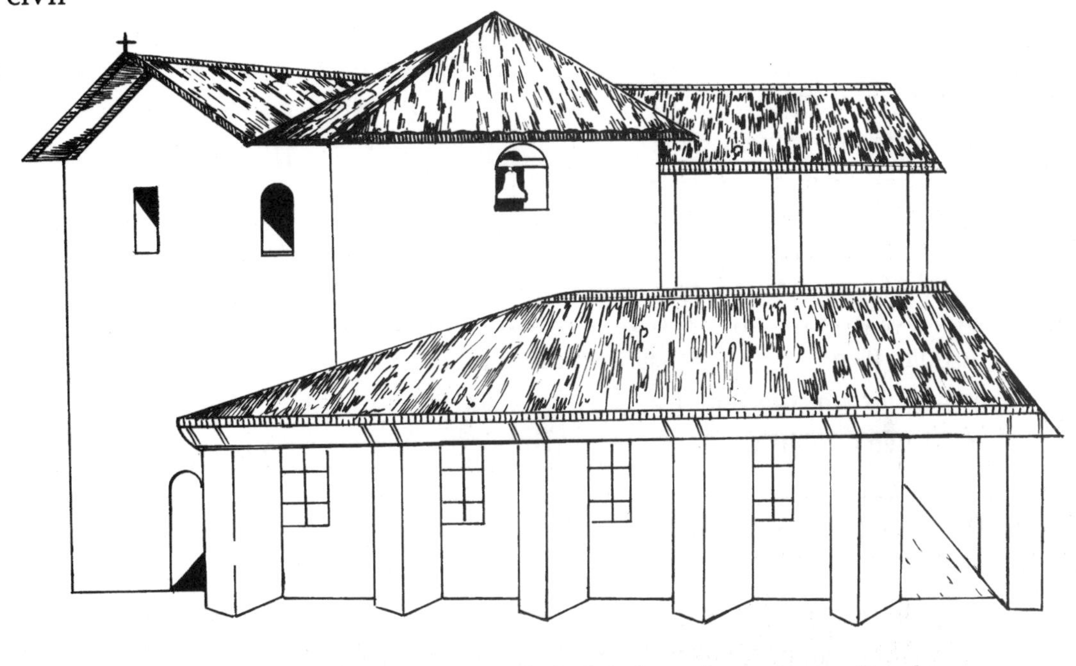

Mission San Fernando Rey was involved in military operations on several occasions. It was the military headquarters for the governors of California from 1833 until 1846, and the American John C. Fremont made it his headquarters after he captured it from the Mexican soldiers in 1847, during the Mexican-American War.

Ten years after Fr. Ibarra left Mission San Fernando Rey, the distribution of its property was complete. The corrupt Governor, Pio Pico, leased the land to his brother Andres and later sold it to another purchaser, with half ownership going to Andres. For several years, Andres used the hospice of the mission as his summer home. ❖

San Fernando Rey de España

Name ______________________________

Date ______________________________

WORD SEARCH PUZZLE

The 17th of 21 Spanish/Catholic Missions

Note: You will have to read page 153 in order to find some of the words that fit into the clue sentences below.

Write the answers from the clue sentences by the corresponding numbers **before** you complete the puzzle.

1. ____________________
2. ____________________
3. ____________________
4. ____________________
5. ____________________
6. ____________________
7. ____________________
8. ____________________
9. ____________________
10. ____________________
11. ____________________
12. ____________________
13. ____________________
14. ____________________
15. ____________________
16. ____________________
17. ____________________

Q	C	H	P	O	X	U	M	E	N	C	R	O	A	C	H	M	E	N	T
H	H	A	G	J	Z	G	L	H	E	A	D	Q	U	A	R	T	E	R	S
M	V	G	T	N	O	Y	H	M	K	P	R	O	D	U	C	T	I	O	N
X	E	M	A	R	K	E	T	X	T	F	T	Y	O	G	R	X	R	J	E
R	D	R	L	N	M	I	S	Z	O	V	P	O	P	E	E	O	D	T	D
W	G	I	C	P	R	W	R	V	R	C	P	N	I	C	I	E	A	N	X
D	P	O	S	H	X	M	H	X	G	Q	X	W	I	R	D	I	A	Y	J
T	R	R	D	T	A	B	C	Q	B	Q	L	P	E	A	D	N	R	J	Q
L	I	A	O	F	I	N	P	P	K	T	S	T	R	E	I	A	C	L	C
Y	I	R	I	P	A	N	D	C	E	O	N	G	M	D	N	C	D	D	M
V	W	Y	O	N	E	T	G	I	H	I	E	M	R	I	M	E	P	Q	N
C	C	A	T	N	A	R	H	U	S	D	I	E	D	Q	H	L	K	X	C
B	J	F	Y	Q	W	G	I	E	I	E	F	R	M	A	A	B	P	W	Q
W	C	H	Z	K	Z	O	E	T	R	S	O	H	E	Z	W	F	L	Y	L
W	Q	B	J	J	B	H	R	T	Y	A	H	H	S	H	I	Z	F	W	N
W	C	C	D	B	E	H	H	K	R	H	A	E	D	P	R	Q	M	Q	S
B	X	R	N	F	U	D	D	T	F	D	Q	B	D	O	O	N	O	C	E
Y	B	M	Z	E	B	V	X	D	V	V	R	C	B	E	E	V	L	A	S
Y	O	K	V	E	V	E	J	L	S	U	U	D	J	U	O	Z	C	C	H
H	W	Y	J	I	G	O	F	D	H	I	M	P	R	E	S	S	I	V	E

1. Gov. Pio Pico ________ Mission San Fernando Rey more than any other mission by turning it into a stable.
2. A special room was built for ________ visitors.
3. Fr. Lasuén established the mission south of the first site because it was barren and had poor ________ .
4. The ________ of mission land and property came from growing number of settlers to Los Angeles.
5. The wealth of Mission San Fernando was not ________ among the California missions.
6. This mission was named after King ________ III of Spain.
7. Francisco Reyes was the ________ of the first child baptized at the mission.
8. The mission supplied the military ________ at Los Angeles with fruits and vegetables.
9. The construction of the "long house" was the answer to the need for ________ space at the mission.
10. As with other inland mission, success at San Fernando Rey was almost ________ .
11. The most ________ part of San Fernando Rey is the Long Building.
12. The church's ________ has native designs painted in bright colors.
13. The Mission House has twenty rooms that are decorated with ________ and tile floors.
14. The nearby pueblo of Los Angeles was the main ________ for the mission's products.
15. Like Soledad, San Fernando had a ready market for selling its________ .
16. As the population of the neophytes decreased, so did the ________ of the mission's merchandise.
17. The native people were vital to the ________ and success of the mission.

San Fernando Rey de España

Name ______________________

Date ______________________

The 17th of 21 Spanish/Catholic Missions

The Mission Today

After Mission San Fernando Rey fell victim to secularization and Governor Pio Pico's actions, the mission was **degraded** even more — far more than any other mission. In 1888, the mission property was used as a warehouse and stable, and the patio was even used as a pig farm. In 1896, a concerned member of the Landmarks Club, Charles Fletcher Lummis, took interest in the future of the mission. He began efforts to reclaim the mission property and the fortunes of San Fernando improved. On August 4, 1916 (called *Candle Day*) about 6,000 supporters of the mission bought candles for $1 each and then marched through the arches of the Long Building to show their support for restoring the mission.

In 1923, the church returned to the mission and from that point on the restoration on Mission San Fernando Rey made great progress. The same year, the mission became an active church again under the Catholic Order of Oblate Fathers, and the original church building was once again used for Mass. During the 1930s restoration to the Long Building, chapel, and quadrangle continued to progress. The severe earthquake of 1971, however, damaged the church beyond repair. Three years later a replica of the original building was built.

Amazingly, the Long Building survived over the years of weather and abuse and is today the largest adobe building in California. It is also the largest original structure remaining from the mission era. Restored rooms of the Long Building display a rich assortment of mission relics. The great wine press and the smoke room show no signs of deterioration. The hospice still contains furniture and other items showing how the visitors lived.

The buildings also contain a **dilapidated** organ brought to the mission in later years but still used today. A huge altar that was brought from Spain is over 400 years old. The altar was originally 45 feet high and 47 feet wide, and the sections of it completely covered the walls in two of the largest rooms in the mission. The structure is decorated with a massive amount of wood carvings representing numerous vines and leaf designs. Some stick out from the face of it so far that it is a wonder they have not been broken off over the years. The entire sculpted structure is covered in beautifully ornate gold leaf. The carved vines flow around large panels of oil paintings, about five feet wide and seven feet high, that visually relate the story of the Holy Family. In 1991, the only surviving artifact from the original mission altar was installed in the church. It is a life-size statue of St. Ferdinand.

The bell tower has incorporated five of the original mission bells that are operated automatically. In the large park across from Mission San Fernando Rey visitors can see the old soap works, the large, star-shaped fountain and a large reservoir used in the original water system. One side of the restored quadrangle has been turned into a museum and workshop. As in the days of old, visitors are always welcome at Mission San Fernando Rey de España. ❖

San Fernando Rey de España
15151 San Fernando Mission Blvd.
Mission Hills, CA 91345
Phone: 818.361.0186
Museum Phone: 818.365.1501

San Fernando Rey de España

REVIEW QUESTIONS

Name ______________________

Date ______________________

Write the correct answer in the space provided.

1. Mission San Fernando Rey was founded ____________ years ago, on ____________ and is named after ____________.

2. Mission San Fernando Rey's success and ____________ depended on the ____________ people who worked at the mission.

3. The mission had a prosperous business in making and selling ____________, ____________ to the nearby pueblo of ____________.

4. The Long Building survived over the years of ____________ and ____________ and is today the largest ____________ structure in California. It also the largest ____________ structure remaining from the ____________.

5. Why was the *Mission House* built?

   ____

6. Explain why Fr. Ibarra left the mission. What would you have done?

   ____

   ____

   ____

   ____

   ____

7. Explain why you think Gov. Pio Poco could get away with being corrupt.

   ____

   ____

   ____

   ____

   ____

8. Today, what can visitors see in the park across the street from the mission?

   ____

   ____

☆☆ Bonus Activity

Use another resource and write a report on one of the people mentioned in this section, Native people of the Los Angeles region, soap making, history and/or process of gold-leafing wood or shoe making, or the Mexican-American War.
Draw maps and pictures for your report.

Mission #18

San Luís Rey de Francia

Founded June 13, 1798

Print the names of the missions on the correct lines. (You may need to look back at a previously finished section/map.)

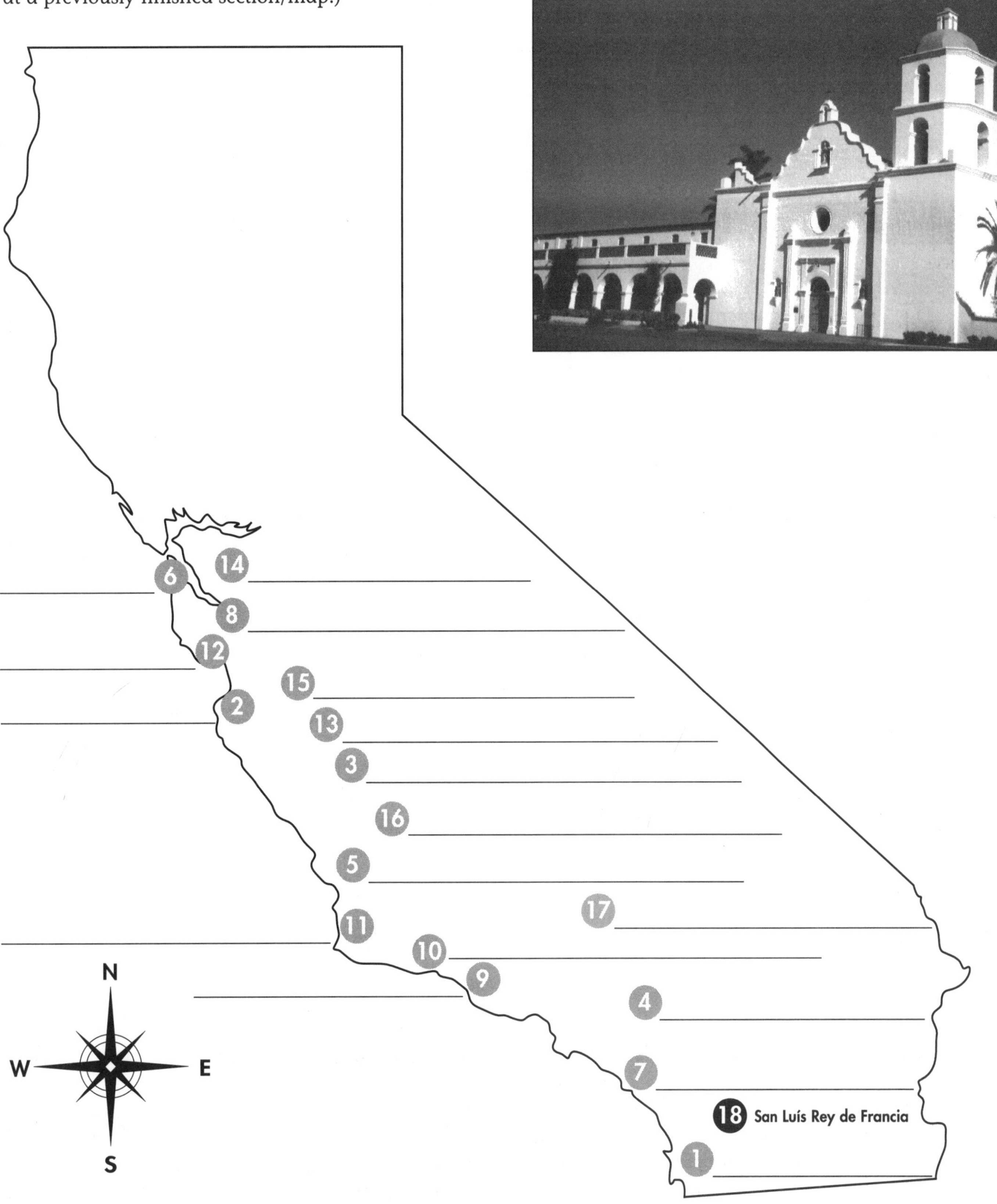

New Words to Learn:

Find the words in the glossary or a dictionary and write the meanings on the line.

1. **affluent:** ______________________________
2. **octagon:** ______________________________
3. **seminary:** ______________________________
4. **Vatican:** ______________________________

① ______________________________

Mission #18 — Founded June 13, 1798

Layout of the Mission Grounds

5 ②

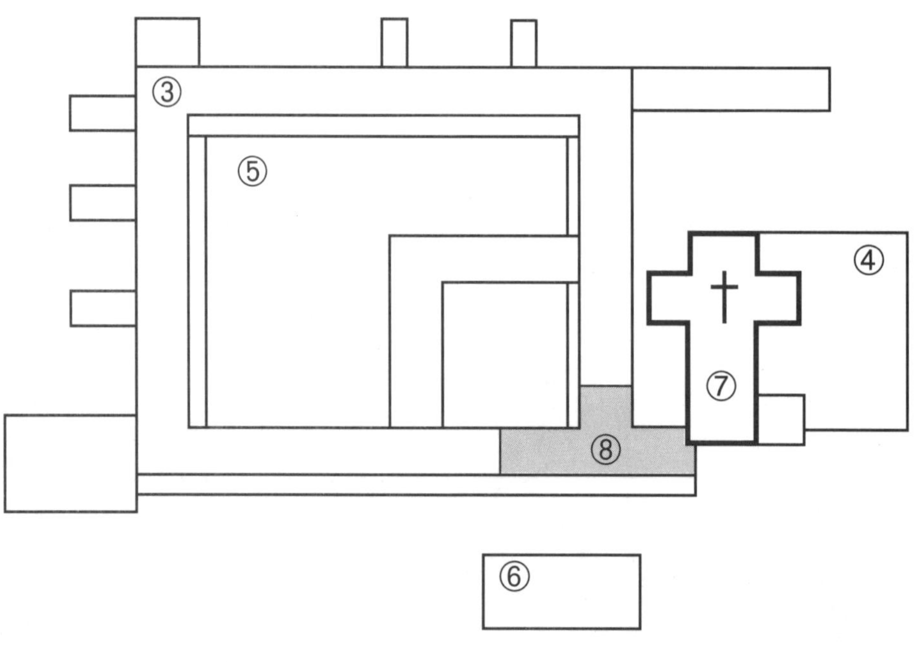

This diagram was taken from a model of the original mission.

San Luís Rey de Francia

Name ______________________

Date ______________________

Named for King Louis IX of France, born in 1215. He became King at the age of 11 when his father died. He led two crusades, one in Egypt in 1248 and another in Tunis in 1270, where he died of typhus.

The 18th of 21 Spanish/Catholic Missions

Design of the Mission

Church: (approximate outside measurements) 180 feet long, 36 feet wide, and 33 feet high. The church is built with adobe and faced with burnt brick. The roof is tile.

Design:
This is one of only two missions built in a cruciform, or cross, design. (The other built in this design is Mission San Juan Capistrano.) The cross design is formed by a long nave, used as the chapel, that is crossed by a shorter **transept** with two side altars. (See the diagram on page 156.) Directly above the crossing is an **octagonal** domed ceiling made of wood. Centered in this area is a smaller glass dome to let in light. (This is the only mission with a smaller glass dome of this type.) The interior, including the ceiling beams and pillars along the walls, is painted with brightly colored, native designs.

Walls: The thickness of the walls varies anywhere from six to nine feet.

Campanario:
The bell tower is a square-based, single dome that also served as a lookout from where guards could warn the mission of approaching visitors or signal the workers in the fields.

Mission Compound:
The main buildings of the mission's quadrangle covered about six acres, and were built around a 500-foot square patio. There were more than 200 arches along walkways adjacent to the buildings. These arches led to storage rooms, workshops for carpenters and workers making soap and candles, spinning yarn and weaving, as well as kitchens and the infirmary. The wing used for the padres' quarters had a second story with rooms that opened onto a balcony along the front.

Mission Grounds:
During the height of its prosperity, Mission San Luís Rey owned 30 square miles where 27,000 head of cattle, 26,000 sheep, and 2,000 horses grazed. The mission also raised a number of pigs, goats, ducks, chicken, and geese. There were also groves of olive and orange trees, large fields for growing wheat and vegetables, and vineyards for grapes that produced a variety of fine wines.

Water System:
Water was brought to the mission from a nearby river via 12 underground pipelines constructed of burnt brick. Drinking water was purified by filtering the water through charcoal. Water from springs flowed from the mouths of two statues and ran into a large lavandería in front of the mission. The women did the laundry in this fountain and then the water flowed into the fields for irrigation.

Do these things using the map provided. (Use the map on page 156.)

1. Write **Mission San Luís Rey de España** ①, **cattle brand** ②, **workshops** ③, **cemetery** ④, **patio** ⑤, **soldiers' quarters** ⑥, **church** ⑦, and **padres' living quarters** ⑧ by the correct number.
2. Do your best job if you color the map.

San Luís Rey de Francia

Also known as "King of the Missions"

Name ______________________________

Date ______________________________

The 18th of 21 Spanish/Catholic Missions

Early History

In the southern part of Alta California, Fr. Fermín Lasuén, president of the missions, was not very anxious to close the gaps along El Camino Real. After he dedicated Mission San Miguel he took three months to establish Mission San Fernando Rey. It was another six months before he arrived in the area between Missions San Diego and San Juan Capistrano. He did not take the original recommendations given him for the site of Mission San Luís Rey, because he thought it would be too far off the route of *The King's Highway*. Instead, he chose the site that was originally planned for Mission San Juan Capistrano. On June 13, 1798, he dedicated the 18th mission along the highway and named it San Luís Rey de España, after King Louis IX, of France, who lived in the 13th century.

The timing was perfect for the founding of this grand mission which is also known as the *"other San Juan."* Although it was started rather late as the missions went, it became the largest and wealthiest of all the missions. From its very first days, everything seemed to successfully fall into place. The Indians living in the area seemed anxious to become a part of the mission's operations, and understood the definite economic advantages it could play in their lives.

Unlike his usual practice of immediately leaving after a mission dedication, Fr. Lasuén remained for about six weeks to help supervise the construction of the church and other buildings. It had been several years since a mission was established in the south and he took the knowledge and experience he gained in the north and utilized it on Mission San Luís Rey.

It is important to note here that after the first 15 years in the development of the mission system, most of the California missions reflected the personalities and abilities of the padres who were first in charge of them. Most of the Franciscan padres were far more concerned about converting the native people to the Catholic faith and their well-being than they were about the natural resources and wealth of the missions. The missions that Fr. Serra left behind were meager shelters, made of mud and brushwood, that were constructed to serve as places where converted natives could come and worship. It was Fr. Lasuén who gave directions about where the magnificent church at Mission Carmel stands near the grave of Fr. Serra, as well as Frs. Lasuén, Crespi, and Lopez. It was Fr. Lasuén who gave all of the missions the great buildings by which they are known today. After him came many gifted padres, but none was more able or talented than Father Antonio Peyri. He was the father in charge of Mission San Luís Rey for 33 years. He left behind this grand mission as a monument to his abilities and the mission system as a whole.

At the height of its prosperity, Mission San Luís Rey was not only the most **affluent** mission in California, but most likely in all of the Spanish Americas (Central and South America). As the population of the neophytes grew in the settlement, Fr. Peyri displayed his organizational skills and soon developed an endless number of successful industries. Fr. Peyri had an exceptional knowledge and understanding of architecture. Construction at the mission continued without interruption. As one project came to an end another would be started. He drew plans and supervised the construction of the buildings, the intricate aqueduct system, a charcoal-filtered water system that purified the drinking water, large open-air laundry and bathing facilities, an irrigation system, and extensive gardens and orchards.

San Luís Rey de Francia

Name ______________________________

Date ______________________________

The 18th of 21 Spanish/Catholic Missions

The vast mission quadrangle extended 500 feet on each side. The church is made of adobe and burnt bricks. One side formed part of the exterior wall of the mission and the other side faced the huge patio. The other buildings of the quadrangle used for the monastery, infirmary, bachelor dormitory, young girls' dormitory, and workshops also faced the patio and were connected by arched walkways. Outside the mission buildings were vast orchards and gardens used to feed the inhabitants a variety of fruits and vegetables. In 1831, the Mission San Luís Rey reported having about 26,000 head of cattle, 25,500 sheep, and 2,150 horses. It also reported to have produced 395,000 bushels of grain and 2,500 barrels of various wines.

Under Fr. Peyri's supervision, construction on the large church that stands today was started in 1811 and finished in 1815. (Remember that the great stone church of Mission San Juan Capistrano, as well as other missions, was totally destroyed by an earthquake in 1812.) The church is the most elaborate architecturally and one of the most interesting of all the missions. The design is in the form of a cross (cruciform) and similar to the destroyed church at San Juan Capistrano. (See the description on page 157 for more details about the church design.)

In addition to Fr. Peyri's accomplishments on the mission, he was one of the few Franciscan padres who went out of his way to be friendly to the civilian officials and Spanish military personnel. The amount and regular supply of goods contributed by the mission to the military presidio were interrupted during the conflicts between Mexico and Spain. However, after the conflict was resolved, Fr. Peyri increased the mission's contributions to show open support of the new **regime**. His friendly cooperation, however, was to no avail after the arrival of Mexico's Governor Echeandia. The Governor led the natives to believe that they would be able to prosper from the mission without continuing to work. As soon as they believed this, the discipline and respect broke down, which soon led to no work being done. Fr. Peyri was so discouraged and disappointed by the actions of the Mexican authorities that he began preparing to return to Spain, after going to the **Vatican** in Rome, Italy.

In 1832, he left the mission in the middle of the night to catch the ship to Spain. He was so well liked that when the Indians living at the mission learned of his leaving, more than 500 rushed to the harbor in San Diego to try to stop him from leaving. When they arrived, however, the ship was already putting out to sea. The padre took with him two young native boys, his favorites, and they enrolled in a Catholic **seminary** when they arrived in Rome, Italy.

This picture shows Mission San Luís Rey de Francia in near ruin in the late 1800s.

San Luís Rey de Francia

Name ____________________

Date ____________________

The 18th of 21 Spanish/Catholic Missions

The authority of the remaining padres was taken away by Mexican officials through secularization. All they could do was helplessly stand by and watch the deterioration of the mission system and the great structures take root. One by one the ranchos and other mission properties were divided among the relatives and friends of Pio Pico. One rancho alone, that he and his brother Andres Pico took title of, was 90,000 acres in size. By 1846 mission life had disappeared, but final sale of Mission San Luís Rey's buildings was defeated when John Fremont, acting for the United States, took possession of "the King of the Missions," San Luís Rey.

After the Franciscan friars left the missions, the Indians learned the true intentions of the Mexican and then U.S. authorities. The systematic taking of Indian lands began and they were removed from one location after another, until finally, in 1903, they were forced to settle on the Pala Reservation. This move was to be only temporary, until an area could be found that could support the Native Californians and give them a better standard of living. Any attempt to settle the natives in other regions brought strong objections from white settlers who did not want to share any part of the available lands. To the discredit and shame of the U.S. Government, the people of the Pala Tribe are still living on the "temporary" site. (The site is about 20 miles east of Mission San Luís Rey.)

The church grounds, San Antonio de Pala, on the Indian reservation in Pala.

On March 18, 1861, President Abraham Lincoln returned the California missions to the Catholic Church. The original decree, signed by President Lincoln, to return the missions to the church is in the possession of Mission San Luís Rey de España. ❖

Scrambled Sentences

Write the unscrambled sentence on the line below the scrambled sentence. (Use capital letters and punctuation.)

1. water filtering was purified by through the water drinking charcoal

____

2. the height mission of its san at luís the most was affluent in rey california prosperity

____

3. father missions known by lasuén gave great all of the the buildings they are which

____

4. authority padres the of was officials taken through away by mexican secularization the

____

San Luís Rey de Francia

Name ______________________________

Date ______________________________

The 18th of 21 Spanish/Catholic Missions

The Mission Today

The neglect of the "King of the Missions" began when it was sold in 1833, and continued even after President Lincoln returned the mission to the Catholic Church. For over half a century, except for occasional military occupations, it was abandoned and left to the mercy of the weather and elements. By 1892 most of the mission's buildings around the patio had collapsed, the dome of the church had fallen, and San Luís Rey was in a terrible state of disrepair. It was this year that the mission's fortunes turned toward the better. Two Franciscan friars from Mexico asked for and received permission from the Church to restore the mission and use it as a college for training new priests. They erected a two-story frame building across from the church and on May 12, 1893, rededicated Mission San Luís Rey. Fr. Joseph O'Keefe dedicated 19 years to its restoration. Fountains were uncovered, bells were hung again, and old treasures and artifacts were found and returned to the mission.

The mission has an excellent museum where a kitchen, workshop, and padre's bedroom were recreated to show everyday life on a mission. Some of the items on display were brought to California by Fr. Junípero Serra, founder of the first missions. A pepper tree that was planted in 1830 grows in the middle of the courtyard. Some believe it was the first pepper tree in California. Mission cooks used the ground peppercorns for seasoning.

Completed in 1950, restoration of Mission San Luís Rey recaptured much of its original splendor and character. To the right of the entrance is a room with a domed ceiling. This was originally the *Mortuary Chapel*, where people living on the mission could go to **mourn** for somebody who had died. Today this small chapel is called the *Chapel of the Madonna.* The church has remained as it was when it first held services. Only the roof had to be replaced; the walls and arches along the walkways stayed intact. Today the church is used as a parish church. The buildings are painted a brilliant white. Visitors can see the original copper baptismal font, wooden pulpit, and a statue of Louis IX, for whom Mission San Luís Rey de España was named. ❖

Mission San Luís Rey
4050 Mission Avenue
Oceanside, CA 92057
Phone: 760.757.3651

San Luís Rey de Francia

Name ______________________

Date ______________________

REVIEW QUESTIONS

Write the correct answer in the space provided.

1. Mission San Luís Rey was founded ______________ years ago, on ______________ and is named after ______________.

2. Mission San Luís Rey was also known as ______________ and ______________.

3. Most of the Franciscan padres were more concerned about ______________ the native people to the ______________ and their ______________ than they were about the ______________ and ______________ of the missions.

4. Explain how Fr. Peyri made Mission San Luís Rey the most affluent mission in all of the Spanish Americas.

5. What happened in 1892 to better the fate of the collapsed mission?

6. Explain how and why Fr. Lasuén chose the site for Mission San Luís Rey.

7. Explain the true intentions of the Mexican and U.S. authorities.

☆☆ **Bonus Activity**

Use another resource and write a report on one of the people mentioned in this section, pepper trees, the Pala Indian nation, specific or general U.S. treaties with California tribes, the Catholic Pope, the Vatican, Italy, Egypt in the 1200s, France, the Crusades, or the Mexican revolution with Spain. Draw maps and pictures for your report.

Mission #19

Santa Inés

Founded September 17, 1804

Print the names of the missions on the correct lines. (You may need to look back at a previously finished section/map.)

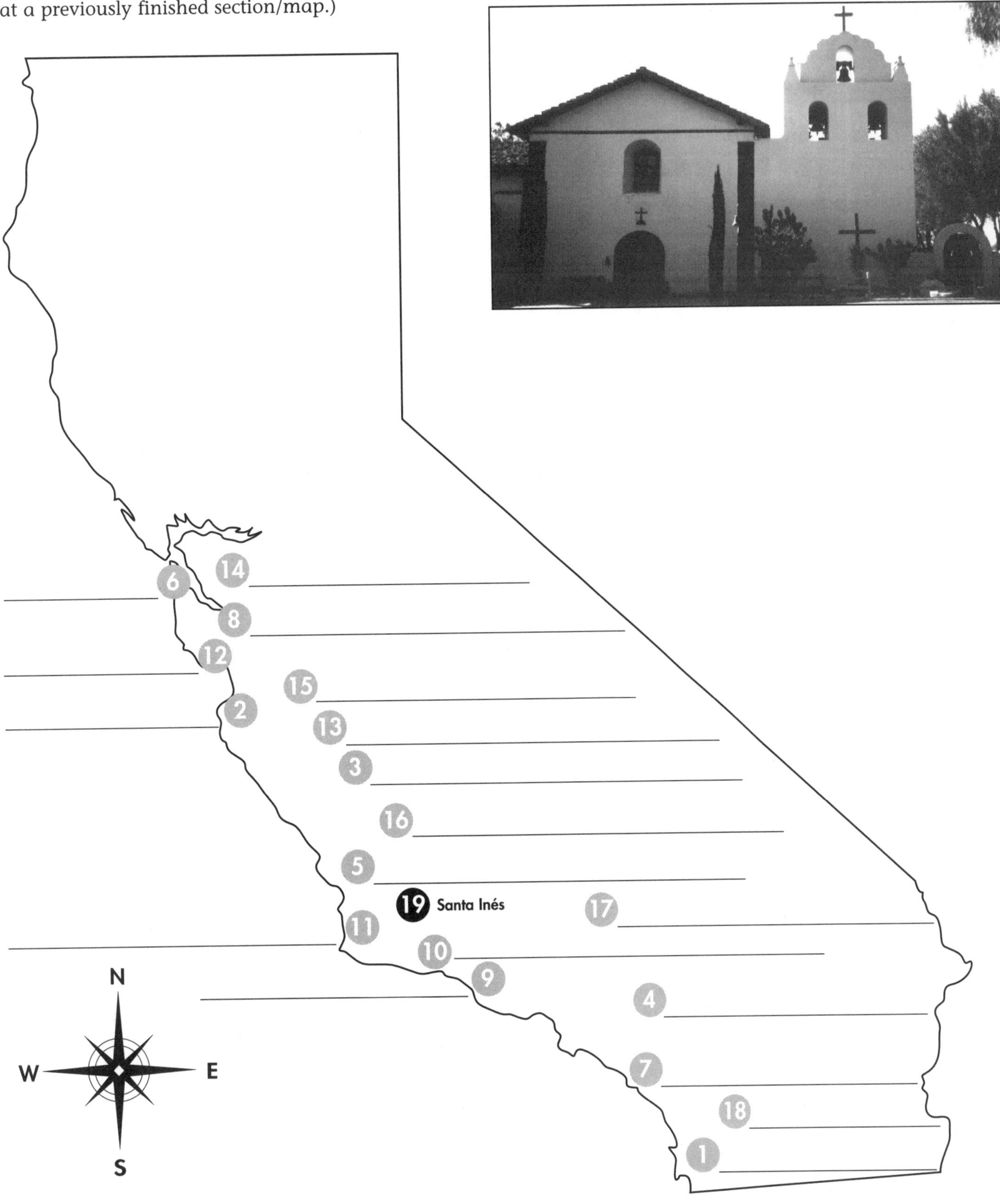

New Words to Learn:

Find the words in the glossary or a dictionary and write the meanings on the line. (You know most of the words in this section!!!)

1. **evade:**____

2. **missal(s):** ____

① ____

Mission #19 — Founded September 17, 1804

Layout of the Mission Grounds

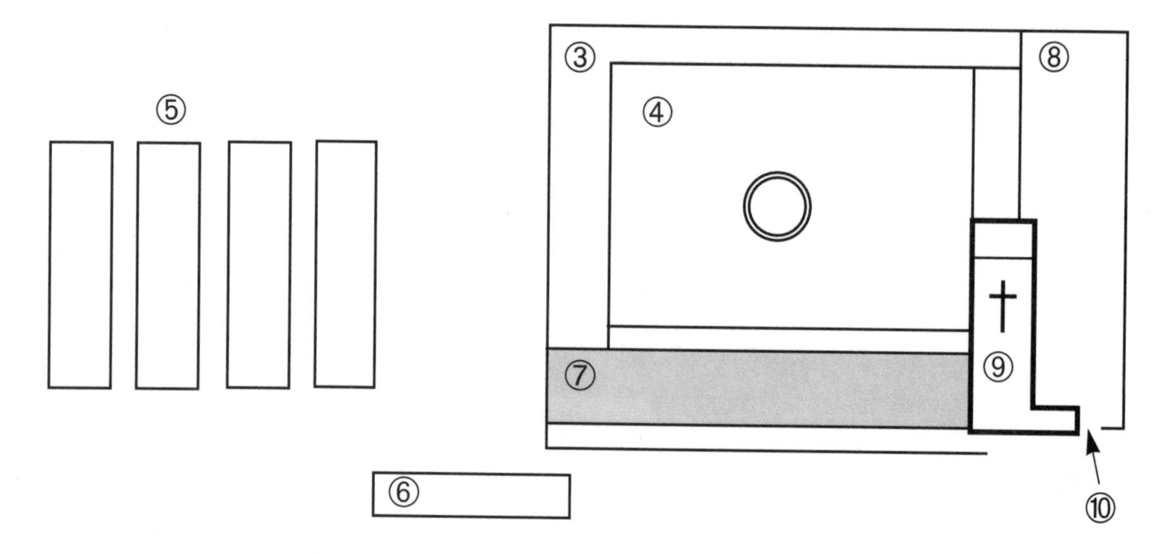

Mission compound grounds, about 1812.

Santa Inés

Named after Saint Agnes, a 13 year old Roman girl who was executed for believing Jesus Christ was the Son of God. This was in 304 A.D. during the persecution of Christians by the Roman Emperor, Diocletian.

Name ______________________

Date ______________________

The 19th of 21 Spanish/Catholic Missions

Design of the Mission

Church: (approximate outside measurements) 163 feet long, 37 feet wide, and 26 feet high.

The church is made of adobe and faced with brick. The bricks are held together with lime mortar made of seashells. It has a tile roof and floor.

Design:

The classic mission architectural style was designed by Father Francisco Javier de Uría. He borrowed some design features from other missions, such as San Gabriel and San Luís Rey. The entrance has two carved wooden doors, with a small arched window directly above the doors. The beams and rafters supporting the roof are made of pine, sycamore, and oak tree, and are held together with strips of rawhide. The timbers were brought to the mission from the mountains about 45 miles away. The interior walls are painted with murals with native designs and traditional native colors. Some of the walls are painted to look like marble. Dark brown columns are painted on each side of the entrance door.

Walls: The walls are six feet thick with heavy buttresses for added support.

Campanario:

The bell tower is located to the right of the entrance and has three niches where bells hang. There is one bell on top, with two bells symmetrically positioned below the top bell. The bells were cast in 1807, 1817, and 1818.

Mission Compound:

Like the traditional quadrangles of the earlier missions, buildings at Santa Inés form a square around a patio that is 350 feet long on each side. The buildings of the quadrangle were used for living quarters, workshops, storerooms and a guard house. The padres' living quarters extend from the church, from the front of the quadrangle, and have a porch with a series of 22 arches. A walkway on top of the porch (similar to the one at Mission San Luís Rey) served as a balcony for the second story rooms. The Chumash Indians working at the mission were especially noted for their craftsmanship with leather and metal. They made elaborate saddles and decorated them with silver. They also made candlesticks and other merchandise from silver and copper. Santa Inés was also used as a center for educating the Indians living at the mission.

Mission Grounds:

The mission grounds were blessed with rich, fertile soil that was excellent for growing crops. The mission grew enough food to support itself and to sell some to the presidio at Santa Bárbara. The grazing land supported about 13,000 head of livestock. About 450 mission workers lived at the mission and were housed in barracks outside the mission quadrangle. The mission also had a water-powered grist mill where corn and wheat were ground. The elaborate water system brought water to the mission from the mountains several miles away through underground clay pipes and stored it in two reservoirs.

Do these things using the map provided. (Use the map on page 164.)

1. Write **Mission Santa Inés** ①, **cattle brand** ②, **workshops** ③, **patio** ④, **workers' barracks** ⑤, **granary** ⑥, **padres' living quarters** ⑦, **cemetery** ⑧, **church** ⑨, and **bell wall** ⑩, by the correct number.

Santa Inés

Also known as "Mission of the Passes" or "The Hidden Gem of the Missions."

Name ______________________

Date ______________________

The 19th of 21 Spanish/Catholic Missions

Early History

The last of the southern missions and the 19th along El Camino Real, was founded by Father Estévan Tápis on September 17, 1804. (He had been elected superior of the missions after the death of Fr. Lasuén in 1803.) The Franciscan missionaries had been concerned about reaching the native people living east of the hills behind Mission Santa Bárbara with their message of Christianity. In order to make reaching them easier, Mission Santa Inés was founded on a site about 45 miles northeast of Mission Santa Bárbara. By this time the Indians were well aware of the missionary efforts and when the Franciscan padres set the altar in the field, about 200 natives were present to receive the blessing, and more than 20 children were baptized on that founding day.

Fr. Tápis had great hopes for Mission Santa Inés to become as successful and prosperous as many of the other missions. The mission operated less than 32 years and the largest neophyte population it ever recorded was only 768. It never had more than 10,000 head of livestock; and it harvested more than 10,000 bushels of grain only twice. Santa Inés was never considered a poor mission, yet it never met the padres' expectations, especially since such a great number of native people lived near the mission.

After almost eight years of construction, the mission buildings were near completion. The church was impressive, and could be seen from several miles away. In 1812, misfortune struck the mission in the form of a huge earthquake that destroyed the buildings. It took an additional five years for the reconstructed church to be dedicated. An aqueduct system was built by the mission neophytes that brought water from a stream several miles away. The water traveled through ditches and clay pipes into two large reservoirs (which still can be seen) near the mission. By 1820, the mission had productive orchards and it began to prosper, however, trouble would soon come to the mission.

This picture shows Mission Santa Inés in the late 1800s.

Santa Inés

Name ______________________

Date ______________________

The 19th of 21 Spanish/Catholic Missions

Starting in 1810, the military forces in California rarely, if ever, received supplies from Mexico or Spain. Therefore the commanders became increasingly more dependent upon the missions for obtaining their supplies. After all, the military was there primarily to protect the missions and the Franciscans. After Mexico gained her independence from Spain in 1821, the cost to support the soldiers increased as well. With the increase in support also came an increased amount of labor from the Indian workers in order to produce the increase in goods. The natives resented the new demands for their labor while they watched the soldiers sit idle much of the time. They also resented being abused by the soldiers. In addition to these problems, the new governor encouraged the Indians to ignore the orders of the padres. He also urged his soldiers to take over the leadership of the missions. In February of 1824, after a soldier had beaten a neophyte for some minor incident, a group of well-armed Indians attacked the mission guard and set fire to several of the buildings. After the Indians realized that the fire was about to destroy the church, they quit fighting and helped to put the fire out. All of the workshops and soldiers' barracks were completely destroyed. Even though the native revolt was not directed against the fathers, Indian relations were never the same.

This is the entrance to the path of the 14 Stations of the Cross. It's hard to see, but it says, "El Calvario" above the entrance.

In the summer of 1836, most of Mission Santa Inés and its properties were transferred into the hands of civil administrators and, except for the short rule of Governor Micheltoreña from 1842 to 1845, the mission fell upon bad fortune. Gov. Micheltoreña was in constant conflict with the authorities wanting secularization of the missions. He tried to restore the administration of the missions back to the Franciscans, but his efforts were for the most part ignored. These efforts did benefit a few of the missions, however, and Mission Santa Inés was one of them.

Governor Micheltoreña and the Catholic Bishop of California entered into a successful legal agreement that was designed to **evade** the Secularization Act. The governor returned 36,000 acres of land that belonged to Mission Santa Inés, not to the mission but gifted it to the Catholic Church for the purpose of starting a religious college. It opened in 1844, becoming California's first college — The College of Our Lady of Refuge. When the new governor, Pio Pico, had sold the last of the mission lands in 1846, he had not been able to **seize** the 36,000 acres of college land. This agreement between the governor and the bishop saved Mission Santa Inés from complete ruin. The college later moved and remained as an active seminary only until 1881. It was first operated by the Franciscan Order and then by the Christian Brothers. The church eventually had to sell the land to private owners because of the success of other schools in the area. ❖

Santa Inés

Name ______________________________

Date ______________________________

The 19th of 21 Spanish/Catholic Missions

QUOTEFALLS PUZZLES

Here's how to complete these puzzles.

Write the letters in the squares below them in order to solve the *Quote Falls Puzzles* correctly. One sentence from the pages of this mission was used to create each of the puzzles. We tried to use exact quotes, but most often had to omit or add certain words, or combine a couple sentences together in order to make the puzzles shorter and/or fit correctly. Cross off the letters as you use them in order to keep track of the ones you have not used. Note that a gray square separates words, and some words are continued onto the next line.

Puzzle #1

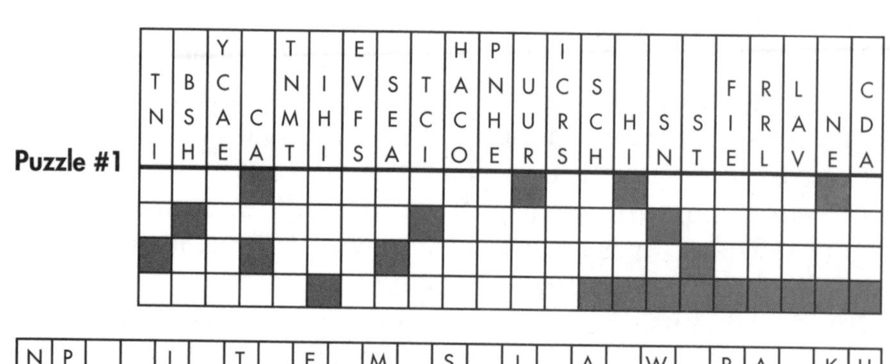

		Y		T		E			H	P		I									
T	B	C		N	I	V	S	T	A	N	U	C	S				F	R	L		C
N	S	A	C	M	H	F	E	C	C	H	U	R	C	H	S	S	I	R	A	N	D
I	H	E	A	T	I	S	A	I	O	E	R	S	H	I	N	T	E	L	V	E	A

Puzzle #2

N	P			I		T		E		M		S		I		A		W		R	A		K	H
I	E			F	H	U		T	E	E	I	H	E	R	R	N	N	T		M	E	N	A	O
T	H	E	A	C	T	R	H	L	H	A	I	R	N	D	I	A	F	S	E	M	E	T	N	I
T	G	D	W	T	O	H	M	A	S	H	T	I	S	C	O	A	N	D	S	W	O	R	S	L

Puzzle #3

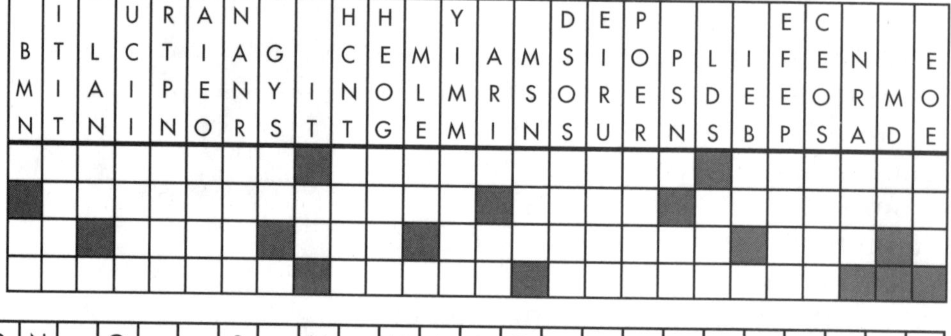

	I		U	R	A	N			H	H		Y			D	E	P				E	C			
B	T	L	C	T	I	A	G		C	E	M	I	A	M	S	I	O	P	L	I	F	E	N		E
M	I	A	I	P	E	N	Y	I	N	O	L	M	R	S	O	R	E	S	D	E	E	O	R	M	O
N	T	N	I	N	O	R	S	T	T	G	E	M	I	N	S	U	R	N	S	B	P	S	A	D	E

Puzzle #4

	U	T	N	R	N		O			S		N		M	I	I	T			N							
A	O	O	I	O	T	O	T	I		I	C	H	E	L	I	C	R	G	W	I	E	C		T		R	
G	A	V	E	O	R	I	N	F	E	C	O	E	A	N	T	S	N	E	O	S	S	H	A	L	A	I	N
Z	C	T	H	S	N	A	R	T	M	T	H	W	F	L	T	O	S	I	N	A	T	W	U	S	H	E	I

Puzzle #5

		O		E	O									E	T	E	H		N	I							
H		W	L	G	D	E	E	O	I	O	R	E	A	R	A	F	O	O	L	H	E		C	S	U	R	C
T	H	L	H	L	R	G	T	R	N	N	S	C	R	C	T	T	D	R	T	D	C		F	I	S	S	O
N	C	E	A	N	E	V	E	I	T	T	H	T	A	L	I	U	R	N	E	I	A	M	I	H	R	I	T

Santa Inés

Name ______________________

Date ______________________

The 19th of 21 Spanish/Catholic Missions

The Mission Today

For the most part, the mission's church remained opened, and in 1882, a clever padre living at the mission invited the Donahues, the family of a stone mason to live at Mission Santa Inés. It was not long after this that the restoration of the buildings began and there was a notable improvement in their appearance. Fr. Alexander Buckler began a restoration program in 1904 and it continued until his death in 1930 — even after the Capuchin Franciscan Fathers were placed in charge in 1923.

The bell campanario was weakened over the years by neglect and heavy rain storms and finally fell due to an earthquake in March of 1911. Fr. Buckler replaced the tower with a shell-like wood and plaster structure. It was not an impressive structure close up, but gave the outward appearance of the old structure with very little money. It served its purpose until 1949 when the William Randolph Hearst Foundation gave the mission $500,000 for further restoration. Part of this money was used to build a solid concrete campanario, which now houses the bells Santa Inés has acquired over the years. The balcony walkway, which had been roofed over since 1817, was discovered and restored.

Five Franciscan friars are buried under the tile floor of the mission church. Many of the original designs on the walls were painted over in attempts to "clean up" the church interior, however, most if not all, have been uncovered and restored to their original state, like much of the other decorations. There are several wooden statues placed throughout the church, but the place of honor, the center of the altar, was reserved for Saint Agnes, for whom the mission is named and dedicated. This rendition of the Virgin and **Martyr** is believed to have been created by one or more native artists who lived at the mission.

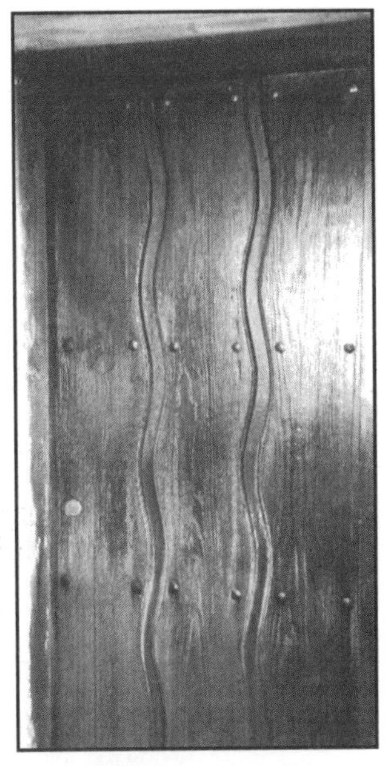

This is a picture of a *River of Life door*, found in most of the missions.

The historical museum in the residence wing of Mission Santa Inés is one of the best in the mission chain. The excellent condition of many of the items comes from the dedication and hard work of Fr. Buckler's housekeeper and niece, Mary Goulet. Miss Goulet spent five years repairing and documenting old ritual garments. There is also a display of Latin **missals** and handmade parchment music books, some that are older than the mission itself. Many original paintings hang on the walls.

Mission Santa Inés is an active church, still served by the Capuchin Franciscan Fathers. In 1972 the mission gardens were restored in the shape of a cross, with a fountain the middle. Eighteen of the 22 arches along the residence building have been rebuilt. The ruins of arch number 19 can be seen.

The old wooden doors of Mission Santa Inés have curved designs carved into them which are similar to those of other missions along El Camino Real. These curved designs symbolize the *River of Life* and were etched into the doors to remind all those who enter of God's abundant grace and provision on earth and throughout eternity through His Son, Jesus Christ. ❖

Mission Santa Inés
P.O. Box 408
1750 Mission Drive
Solvang, CA 93463
Phone: 805.688.4815

Name ______________________

Date ______________________

REVIEW QUESTIONS

Write the correct answer in the space provided.

1. Mission Santa Inés was founded ____________ years ago, on ____________ and is named after ____________.

2. The Franciscan ____________ were concerned about reaching the native people east of the hill behind ____________ with their message of ____________. To make it easier to reach, the native population ____________ was founded.

3. Santa Inés never met the ____________ of the mission padres.

4. The ____________ foundation donated $500,000 to the church for ____________.

5. Explain how the governor and Catholic Bishop tried to evade the consequences of the Secularization Act.

____

____

____

____

6. Describe the wooden doors and the meaning of the carvings.

____

____

____

____

7. Write how you would have felt toward the Spanish military if you lived at Mission Santa Inés.

____

____

____

____

☆☆ Bonus Activity

Use another resource and write a report on one of the people mentioned in this section, Saint Agnes, Jesus Christ, the history of Christian persecution and/or martyrs, the Fourteen Stations of the Cross, the Cross of Calvary, the Roman Empire, Roman emperors in general and/or Diocletian, native people to the southern California region, or William Randolph Hearst and/or his foundation. Draw maps and pictures for your report.

Mission #20

San Rafael Arcángel

Founded December 14, 1817

Print the name of the mission on the correct line. (You may need to look back at a previously finished section/map.)

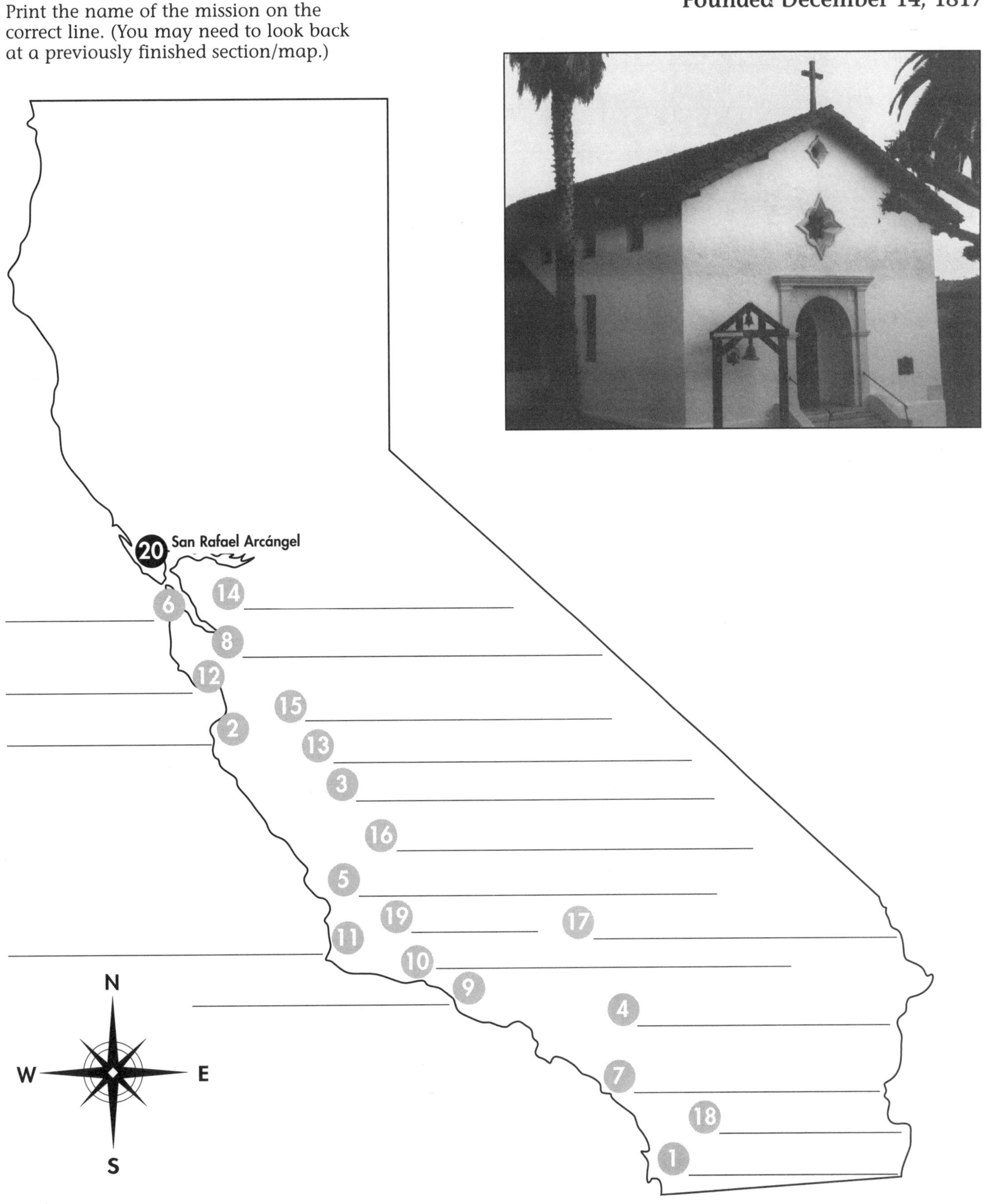

New Words to Learn:

Find the words in the glossary or a dictionary and write the meanings on the line.

1. **bleak:** ______________________________
2. **immunity**(ies): ______________________________
3. **invalid:** ______________________________
4. **patronage:** ______________________________
5. **perpendicular:** ______________________________
6. **philanthropy:** ______________________________
7. **sanitarium:** ______________________________

① ______________________________

Mission #20 — Founded December 14, 1817

Layout of the Mission Grounds

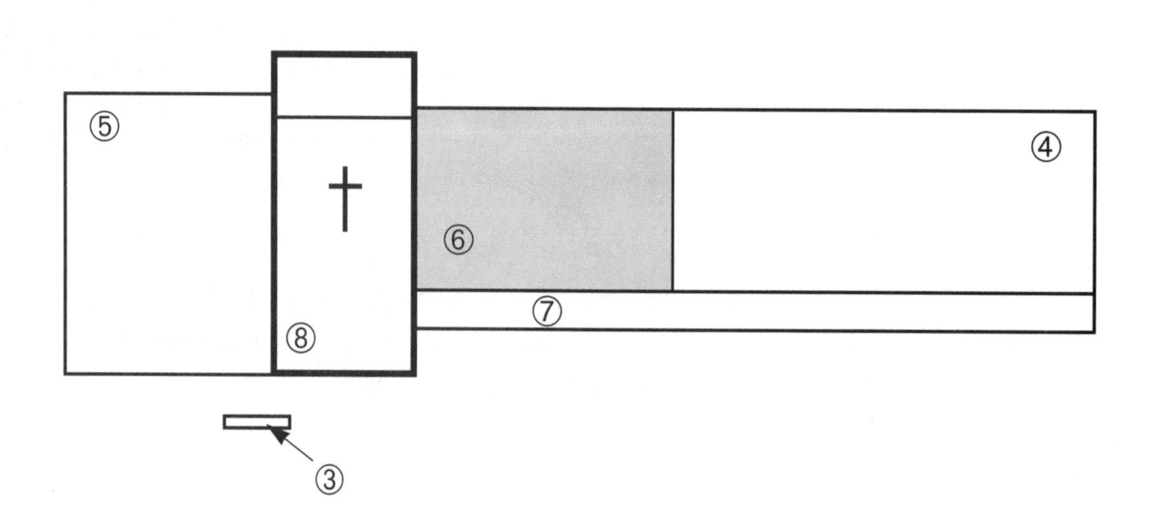

This diagram shows the mission buildings in 1812.

San Rafael Arcángel

Name ______________________________

Date ______________________________

Named for one of the three archangels named in the Bible. Rafael means "God heals." He is the patron saint of travelers, of joy, and against sickness and disease.

The 20th of 21 Spanish/Catholic Missions

Design of the Mission

Mission House: (approximate outside measurements) 88 feet long, 42 feet wide, and 18 feet high.

Unlike every other mission along El Camino Real, the church was not the first building constructed at San Rafael. This mission was established as a branch of Mission San Francisco de Asís (Dolores) to serve as a **sanitarium** for sick mission workers. (Note what the name of the mission means.) The mission house had storerooms, a kitchen, and living quarters which were actually part of the hospital facilities. A year later the church was built on one end of the mission house.

Design:

The mission house was plain and built of adobe. It was bordered on one side by a long porch. The porch was held up by square posts and had a thatched roof. The plain style church was built **perpendicular** to the mission house. Above the church's entrance was a star-shaped window which was modeled after the Moorish styled star at Mission Carmel. Like the mission house, the church was constructed of adobe. The baptistry was a small lean-to at one side of the church.

Campanario:

Mission San Rafael never had a bell tower or bell wall. Four small bells were hung on a simple wooden frame just to the right of the front entrance.

Mission Grounds:

The traditional mission quadrangle was never built at San Rafael. A colony of huts built by natives surrounded the mission house. At first, the main purpose of the mission was a healing ministry. With the number of new settlers and soldiers coming to San Francisco, came new diseases not known by the native Californians. With this exposure, many natives became ill. The damp and foggy weather at Mission Dolores, in San Francisco, added to their slow recovery. Mission San Rafael, however, was in a location that was sunny and sheltered and helped in the recovery of the victims. Mission San Rafael (a hospital) was, at first, solely supported by Mission Dolores. It did not take long, however, before the native workers at San Rafael were raising a small heard of cattle and harvesting more crops than they actually needed for themselves. The mission also had several workers who were very skilled in other trades, especially boat building. Mission San Rafael was one of the few missions whose inhabitants built boats.

Do these things using the map provided. (Use the map on page 172.)

1. Write **Mission San Rafael Arcángel** ①, **cattle brand** ②, **bells** ③, **hospital** ④, **cemetery** ⑤, **padres' living quarters** ⑥, **porch** ⑦, and **church** ⑧ by the correct number.
2. Do your best job if you color the map.

San Rafael Arcángel

One of three mission named for angels.

Name ______________________

Date ______________________

The 20th of 21 Spanish/Catholic Missions

Early History

When white settlers and Spanish soldiers began to settle in California, they brought with them several diseases that native Californians were exposed to for the first time. The **immunities** of the natives were not built up against the new diseases and many of the Indian people caught these illnesses and even died. In addition to the new diseases brought to the area by the white settlers, the damp and foggy weather where Mission San Francisco de Asís (Mission Dolores) was built added to the long recovery periods for many of the sick Indians living at the mission. The bad weather caused hundreds to die instead of recovering.

After becoming aware of the affects of the weather, the Father Prefect (head padre), Fr. Sarría, discussed a plan with other padres for moving the weaker and sickest neophytes from Mission Dolores to a site with warmer climate on the north side of the bay. The area was protected from the wind and fog by a mountain range. Fr. Sarría feared that the Indian patients would not be able to withstand the influences of the pagan ranchers and hunters who lived in the wilderness of the northern bay side region. For these reasons, Fr. Sarría wanted to wait before making his decision. However, when Fr. Luís Gil from Mission La Purísima — the only padre with some medical training — volunteered to oversee the establishment of the sanitarium, Fr. Sarría gave his approval of the plan.

On December 14, 1817, the sanitarium was founded under the leadership of Fr. Gil and the **patronage** of San Rafael Arcángel, God's angel of bodily healing. Several **invalid** and sick Indians were transferred from Mission Dolores to the new settlement at San Rafael. Along with a few converted natives from the area, a new neophyte community was formed. By the end of the first year, it had a population of more than 300 and quickly became self-supporting, yet was not given full mission status until 1822.

The outward appearance of the new settlement was simple. Unlike every other mission, the first building constructed was not a church, but instead a mission house. The building was 87 feet long and 42 feet wide, and divided into several rooms which served as hospital, chapel, storeroom, and monastery. Because it was only a branch of Mission Dolores, all of its records and statistics were included as part of Dolores, including the number of converted natives.

Fr. Gil served at the hospital for two years until the administration of the branch was placed in the hands of Fr. Juan Amoros. This padre had a character of great zeal and energy. Under his administration and example the neophytes turned to a more industrious way of life. There are stories told of him taking long trips into the northern wilderness in search of new converts, and surprisingly would often bring back one or two to live at the settlement.

It was not too many years after the founding of the sanitarium at San Rafael that it became a thriving, self-supporting community, with more than 1,000 neophytes living there. On October 19, 1822, San Rafael was recognized by the Franciscans as an independent mission and was declared independent of Mission Dolores. The next year, Fr. Amoros and other mission padres heatedly discussed the possibility of abolishing both missions at San Francisco and San Rafael and in turn build a new mission at Sonoma. The future of both missions looked **bleak** until it was decided that they would maintain a mission at all three locations.

San Rafael Arcángel

Name ______________________________

Date ______________________________

The 20th of 21 Spanish/Catholic Missions

A secondary reason that Mission San Rafael was founded was because the Russians had established a fur trading outpost at Fort Ross in 1812. The Spanish crown did not want them expanding their territory any further south into Spanish territory.

The pride of becoming a full-fledged mission was a springboard for San Rafael to become as successful and prosperous as possible. The herds of livestock grew rather rapidly, as well as the number of acres it used to produce agriculture goods. San Rafael soon became noted along the mission chain and the region for growing high quality pears. The timing of gaining full mission status was, unfortunately, too late for San Rafael. It acquired its independence near the end of the mission period and political and social disturbances were almost always a concern of the padres at the mission.

Fr. Amoros passed away after 13 years at Mission San Rafael. He worked tirelessly for the welfare of the native converts at the mission and for his religious beliefs. It was 1832 when the mission workers and companions lain him to rest and shortly afterwards the mission was turned over to the Zacatecan Franciscans to run. The new padre in charge was Father José Mercado. He had a violent temper and disliked any outside interference questioning him or his authority to run the mission. It was not too long before he was having a heated conflict with General Mariano Vallejo, the commandante of the San Francisco Presidio who used his rank to always butt into the affairs of all the missions in the region. Unfortunately for the Fr. Mercado, his uncompromising, iron-rule nature led him into violent behaviors that the general eventually used against the friar. Unlike most of the padres trying to convert the natives to Catholicism, Fr. Mercado did not tolerate natives who did not submit to his authority (or at least the authority he thought he had). The padre once organized and armed a number of his neophytes and sent them against a group of natives who had rejected his efforts to convert them. The neophytes came upon the group of unarmed people and killed several of them. This act of violence triggered most of the natives in the outlying areas not to trust or befriend any white people. The Spaniards in the area protested this act of rage. General Vallejo brought Fr. Mercado's actions to the attention of Governor Figueroa who almost immediately got Fr. Mercado removed from Mission San Rafael.

San Rafael was the first of the California missions to be secularized — soon after Fr. Mercado's removal. Coincidently (or maybe not), General Vallejo became the mission's new official administrator. It was not long after he took control that all of the mission's livestock was transferred to his own huge ranchos; and soon after the livestock showed up most of the mission's equipment and supplies also found the way to his property. Even the fruit trees and grape vines were dug up and taken to his property. This was a huge undertaking and required a lot of labor. Ironically, the neophytes were hired to do the work.

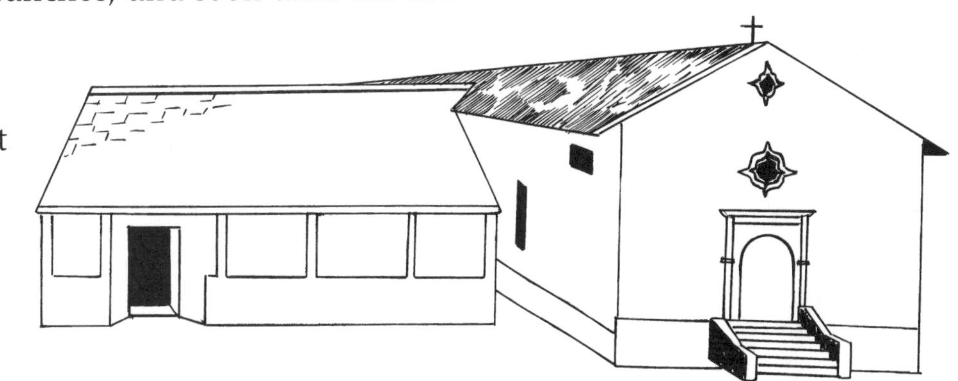

San Rafael Arcángel

Name ____________________

Date ____________________

The 20th of 21 Spanish/Catholic Missions

After Vallejo became the undisputed authority in the region north of San José, he often gave his friends and soldiers under his command land grants. To understand why Vallejo was such a bitter enemy of the missions remember this; he was greedy and that, under Spanish law, the missions held their lands only *for* the converted natives. He was an enemy of the Indians because they essentially owned the land; he was an enemy of the Church because the Church supported the idea that the natives possessed the land.

Men like Vallejo were unable or unwilling to spend the long years and countless number of working hours that is always required to build up and develop the land. The agricultural and livestock wealth existing in California when they arrived was the result of the mission system. The only way they could get this wealth was to take it from the mission — and ultimately from the converted natives. The Mexican Secularization Act, without provisions for protecting the Indians, was a solution to satisfy their greed and they willingly adopted it. One of the sad results of secularization, however, is the fact that, with rare exception such as General Vallejo, most of the men "grabbing" the lands from the missions had no idea how to work it once they got it. ❖

KrissKross Puzzle

Directions for Solving KrissKross Puzzles:

Start with either the longest or shortest word from the list of word. Write the word in the correct place. Then fill in the next word that KrissKrosses the first word, counting the number of squares and then matching the number of letters and/or the correct letter where they KrissKross.
For less confusion, mark the words off the list as you use them.

HUTS
BOATS
FOGGY
GREEDY
HEALING
DISEASES
HOSPITAL
RUSSIANS
ZACATEAN
ARCHANGEL
CHARACTER
COMMUNITY
SPANIARDS
VOLUNTEER
SANITARIUM
STATISTICS
WILDERNESS
INDEPENDENT
AGRICULTURAL
SECULARIZATION

San Rafael Arcángel

Name ______________________

Date ______________________

The 20th of 21 Spanish/Catholic Missions

The Mission Today

All of the buildings at Mission San Rafael were completely destroyed over the years. Historians have no actual plans to show how the compound was laid out. In 1949 a replica of the mission church was constructed with money donated by the Hearst Foundation. The replica was built based on pictures found of the exterior of the original church and on descriptions written about it.

The mission people visit today is located near the original site, however, it is oriented in the opposite direction. This church replica faces the mountains, whereas, the original church faced the bay. It is located on the property of a newer, larger church, St. Raphael's Church, which serves as the parish church. The new Mission San Rafael is constructed of concrete plastered to look like adobe bricks. The designers included some exterior features of the original church, like the star-shaped window above the entrance, modeled after that of Mission Carmel. Bells hung from a simple wooden frame in front of the entrance.

The interior design is a more modern one, with only a few old mission-style features, such as an arched sanctuary and deep-set windows as part of the plan. Some paintings of original missions are displayed in the small museum that is attached to the church. There are also a few statues and art objects from the original Mission San Rafael, as well as objects from some of the other California missions. ❖

This is the mission building replica.

This photo shows the newer, larger St. Rafael's Church on Easter Sunday.

Mission San Rafael Arcángel
1104 – 5th St.
San Rafael, CA 94901
Phone: 415.456.3016

San Rafael Arcángel

Name ______________________

Date ______________________

Review Questions

Write the correct answer in the space provided.

1. Mission San Rafael was founded ______________ years ago, on ______________ and is named after ______________.

2. What does "Rafael" mean? ______________

3. At first, the main purpose of the mission was a ______________.

4. Historians have no ______________ of how the compound was laid out.

5. The mission had natives who were very skilled in ______________.

6. Unlike every other mission, the first building ______________ at Mission San Rafael was not a ______________.

7. Explain the reasons many of the Indians living at the Mission Dolores died.

8. Explain why Fr. Gil volunteered to go to San Rafael, and how he helped the settlement grow into an independent mission.

9. Explain why General Vallejo supported the Secularization Act.

☆☆ **Bonus Activity**

Use another resource and write a report on one of the people mentioned in this section, archangels, Biblical accounts of healing, boat building process and/or history, a native tribe to the area (No. California), a general or a specific disease, Spanish exploration or expansion, the history and/or comparison of Easter Sunday and Passover, or William Randolph Hearst (the Hearst Foundation), or **philanthropy** in general. Draw maps and pictures for your report.

Mission #21

San Francisco de Solano

Founded July 4, 1823

Print the name of the mission on the correct line. (You may need to look back at a previously finished section/map.)

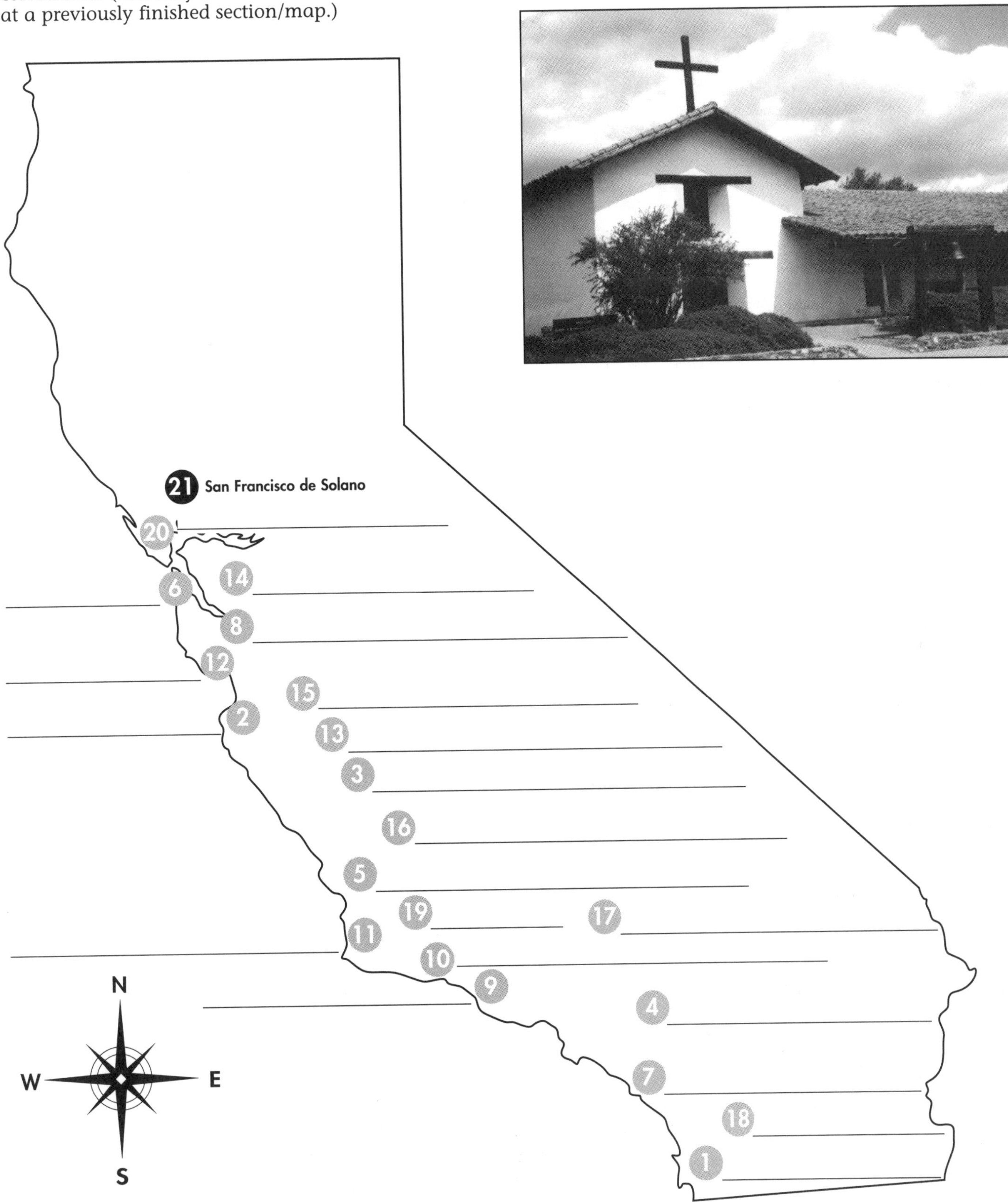

New Words to Learn:

Find the words in the glossary or a dictionary and write the meanings on the line.

1. **asinine:** ______________________________
2. **authoritarian:** ______________________________
3. **cupola:** ______________________________
4. **curtail:** ______________________________
5. **deject**(ed)**:** ______________________________
6. **enterprise:** ______________________________
7. **expel:** ______________________________

① ______________________________

Mission #21 — Founded July 4, 1823

Layout of the Mission Grounds

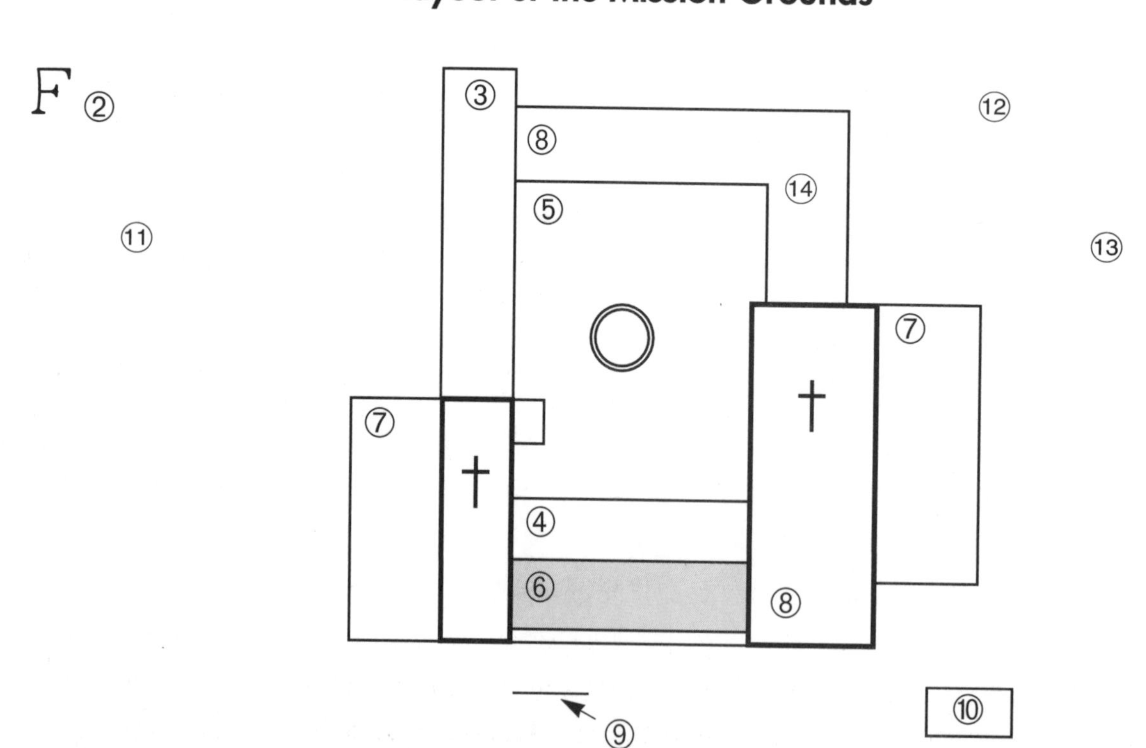

This diagram shows the mission compound about 1832

San Francisco de Solano

Name ______________________

Date ______________________

Named in honor of St. Francis Solanus, who was born in 1549, in Montilla, Spain. He became a Franciscan missionary to South America. He learned the languages of the Native American Indians very quickly.

The 21st of 21 Spanish/Catholic Missions

Design of the Mission

Church: (approximate outside measurements) 106 feet long, 25 feet wide, and 18 feet high.

The first church was made with wood and whitewashed with mud and officially dedicated in 1824. It was used only three years. The first church was replaced by a larger church made of adobe on the other side of the compound. This second church was completed in 1833, and destroyed due to decay. Restoration was based on a church built on the original site in 1840, after the Franciscans left.

Design:

All of the churches were apparently plain in style, without any distinguishing characteristics. The 1840 church was built from adobe and decorated on the exterior by wooden beams above the entrance and windows. The entrance and windows were recessed (set in) from the walls. Like most of the other missions, the interior was most likely painted in native Indian colors and designs.

Walls: The walls of the 1840 church were 105 feet long and 23 feet wide.

Campanario:

There was no bell tower or bell wall in any of the churches. A single bell was hung from a wooden frame in front of the church. The Russian settlement at Fort Ross gave the mission its first bell. Another bell that hung at the mission was made in Mexico in 1829.

Mission Compound:

The monastery building was the long structure in front of the mission compound. It provided the living quarters for the mission staff. It had a covered porch that was supported by square, wooden posts, rather than a series of arches that was typical of many of the other missions. The quadrangle also had storerooms, workshops, women's living quarters, a granary, kitchens, and a guardhouse — all of which surrounded a patio area. Mission workers were skilled craftsmen, especially in weaving cloth.

Mission Grounds:

Mission Solano was never as prosperous as many of the other missions. Because it was established near the end of the Franciscan mission system era, it did not have time to develop and prosper like many of the other missions. It did, however, have more than 10,000 acres of property where it grew grapes, fruit, grains, and raised livestock. There were kilns to fire roof tiles, which it used and sold. Another reason it did not grow very quickly is that it was not well managed by Fr. Altimira the first three years of its existence. Father Buenaventura Fortuni replaced Fr. Altimira and is credited with the limited success of the mission.

Do these things using the map provided. (Use the map on page 180.)

1. Write **Mission San Francisco de Solano** ①, **cattle brand** ②, **workshops** ③, **padres' living quarters** ④, **1st cemetery** ⑤, **2nd cemetery** ⑥, **patio** ⑦, **women's quarters** ⑧, **laundry pool** ⑨, **firing kilns** ⑩, **orchards** ⑪, **vineyards** ⑫, **grist mill** ⑬, and **storerooms** ⑭, by the correct number.
2. Do your best job if you color the map.

San Francisco de Solano

Also known as "Sonoma Mission"

Name ____________________

Date ____________________

The 21st of 21 Spanish/Catholic Missions

Early History

The Spanish crown was worried that Russian explorers would extend their California holdings further south. To **curtail** Russian expansion, the Spanish laid plans to establish missions to extend north almost to the Russian settlement at Fort Ross. These new northern missions were to be established at Sonoma, Santa Rosa, and Napa with a presidio to protect the new settlements to be established a Bodega Bay.

The changes being made in California from Spanish rule to Mexican rule (because of Mexico's independence from Spain) not only caused many civil disruptions, it also caused military, civilian, and missionary leaders to be divided on many issues. Many of these leaders were hoping to become governor of the Mexican territory. The Franciscan padres were also divided in their loyalties. Some were remaining loyal to Spain, while others were aligning with the authorities in power in Mexico. In addition to making loyalty commitments, the fathers in charge of the individual missions were more and more making decisions, taking actions, and dealing with problems at their particular mission, rather than consulting with the mission presidente, Fr. Vicente Sarría, Fr. Senan's successor, or the authorities in Mexico. It was in this turmoil and climate that the mission in Sonoma was to be established.

At this time, a young Franciscan padre was stationed at Mission Dolores. He came from Spain, was fairly new to California, full of evangelistic energy, and was anxious to convert as many Indians to Christianity as possible. His name was Fr. Altimira. With a desire to convert souls, and after watching Fr. Amoros at San Rafael be so successful, he felt that Mission Dolores, near the San Francisco Presidio, was not the right place to make converts. He noted that there were only about 50 able-bodied Indian neophytes surviving at Dolores, women were doing men's work, and the mission could not survive like this. The people living in the area, for the most part, had already heard the missionary message. He felt Dolores was dying as an **enterprise**.

Therefore, he developed a plan to close the missions at Dolores and San Rafael, and combine all of their assets into one large, prosperous mission north of San Rafael. Without ever asking for approval or permission from Fr. Presidente Senan, Fr. Altimira went to Governor Arguello with his plan. The governor saw his plan as a convenient way of expanding Spanish settlements farther to the north in Alta California. With the Governor's approval, Fr. Altimira went north of San Rafael and found a great location. On July 4, 1823, the Franciscan padre and his party raised a small cross on the site in Sonoma and transferred the name *San Francisco* to the new mission. Only when he returned to the "old" San Francisco Mission at Dolores did he notify his supervisors of what he (and the Governor) had done.

This is a typical mission kitchen with a beehive oven.

San Francisco de Solano

Name ______________________

Date ______________________

The 21st of 21 Spanish/Catholic Missions

Fr. Vicente Sarría was shocked and angry at the young padre's actions and interference into mission affairs. Nevertheless, he agreed to a compromise. Both missions San Francisco de Asís (Mission Dolores) and San Rafael would remain, and Fr. Altimira could go to Sonoma, but the mission would be named San Francisco de Solano and have full mission status.

Fr. Altimira was determined to prove the merit of his new mission. A small, plain wooden church, covered inside and out with whitewashed mud, was the first building constructed. It was officially dedicated on April 4, 1824. There were no gifts given by other missions, except for Dolores, which gave a contribution of some livestock. Several neophytes were persuaded to join him to help with the work. Surprisingly, the Russians at Fort Ross turned out to be friendly neighbors and unexpectedly donated many useful articles to the new mission, as well as bells made in Russian design. The second building constructed at the compound was a long adobe wing used for living quarters. (This building is still standing.) A vineyard, orchard, and garden were planted. The mission workers began to manufacture roof tiles, adobe brick, and make soap and hide tanning. With all this is place, Fr. Altimira had everything he needed to succeed, with the exception of leadership abilities.

He treated the neophytes harshly and unfairly. In protest, many of them ran away or returned to their former missions or settlements. Some of the Indians revolted against the padre and the mission system. After a short two years of running the mission, Fr. Altimira fled for his safety to Mission San Rafael. Feeling angry and **dejected**, he eventually had himself transferred to Mission San Buenaventura in 1826. He was replaced at Solano by Fr. Buenaventura Fortuni, under whose leadership the mission reached its height of prosperity.

The Mission remained under the authority of the Spanish Franciscans until 1833, when the Zacatecan Order of Franciscans took over the leadership with Father José Gutierrez in charge. A large adobe church was completed in 1833. It formed the eastern side of the quadrangle. But by this time, however, the political changes in California were so evident that the mission had no chance of developing like the typical missions that came before Solano.

Lieutenant Mariano Vallejo, commander of the San Francisco Presidio, constantly challenged the authority of the mission padres over the neophytes. He wanted to cause division between the Indians and friars, and did it rather successfully. Fr. Gutierrez, who was an **authoritarian**, tried to strengthen his control over the natives by beating them into submission. This **asinine** tactic backfired, however, and added to the unrest at the mission; and eventually led to its secularization the next year (1834).

This 1938 photo shows the mission after the restoration projects of 1911 and 1926.

San Francisco de Solano

Name ______________________________

Date ______________________________

The 21st of 21 Spanish/Catholic Missions

Governor José Figueroa was concerned about the Russian settlement on the northern coast of California at Fort Ross — even though it had been there since 1812. He assigned Lt. Vallejo the task of colonizing the area surrounding Bodega Bay and Fort Ross. He founded the pueblo of Sonoma in 1835, a year after the mission had been secularized, and he was made chief administrator of the mission. As soon as the missions were formally turned over to Vallejo (now promoted to General) he distributed all of the best properties of the mission to his ranchos. He announced that these lands were being held by him only for the benefit of the mission natives. However, when the officials arrived to appraise these Indian lands, General Vallejo did not let them onto the properties.

With the founding of Sonoma, the old mission chapel became a parish church and was used until 1880. The mission's large chapel decayed so rapidly that in 1840 General Vallejo had the present chapel built, probably using the bricks and wood from the old chapel. He added a wooden **cupola** on top during alterations in 1858–1860.

The Russians moved from Fort Ross in 1841, partly because they had trapped most of the sea otter in the area, and partly because of General Vallejo's effort to colonize the region. General Vallejo believed that California should no longer be part of Mexico, but rather become part of the United States. The growing number of Americans in the area feared that Mexico would **expel** them from California. Without knowing that the United States had already declared war on Mexico (the Mexican-American War), on June 14, 1846, a small band of settlers seized the Mexican headquarters in Sonoma, took General Vallejo prisoner and raised a simple flag displaying a red star near the top, a red stripe along the bottom, and a grizzly bear in the middle. The words, *California Republic* were written on it. This became known as *The Bear Flag Revolt*, and was led by Ezekiel Merritt and William B. Ide. They declared that California was an independent republic. The Republic of California lasted for 23 days, until July 7th, when Commodore John Sloat raised the American flag, declaring California part of the United States. General Vallejo was released and later played a major role in California becoming a state in 1850. ❖

Quotefalls Puzzle

Read the directions on page 168 if you do not know how to solve this puzzle.

N		L	I	T	H										R		R		O		F	I							
U	E	M	I	K	H	E	O		Y	B	S	E	C	O	I	H	G		L	H	E	V	R		N	T			
R	A	T	G	S	E	I	M	N	S	T	B	T	E	I	T	E	B		T	R	H	E	R	E	T	T	H	E	S
S	N	N	I	V	S	S	R	O	G	U	U	I	A	T	N	T	E	O	T	T	I	E	E	I	D	O	O	R	T
U	B	F	A	T	E	E	N	B	H	I	T	O	F	R	T	N	Z	A	C	K	O	M	D	R	P	A	D	S	E
						■					■			■				■						■					
	■							■										■						■			■		
								■				■								■					■				■
							■			■								■					■					■	
									■				■			■										■	■	■	■

San Francisco de Solano

Name ______________________

Date ______________________

The 21st of 21 Spanish/Catholic Missions

The Mission Today

Mission Solano fared badly during the time of the Mexican-American War and when California was becoming a state. The mission buildings were eventually sold in 1881 and then used as a barn, winery, and blacksmith shop. With the money from the sale, a small modern church was built, and the mission continued to decay. The only thing that saved the mission buildings from total destruction was that the Historic Landmarks League purchased the property in 1903. The League turned the mission over to the state in 1906. An earthquake in 1906 caused severe damage to the chapel and the rest of the buildings. Restoration of the chapel from 1911 to 1913 allowed for the rebuilding of a church. The new church was built as a replica of the 1840's church that General Vallejo built. The mission property was given to the State of California by the League in 1926. Further restoration took place in the 1940s. It now forms part of the public plaza.

The altar of the church looks as it did during its first years. The floors are uneven and have no pews, just as it was then. The natives attending mass either stood or sat on the floor. The property is now the Sonoma Mission State Historic Park, which consists of the reconstructed church and the living quarters wing. (This wing is the only part of the original mission.) Part of the wing has been turned into a small museum. The church is not used for religious purposes on a regular basis. As one of the first State Historical Monuments the buildings are maintained by the State Department of Parks and Recreation.❖

Sonoma State Historic Park
(Mission San Francisco de Solano)
P.O. Box 167
20 East Spain Street
Sonoma, CA 95476
Phone: 707.938.1519

San Francisco de Solano

Name ______________________

Date ______________________

REVIEW QUESTIONS

Write the correct answer in the space provided.

1. Mission San Francisco de Solano was founded ____________ years ago, on ____________________ and is named after ______________________.

2. What was St. Francis Solanus? ______________________

3. The Spanish ____________ was worried that ______________ explorers would extend their California holding further south, so they made plans to establish missions in ____________, ______________, and ____________.

4. The ________________________ gave the mission to the state in 1926.

5. Mission Solano was never as ____________ as many of the other missions because it was established near the end of the mission ______________.

6. How did the Russians surprise the leadership of the missions?

____

____

____

7. Explain Fr. Altimira's plan for Missions Dolores, San Rafael, and Sonoma.

____

____

____

____

____

____

8. Explain how and why Fr. Altimira's left the mission.

____

____

____

____

____

☆☆ Bonus Activity

Use another resource and write a report on one of the people mentioned in this section, Mexican-American War, history/process of blacksmithing, the Historic Landmark League, boat building process and/or history, a native tribe to area (No. California), Russia or Russian exploration in North America. Draw maps and pictures for your report.

California Missions

Extras

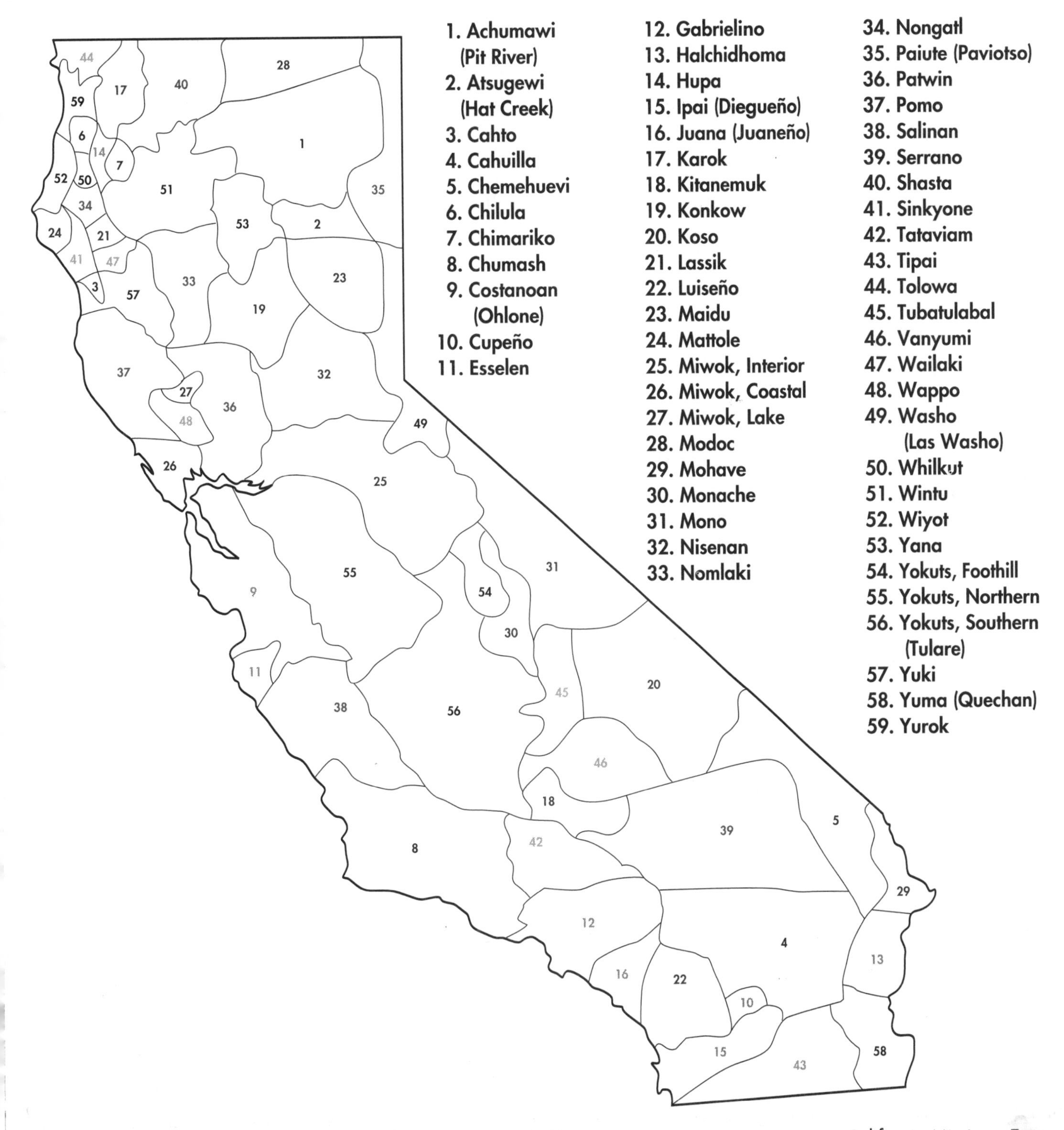

1. Achumawi (Pit River)
2. Atsugewi (Hat Creek)
3. Cahto
4. Cahuilla
5. Chemehuevi
6. Chilula
7. Chimariko
8. Chumash
9. Costanoan (Ohlone)
10. Cupeño
11. Esselen
12. Gabrielino
13. Halchidhoma
14. Hupa
15. Ipai (Diegueño)
16. Juana (Juaneño)
17. Karok
18. Kitanemuk
19. Konkow
20. Koso
21. Lassik
22. Luiseño
23. Maidu
24. Mattole
25. Miwok, Interior
26. Miwok, Coastal
27. Miwok, Lake
28. Modoc
29. Mohave
30. Monache
31. Mono
32. Nisenan
33. Nomlaki
34. Nongatl
35. Paiute (Paviotso)
36. Patwin
37. Pomo
38. Salinan
39. Serrano
40. Shasta
41. Sinkyone
42. Tataviam
43. Tipai
44. Tolowa
45. Tubatulabal
46. Vanyumi
47. Wailaki
48. Wappo
49. Washo (Las Washo)
50. Whilkut
51. Wintu
52. Wiyot
53. Yana
54. Yokuts, Foothill
55. Yokuts, Northern
56. Yokuts, Southern (Tulare)
57. Yuki
58. Yuma (Quechan)
59. Yurok

California Missions
El Camino Real

Name ______________________

Date ______________________

Print the name of the mission on the correct line. (This time do it **without** looking back at any of the other section maps.)

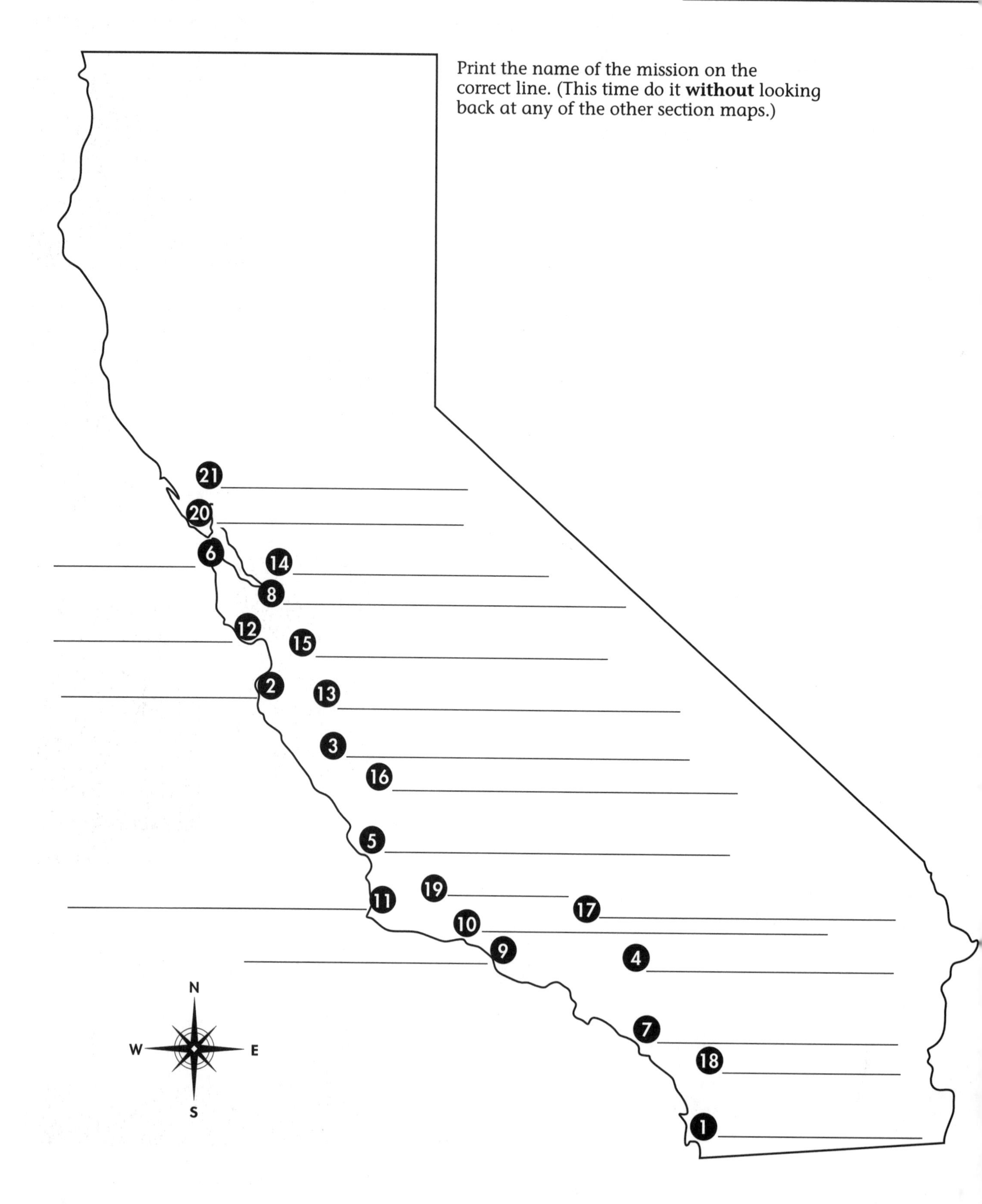

California Missions
Campanarios

Name ______________________

Date ______________________

Print the name of the mission on the line near each bell or campanario.

California Missions
At-A-Glance

Name ______________________

Date ______________________

Print the name of the mission on the line near each bell or campanario.

California Missions
At-A-Glance

Name ______________________

Date ______________________

Print the name of the mission on the line the picture.

____

____

____

____

______________________ →

______________________ →

____

____

____

____

______________________ →

California Missions
Current Addresses and more.

Name ____________________

Date ____________________

If you contact the any of the missions by mail, always include a self-addressed stamped envelope. If you plan to visit any of the missions in person, it is always helpful if you call the mission before you go and find out their hours of operation and/or if any special events are taking place during the time you want to visit. If they have special events that you might want to attend, then you can plan accordingly. It is also helpful to you to plan your route of travel if you visit more than one of the missions in a day. At the time of this printing, only Mission San Juan Capistrano had a web site for you to visit.

#1 Mission Basilica San Diego de Alcalá
10818 San Diego Mission Rd.
San Diego, CA 92108
Phone: 619.283.7319

#2 San Carlos Borroméo Basilica
P.O. Box 2235;
3080 Rio Road
Carmel, CA 93921
Phone: 831.624.3600

#3 San Antonio de Padua Mission
P.O. Box 803;
Mission Creek Road
Jolon, CA 93928
Phone: 831.385.4478

#4 San Gabriel
537 West Mission Drive
San Gabriel, CA 91776
Phone: 626.457.3048

#5 San Luís Obispo de Tolosa
P.O. Box 1461;
728 Monterey Street
San Luis Obispo, CA 93401
Phone: 805.543.6850

#6 San Francisco de Asís *(Mission Dolores)*
3321 16th Street
San Francisco, CA 94114
Phone: 415.621.8203

#7 San Juan Capistrano
Corners of Camino Capistrano and Ortega Highway
P.O. Box 697
San Juan Capistrano, CA 92693
Phone: 949.248.2047
www.missionsjc.com

#8 Santa Clara
Santa Clara University
500 El Camino Real
Santa Clara, CA 95053
Phone: 408.554.4023

#9 Mission San Buenaventura
211 East Main Street
Ventura, CA 93001
Phone: 805.643.4318

#10 Old Mission (Santa Bárbara)
2201 Laguna Street
Santa Barbara, CA 93105
Phone: 805.682.4713

#11 La Purísima Concepción
RFD #102;
(Gift Shop 2295 Purísima Rd.)
Lompoc, CA 93436
Phone: 805.733.7782

#12 Mission Santa Cruz
126 High Street
Santa Cruz, CA 95060
Phone: 831.426.5686

#13 Old Mission (Soledad)
c/o Our Lady of Soledad Parish
P.O. Box 506
36641 Fort Romie Road
Soledad, CA 93960
Phone: 831.678.2586

#14 San José
P.O. Box 3159
43300 Mission Blvd.
San Jose, CA 94538
Phone: 510.657.1797
Fax 510.657.8332

#15 San Juan Bautista
P.O. Box 41
2nd and Mariposa Streets
San Juan Bautista, CA 95045
Phone: 408.623.2127

#16 Old Mission (Mission San Miguel)
P.O. Box 69
775 Mission Street
San Miguel, CA 93451
Phone: 805.467.3256

#17 San Fernando Rey de España
15151 San Fernando Mission Blvd.
Mission Hills, CA 91345
Phone: 818.361.0186
Museum Phone: 818.365.1501

#18 San Luis Rey
4050 Mission Avenue
Oceanside, CA 92057
Phone: 760.757.3651

#19 Santa Inés
P.O. Box 408
1750 Mission Drive
Solvang, CA 93463
Phone: 805.688.4815

#20 San Rafael Arcángel
1104 – 5th St.
San Rafael, CA 94901
Phone: 415.456.3016

#21 Sonoma State Historic Park (San Francisco de Solano)
P.O. Box 167
20 East Spain Street
Sonoma, CA 95476
Phone: 707.938.1519

California Missions
Founding Dates

Name ______________________________

Date ______________________________

Mission	Named For	Date Founded
1. San Diego de Alcalá	St. Didacus from the University of Alcalá	July 16, 1769
2. San Carlos Borromeo de Carmelo	St. Charles Borromeo	June 3, 1770
3. San Antonio de Padua	St. Anthony buried at Padova (Padua), Italy	July 14, 1771
4. San Gabriel Arcángel	St. Gabriel Arcangel of God, announced birth of Jesus	September 8, 1771
5. San Luís Obispo de Tolosa	St. Louis Bishop of Toulouse, France	September 1, 1772
6. San Francisco de Asís (also known as *Mission Dolores*)	St. Francis born in Assisi, Italy in 1182	October 9, 1776
7. San Juan de Capistrano	St. John of Capistrano, Italy	November 1, 1776
8. Santa Clara de Asís	St. Clara born in Assisi, Italy in 1194	January 12, 1777
9. San Buenaventura	Giovanni de Fidanza healed boy, "O! Buena ventura!" (means Good Fortune)	March 31, 1782
10. Santa Bárbara	St. Barbara imprisoned by her father	December 4, 1786
11. La Purísima Concepción	Most Pure Conception	December 8, 1787
12. Santa Cruz	Holy Cross Saint Cross	September 25, 1791
13. Nuestra Señora de la Soledad	Our Most Sorrowful Lady of Solitude (mother of Jesus)	October 9, 1791
14. San José	St. Joseph Husband of Mary, mother of Jesus	June 11, 1797
15. San Juan Bautista	St. John the Baptist	June 24, 1797
16. San Miguel Arcangel	St. Michael Arcangel of God, leader of God's army	July 25, 1797
17. San Fernando Rey de España	St. Ferdinand III from Castille, Spain	September 8, 1797
18. San Luís Rey de Francia	St. Louis IX King of France	June 13, 1798
19. Santa Inés	St. Agnes 13 year old Christian martyr	September 17, 1804
20. San Rafael Arcángel	St. Raphael Arcangel of God (God heals)	December 14, 1817
21. San Francisco de Solano	St. Francis Solanus Missionary to So. America (born 1549)	July 4, 1823

California Missions
Baja California Missions

Name ____________________

Date ____________________

Mission	Date Founded	Current Condition	Religious Order
Loreto	1697	stone – Rebuilt	Jesuit
San Javier	1699	stone – Good	Jesuit
Ligui	1705	tile floor	Jesuit
Mulege	1705	stone	Jesuit
Comondu	1708	stone ruins	Jesuit
La Purísima	1719	stone ruins	Jesuit
La Paz	1720	no remains	Jesuit
Guadalupe (South)	1720	stone foundation	Jesuit
Dolores	1721	adobe ruins	Jesuit
Santiago	1724	no remains	Jesuit
San Ignacio	1728	stone	Jesuit
San José del Cabo	1730	no remains	Jesuit
San Miguel (South)	1730	no remains	Jesuit
Todos Santos	1734	rebuilt – adobe	Jesuit
San Luís Gonzaga	1737	stone	Jesuit
La Pasión	1737	stone ruins	Jesuit
Santa Gertrudis	1752	stone	Jesuit
San Borja	1762	stone	Jesuit
Calamajue	1766	adobe ruins	Jesuit
Santa Maria	1767	adobe ruins	Jesuit
San Fernando	1769	adobe ruins	Franciscan
El Rosario	1774	adobe ruins	Dominican
Santo Domingo	1775	adobe ruins	Dominican
San Vincente	1780	adobe ruins	Dominican
San Miguel de la Frontera (North)	1787	adobe ruins	Dominican
Santo Tomas	1791	stone foundation	Dominican
San Pedro Martir	1794	adobe ruins	Dominican
Santa Catalina	1797	adobe ruins	Dominican
Descanso	1814	no remains	Dominican
Guadalupe (North)	1834	no remains	Dominican

❖ ❖ ❖

California Missions

Historical Time Line

1450 to 1850

Name ____________________

Date ____________________

1450

Columbus discovers America – 1492

1512 – Cortez goes to Mexico

Magellan to Manila – 1521
Trade with Manilla begins

1533 – Cortez goes to Baja California

Cabrillo explores the coasts of – 1542
Baja and Alta California

1596 – Vizcaíño sails up the coast of Baja California

Vizcaíño goes to Alta California – 1602

1615 – Captain Juan de Iturbi explores the Baja Peninsula

Father Kino and the Jesuits explore – 1683
the Baja Peninsula for future missions

1697 – Jesuits found the first Baja Mission

The Franciscans move to Baja – 1768
and the Jesuits leave

1769 – The Franciscans leave Baja for Alta California and establish Mission San Diego de Alcala

Twenty-one missions established – 1769 – 1824
in Alta California

1834 – Secularization of Missions began
Mexico won independence from Spain

1850 – California became the 31st state of the United States (September 9th)

California Missions
Historical Summary

Name ______________________

Date ______________________

The following is written on the walls of the Sonoma Mission:

1. California's mission system began at San Diego where Fr. Junípero Serra founded San Diego de Alcalá in 1769. Fr. Serra was instrumental in starting nine missions before his death in 1784.
2. With the padres came the Spanish soldiers to protect the padres, neophytes, and settlers. Some settlers brought wives from Mexico, others married Native Indian women.
3. Into the wilderness came the Franciscans; with plow and hoe and church bell they settled in this new land.
4. From the beginnings of Christianity there have been missions. California's twenty-one were Catholic. The history of the California missions is beyond any one religious belief denomination. It is part of California's heritage.
5. Beginning with bare earth and the padres' zeal, each mission soon became a walled center of religion and general place of education for the Indians. Most of the missions owned countryside property which surrounded the main building complex.
6. California was the Spanish Crown's last frontier in America. Continuing a century-old system, the California Missions were a first step toward settlement of this frontier. They were to be followed by pueblos and ranchos.
7. Each mission was an oasis, where the travelers could find safety, rest, and refreshments which was a welcome sight treveling in the wilderness of California's countryside.
8. The mission grew from the very soil upon which it stood. Each had its own plan, following the ancient pattern of strong buildings in a fort-like arrangement surrounding an open compound.
9. With materials native to each region and a few simple tools, the padres taught the Indian converts (neophytes) how to build the missions. Using redwood, pine, oak, sycamore, soil, and stone they performed incredible feats of construction.
10. The Franciscans left a heritage and a great tribute to their labors. Catholic services have been restored to most of the missions, and they function as churches and schools, except San Francisco Solano and La Purísima Concepción, which are state properties and preserved historical monuments.
11. Mexico won independence and carried the Spanish idea of secular churches to follow the missions. Some became villages or churches. Some were looted. Some abandoned. Most of the missions deteriorated to a state of ruin from lack of use and/or neglect.
12. Spaced about a day's travel apart, from San Diego to Sonoma, California's missions have been called "The Golden Chain." Twenty-one were founded between 1769 and 1823.

❖ ❖ ❖

Hardships Missions Faced

Name ____________________

Date ____________________

San Diego de Alcalá	Raided 1775	Earthquake 1803	Secularization 1834		Sold 1846	Returned 1862
San Carlos Borromeo de Carmelo	Bouchard Raids 1818	Secularization 1834				
San Antonio de Padua	Secularization 1834	Earthquake 1906				
San Gabriel Arcángel	Earthquake 1812	Native Raids 1834			Sold 1846	Returned 1859
San Luís Obispo de Tolosa	Native Raids 1776	Bouchard Raids 1818	Earthquake 1830	Secularization 1835	Sold 1845	Returned 1859
San Francisco de Asís (Dolores)	Secularization 1834	Native Epidemic 1838	Earthquake 1906			
San Juan de Capistrano	Native Epidemic 1801	Earthquake 1812	Bouchard Raids 1818		Sold 1845	
Santa Clara de Asís	Earthquake 1812, 1818	Mouse Plague	Secularization 1836			
San Buenaventura	Earthquake 1812	Bouchard Raids 1818	Secularization 1836		Sold 1846	Returned 1862
Santa Bárbara	Earthquake 1800, 1812	Native Raids 1824	Secularization 1834		Sold 1846	Returned 1865
La Purísima Concepción	Earthquake 1812	Native Raids 1824	Secularization 1834	Native Epidemics 1844	Sold 1845	
Santa Cruz	Bouchard Raids 1818	Secularization 1834	Earthquake 1857			
Nuestra Señora de La Soledad	Native Epidemic 1802	Secularization 1835			Sold 1846	Returned 1859
San José	Native Raids 1817, 1826, 1829	Secularization 1834			Sold 1846	Returned 1865
San Juan Bautista	Secularization 1835					
San Miguel Arcángel	Serious Fire 1806				Sold 1846	Returned 1859
San Fernando Rey de España	Earthquake 1812	Secularization 1834	Military HQ. 1833-1846			
San Luis Rey de Francia	Secularization 1834				Sold 1846	Returned 1865
Santa Inés	Earthquake 1812	Native Raids 1824	Secularization 1834		Sold 1846	Returned 1862
San Rafael Arcángel	Native Raids 1832	Secularization 1834			Sold 1846	Returned 1855
San Francisco de Solano	Native Raids 1826	Secularization 1834			Sold 1880	

Craft Ideas

Name ______________________

Date ______________________

Making a Mission from Bakers Clay.

Materials:

Salt, flour & water to make bakers clay
Tempra or similar paint for color
Cardboard, wood, or other material for modeling clay around
*Be sure to wrap unused portions or they may become dry

Instructions:

Mix flour, salt and water (the same as making playdough).

Add selected paint about 3/4 of the way through mixing.

Put together the frame of the mission you wish to build. Use a rolling pin to roll the bakers clay and completely cover the frame. Pinch corners and fill in cracks with left over materials to ensure an unbroken finish. (If replicating the current state of a mission, cracks can be added as they appear.) Bake at 325 for two hours.

*Sometimes when modeling a complicated mission it is best to bake the building frame as separate rooms and then mold together with saved clay. (Small amounts of clay will dry at room temperature.) Let pieces cool or be careful when assembling...they're hot!

❖ ❖ ❖

Making Adobe Bricks:

Materials:

Adobe clay
Sand
Water
Straw or other similar material to add to adobe clay for strength
Boxes (The size will depend on the size bricks you wish to make. Match boxes work well for small projects, or you can make larger wooden boxes if desired.)

Instructions:

Mix the materials, 1 part sand to 3 parts clay. Add water to allow for an easily workable substance. Begin to fill molds and add straw as you go. After all molds have been filled, allow to dry overnight. Seal extra adobe in a plastic bag. After drying molds, remove your bricks and bind together using left over clay.

If molds are limited in number, the drying process might need to be repeated to make enough bricks for a mission. The molds should be lined with tin foil to prevent the soil from sticking to the molds.

❖ ❖ ❖

Name ______________________

Date ______________________

Making a Diorama.

Materials:

Shoe box or small cardboard box
Scissors and glue
Colored paper, sponges, twigs
Paint
(Those little fuzzy pipe cleaner thingies and magazine pictures can also be used to add color to this project.)

Instructions:

Select a mission to replicate.

Cut the necessary pieces for your mission from construction paper or light cardboard. With the box facing you, construct the building or bell wall of the mission you have chosen. Leave room for the mission yard.

Cut and assemble, if necessary, the materials which will be used to show how the mission yard could have looked.

Make sure all of the glue is dry before moving the diorama.

*For a more detailed project, try using a flat piece of cardboard or cut out the top side of a box, open side facing you, and figure out how to construct a mission out of toothpicks and glue.

❖ ❖ ❖

Making Relief Maps:

Use either paper maché or a 2 parts flour to 1 part salt and water mixture to create the material necessary for molding your relief map.

Mold map on a large piece of tag board or cardboard and allow to dry.

After maps have dried 24 to 36 hours, color or paint your map. Indicate in colors where the missions would have been and the route which may have been followed by early missionaries while traveling from one mission to another.

Note: Tin foil may also be used in creating your map, but it is harder to color.

California Missions
Craft Ideas

Name ______________________

Date ______________________

Making Paper Mash (or Pulp):

Materials:

Paper (newspaper works well, but any will do)
Pan or bowl big enough to hold all necessary paper and water
Liquid Starch

Instructions:

Paper mash can be used for the entire mission or used as texture to give your mission a more realistic look.

When using paper mash for an entire mission you will need to have a fairly solid structure to mold around (thin cardboard or tag board works well). Begin by assembling and covering the main structures of your mission. Allow time for these pieces to set. Assemble all building structures using the same paper mash, then allow to dry.

You may add texture during the first covering or at any time after completing.

If you are uncertain about measurements "ready-mixed" paper mash can be found at most craft and hobby stores.

❖ ❖ ❖

Making Soap:

Materials:

2.5 lbs. of tallow
One regular can of lye
Water

Caution:

BE VERY CAREFUL WHEN HANDLING THE LYE. IT WILL BURN YOU OR YOUR FRIENDS IF IT GETS ON YOU. *DO NOT 'HORSE' AROUND WHILE HANDLING IT!*

Instructions:

Melt the tallow. Mix half (.5) of the lye into three-fourths (.75) pint of water. After the lye and water are mixed together, mix the melted tallow into the lye-water. Stir everything until it begins to form into soap. Pour the mixture into another container and let it harden. After the soap is hardened, cut it into bars.

❖ ❖ ❖

California Missions

Answer Keys

Historical Background

Answer Keys
Pages 3–16

Section A: pages 3–16

Map Pages 6; 8; 10; 12, and 14: *Teacher Check*

Fill in the blank page 15:

1. **Ferdinand; Isabella**
2. **Spain; Portugal**
3. **Venezuela**
4. **New Laws**
5. **secular; religious**
6. **secularization**

Matching page 16:

7. D
8. B
9. A
10. G
11. C
12. E
13. F

News Headlines Pages 14–19: *Teacher Check*

☆ Bonus Activities: *Teacher Check*

California Missions

Answer Keys
Pages 17–42

#1 San Diego: pages 17-26

Map Page 20: *Teacher Check*

Fill in the blank page 26:

1. **San Diego de Alcalá; Mother; Didacus**
2. **Junípero Serra; Franciscan**
3. **50;000; wine**
4. **Parish; basilica**

Explanation 5-7: *Teacher Check*

☆ Bonus Activities: *Teacher check*

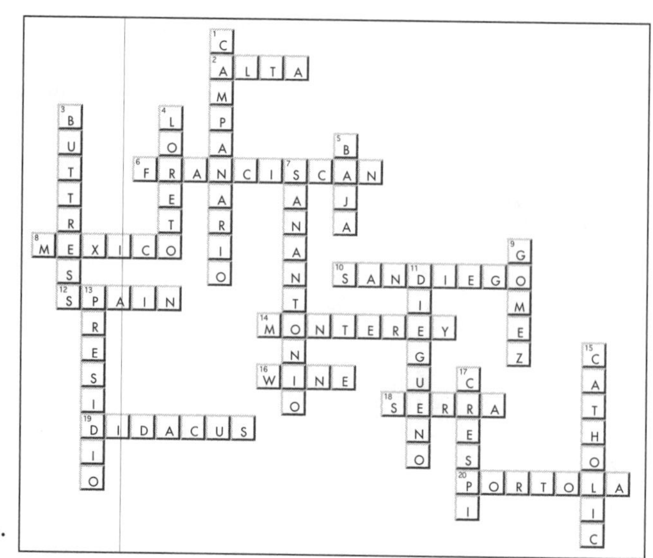

Crossword Puzzle page 24.

#2 Carmel: pages 27-34

Fill in the blank page 34:

1. **June 3, 1770; answers vary; Carmel Mission**
2. **400 miles; month**
3. **(Moorish) star**
4. **Serra; Crespi; Lasuén; Lopez**
5. **El Camino Real**
6. **beautiful; interesting**

Explanation 7-9: *Teacher Check*

☆ Bonus Activities: *Teacher check*

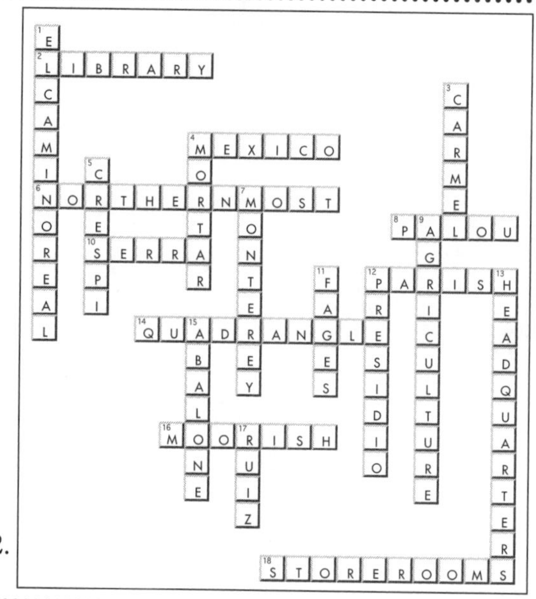

Crossword Puzzle page 32.

#3 San Antonio: pages 35–42

Fill in the blank page 42:

1. **1771; San Antonio de Padua**
2. **oak tree**
3. **aqueduct; grist mill**
4. **cobblestone; barrel vault**
5. **railroad station**

Explanation 6–8: *Teacher Check*

☆ Bonus Activities: *Teacher Check*

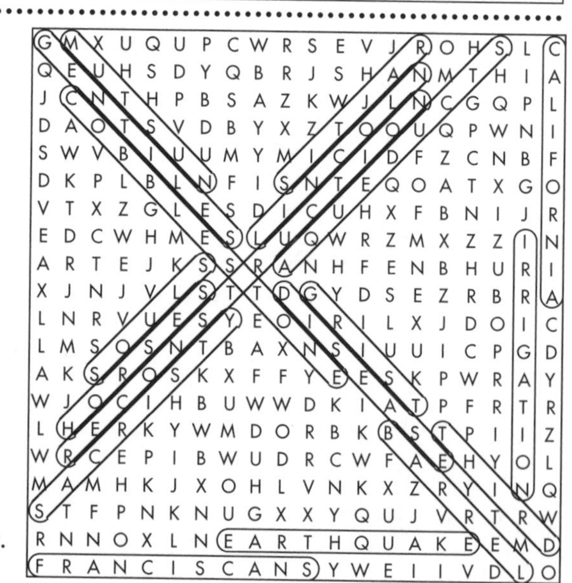

Word Search Puzzle page 40.

#4 San Gabriel: pages 43–50

Fill in the blank page 50:

1. **Pride of the Missions**
2. **Santa Ana (River)**
3. **land route; sea journey**
4. **conversion of Indians Catholicism through baptism**
5. **wealthiest; most prosperous**
6. **day's journey**
7. **1862; Catholic Church**

Explanation 8–10: *Teacher Check*

☆ Bonus Activities: *Teacher Check*

Crossword Puzzle page 48.

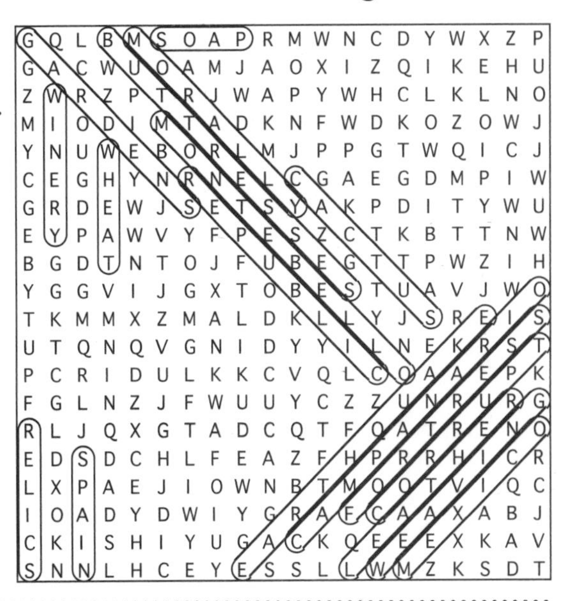

#5 San Luís Obispo: pages 51–58

Fill in the blank page 58:

1. **1772; San Luís Obispo de Tolosa**
2. **tiles**
3. **New England; John Harnett; 1933**
4. **photographs; century**

Explanation 5–8: *Teacher Check*

☆ Bonus Activities: *Teacher Check*

Crossword Puzzle page 56.

#6 San Francisco (Dolores): pages 59–66

Fill in the blank page 66:

1. **1776; San Francisco de Asís St. Francis of Assisi; Dolores**
2. **infirmary; cemetery**
3. **hides; tallow**
4. **earthquake; Mission Dolores Basilica**

Explanation 5–8: *Teacher Check*

☆ Bonus Activities: *Teacher Check*

Quotefalls Puzzles page 64:
(No punctuation or capitals required.)

1. The mission is most often called Mission Dolores.
2. Mission Dolores was a very important shipping center.
3. Dolores never prospered agriculturally or financially like the other missions.
4. The mission system offered the local natives food and protection from their enemies.
5. Saint Francis gave up wealth for vows of poverty, obedience, and chastity, thereby starting the Franciscan Order.

Answer Keys
Pages 67–90

#7 San Juan Capistrano: pages 67–74

Fill in the blank page 74:

1. **7th; 1775; 1776; Great Stone Church**
2. **Father Serra's Church**
3. **larger church; nine; earthquake; 40 (converted) Indians**
4. **hides; shoes**
5. **Charles Fletcher Luminus**

Explanation 6–8: *Teacher Check*

☆ Bonus Activities: *Teacher Check*

Quotefalls Puzzles page 72:
(No punctuation or capitals required.)

1. The campanario held four bells and had a gilded rooster weather vane on top.
2. Stonemason, Isidor Aguilar, incorporated a design into the church structure not found in any other mission.
3. Eight days after dedication, hostile Indians attacked the newly founded mission and killed one of the padres.
4. The stone church took nine years to complete and is the most impressive building along El Camino Real.

#8 Santa Clara: pages 75–82

Fill in the blank page 82:

1. **January 12, 1777; Santa Clara de Asís; Clare (Claire)**
2. **Moraga; San José**
3. **candles; wine; brandy; weaving; Indians (Natives); Catholic**
4. **University of Santa Clara; Jesuits**

Explanation 5–7: *Teacher Check*

☆ Bonus Activities: *Teacher Check*

Crossword Puzzle page 80.

#9 San Buenaventura: pages 83–90

Fill in the blank page 90:

1. **St. Bonaventura; Father Serra; 1782**
2. **Chumash; Channel Indians; boatbuilding; wood carving; baskets**
3. **pears**
4. **The Mission by the Sea or place of canals**
5. **George Vancouver; prosperity or abundance of agricultural products**

Explanation 6–7: *Teacher Check*

☆ Bonus Activities: *Teacher Check*

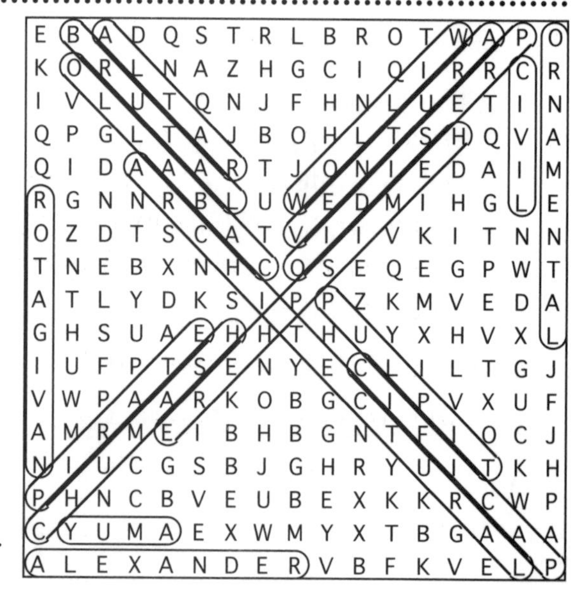

Word Search page 88.

ANSWER KEYS
Pages 91–114

#10 Santa Bárbara: pages 91–98

Fill in the blank page 98:

1. **December 4, 1786; Santa Barbara; Franciscan Order**
2. **Father Lasuén; Father Serra**
3. **bell towers; candelabra; reservoir**
4. **Golden Age**

Explanation 5–7: *Teacher Check*

☆ Bonus Activities: *Teacher Check*

Quotefalls Puzzles page 96:
(No punctuation or capitals required.)

1. The Queen of the missions was the only mission along El Camino Real to be constantly occupied by the Franciscan Order.

#11 La Purísima Concepción: pages 99–106

Fill in the blank page 106:

1. **La Purísima Concepción; Fr. Lasuén; December 8, 1787**
2. **six; seventeen; Chumash; month**
3. **earthquake; 1812; Lompoc**
4. **three; aqueducts (clay pipes) dams; reservoirs**
5. **quadrangle; exit; earthquake**

Explanation 6–7: *Teacher Check*

☆ Bonus Activities: *Teacher Check*

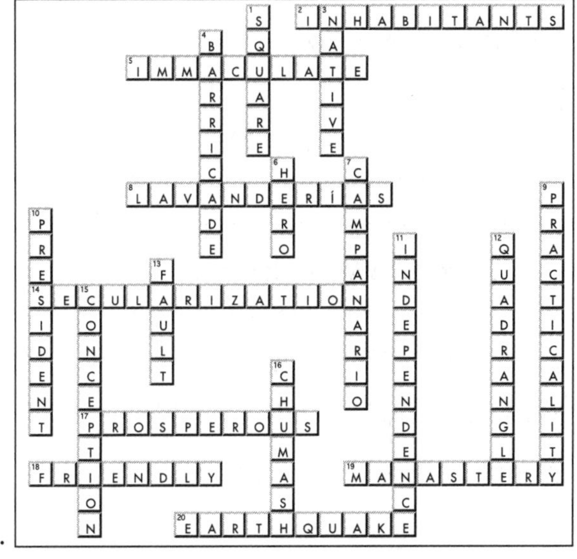

Crossword Puzzle page 104.

#12 Santa Cruz: pages 107–114

Fill in the blank page 114:

1. **Mission Santa Cruz; September 25, 1791; answers vary**
2. **Branciforte; smugglers; roughest**
3. **1840; earthquake; earthquake; 1857**
4. **peace; military**

Explanation 5a–5c: *Teacher Check*

☆ Bonus Activities: *Teacher Check*

KrissKross page 112.

SYMPATHETIC
CONFLICT
HISTORICAL
PUEBLO
PROMOTE
TROUBLEMAKERS
BARRACKS
ERA
ENGINEER
STRIFE
FRONTIER
PERMANENT
MISFORTUNE
NEOPHYTE
FRANCISCAN

#13 Soledad: pages 115–122

Fill in the blank page 122:

1. **13th; El Camino Real (King's Hwy.)**
2. **Gov. Gaspar de Portolá; 1770; answers vary;**
3. **isolated**
4. **hunt; gifts; Spain**
5. **sick; transfer**

Explanation 6–8: *Teacher Check*

☆ Bonus Activities: *Teacher Check*

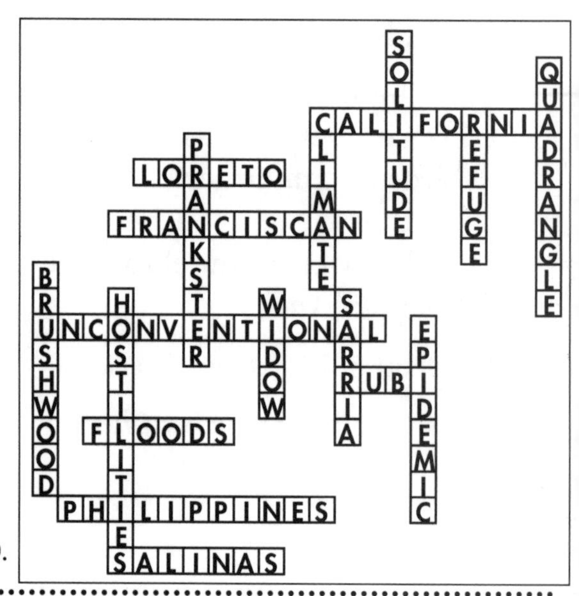

KrissKross page 120.

#14 San José: pages 123–130

Fill in the blank page 130:

1. **14th; El Camino Real; successful; California**
2. **answers vary**
3. **3rd; converted; San Gabriel**
4. **Hayward Fault; earthquake; strongest; California**

Explanation 5–8: *Teacher Check*

☆ Bonus Activities: *Teacher Check*

Scrambled Sentences page 128: (Punctuation and capitals are required.)

1. A new wooden roof was built over the remains for protection from erosion.
2. The padres envisioned Mission San José as a base to control the native Californians.
3. Mission San José had the great fortune of having hot springs nearby.
4. The sale of the mission by was annulled and the property returned to the Catholic Church.
5. Much of the success of the mission was due to the efforts and gifts of Father Durán.
6. The trapper Jedediah Smith stayed at the mission and records show Kit Carson visited it.
7. San José became the most successful mission in northern California.

#15 San Juan Bautista: pages 131–138

Fill in the blank page 138:

1. **June 24, 1797; answers vary; San Juan Bautista; Saint John the Baptist**
2. **San Andreas**
3. **wealthy; agriculture**
4. **three**

Explanation 5–7: *Teacher Check*

☆ Bonus Activities: *Teacher Check*

Crossword Puzzle page 136.

California Missions

Answer Keys
Pages 139–162

#16 San Miguel: pages 139–146

Fill in the blank page 146:

1. **Answers vary; July 25, 1797; The Angel (Arcángel) Michael**
2. **possessions; San Joaquin Valley; neighbors**
3. **blacksmiths; masons; carpenters; soap makers; weavers; leather workers**
4. **best-preserved; decorations; original**
5. **expeditions; mission**

Explanation 6–8: *Teacher Check*

☆ Bonus Activities: *Teacher Check*

Scrambled Sentences page 144:
(Punctuation and capitals are required.)

1. In a period of four months, Father Fermín de Lasuén founded four missions.
2. San Miguel developed an interest in converting the native people living in central California.
3. Friendly natives helped the Franciscans work and set up the mission.
4. Native converts were not treated as slaves who were locked up at night and forced to work.
5. The native people were not forced to adopt the Catholic beliefs, and many did not.
6. San Miguel's property was illegally sold by the dishonest and greedy Governor, Pio Pico.

#17 San Fernando Rey: pages 147–154

Fill in the blank page 154:

1. **Answers vary; September 8, 1797; King Ferdinand III**
2. **prosperity; natives (Indians)**
3. **hides; tallow; saddles or shoes Los Angeles**
4. **weather; abuse; adobe; original; mission era**

Explanation 5–8: *Teacher Check*

☆ Bonus Activities: *Teacher Check*

Word Search page 152.

Q	C	H	P	O	X	U	M	E	N	C	R	O	A	C	H	M	E	N	T
H	H	A	G	J	Z	G	L	H	E	A	D	Q	U	A	R	T	E	R	S
M	V	G	T	N	O	Y	H	M	K	P	R	O	D	U	C	T	I	O	N
X	E	M	A	R	K	E	T	X	T	F	T	Y	O	G	R	X	R	J	E
R	D	R	L	N	M	I	S	Z	O	V	P	O	P	E	E	O	D	T	D
W	G	I	C	P	R	W	R	V	R	C	P	N	I	C	I	E	A	N	X
D	P	O	S	H	X	M	H	X	G	Q	X	W	I	R	D	I	A	Y	J
T	R	R	D	T	A	B	C	Q	B	Q	L	P	E	A	D	N	R	J	Q
L	I	A	O	F	I	N	P	P	K	T	S	T	R	E	I	A	C	L	C
Y	I	R	I	P	A	N	D	C	E	O	N	G	M	D	N	C	D	D	M
V	W	Y	O	N	E	T	G	I	H	I	E	M	R	I	M	E	P	Q	N
C	C	A	T	N	A	R	H	U	S	D	I	E	D	Q	H	L	K	X	C
B	J	F	Y	Q	W	G	I	E	I	E	F	R	M	A	A	B	P	W	Q
W	C	H	Z	K	Z	O	E	T	R	S	O	H	E	Z	W	F	L	Y	L
W	Q	B	J	J	B	H	R	T	Y	A	H	H	S	H	I	Z	F	W	N
W	C	C	D	B	E	H	H	K	R	H	A	E	D	P	R	Q	M	Q	S
B	X	R	N	F	U	D	D	T	F	D	Q	B	D	O	O	N	O	C	E
Y	B	M	Z	E	B	V	X	D	V	V	R	C	B	E	E	V	L	A	S
Y	O	K	V	E	V	E	J	L	S	U	U	D	J	U	O	Z	C	C	H
H	W	Y	J	I	G	O	F	D	H	I	M	P	R	E	S	S	I	V	E

#18 San Luís Rey: pages 155–162

Fill in the blank page 162:

1. **Answers vary; June 13, 1798; King Louis IX**
2. **King of the Missions; The Other San Juan**
3. **converting; Catholic faith; well-being; natural resources; wealth**

Explanation 4–7: *Teacher Check*

☆ Bonus Activities: *Teacher Check*

Scrambled Sentences page 160:
(Punctuation and capitals are required.)

1. Drinking water was purified by filtering the water through charcoal.
2. At the height of its prosperity, San Luís Rey was the most affluent mission in California.
3. Father Lasuén gave all of the missions the great buildings by which they are known.
4. The authority of the padres was taken away by Mexican officials through secularization.

Answer Keys
Pages 163–186

#19 Santa Inés: pages 163–170

Fill in the blank page 170:

1. **Answers vary; September 17, 1804; Saint Agnes**
2. **missionaries; Mission Santa Bárbara; Christianity; Mission Santa Inés**
3. **expectations**
4. **William Randolph Hearst; restoration**

Explanation 5–7: *Teacher Check*

☆ Bonus Activities: *Teacher Check*

Quotefalls Puzzles page 168:
(No punctuation or capitals required.)

1. The mission is still an active church served by the Capuchin Franciscan Fathers.
2. The Chumash Indians working at the mission were noted for their craftsmanship with leather and metal.
3. Military commanders became increasingly more dependent upon the missions for obtaining their supplies.
4. Governor Micheltorena was in constant conflict with the authorities wanting secularization of the missions.
5. The governor returned mission land to the Catholic Church where it started the first college in California.

#20 San Rafael: pages 171–178

Fill in the blank page 180:

1. **Answers vary; December 14, 1817; Rafael the Archangel (Arcángel)**
2. **God Heals**
3. **healing ministry**
4. **actual plans**
5. **boatbuilding**
6. **constructed; church**

Explanation 7–9: *Teacher Check*

☆ Bonus Activities: *Teacher Check*

KrissKross page 176.

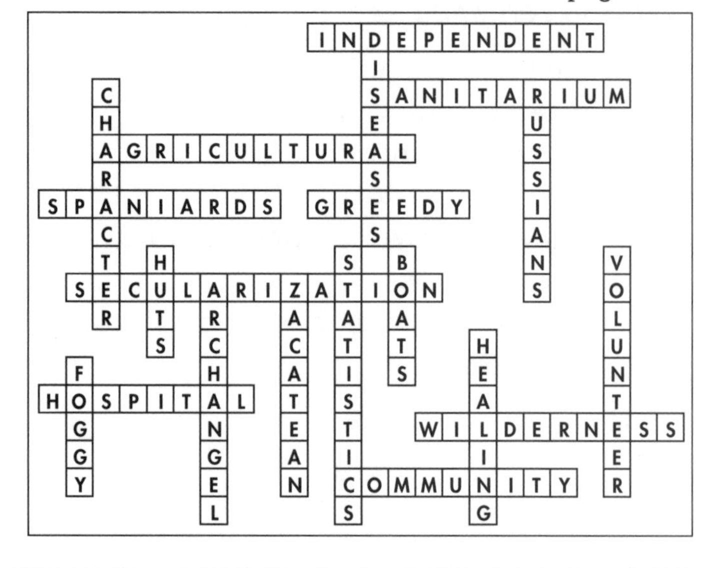

#21 Solano (Sonoma): pages 179–186

Fill in the blank page 186:

1. **Answers vary; July 4, 1823 Saint Francis Solanus**
2. **missionary (to South America)**
3. **crown; Russian; Sonoma; Santa Rosa; Napa**
4. **Historic Landmark League**
5. **prosperous; era**

Explanation 6–8: *Teacher Check*

☆ Bonus Activities: *Teacher Check*

Quotefalls Puzzles page 184:
(No punctuation or capitals required.)

1. Unlike most of the other padres, Father Gutierrez tried to strengthen his control over the natives by beating them into submission, but it backfired.

Barton, Bruce. *A Tree in the Center of the World.* Ross Erickson.
A complete volume of mission folk tales.

Bauer, Helen. *California Mission Days.* Doubleday & Co.
A good old children's book covering the settling, living in and working in the missions.

California Historical Landmarks, Office of Historic Preservation,
California Department of Parks and Recreation. 1990.

California Missions, John Hinde Curteich Inc. Printed in Ireland. 1-800-343-7115.
A color pictorial view of the California Missions.

California Missions Fact Cards, Toucan Valley Publications. 1992.
These *Fact Cards* focus on the physical mission, particularly the buildings.

Castor, Henry. *The First Book of The Spanish-American West.* Albert Micale, Illustrator.
4th Grade–Adult. This resource depicts the Indians and their successors, the explorers.

Copely, James. *The Call to California.* Union Tribune Publishing Co. Grades 7–Above.
This nicely illustrated book tells the story of the 1769 Portolá/Serra expedition
with portions of Father Crespi's diary added for "spice".

DaSilva, Owen Francis. *Music of California.* This book tells of Father Da Silva's success in
teaching the mission neophytes singing through the use of colored music notes.
Mission Santa Bárbara houses many of the music sheets created by Father Da Silva.

Don J. Baxter. *Missions of California.* Compiled from a series of articles from Pacific Gas and
Electric and E. Progress. 1970. Illustrations courtesy of Bancroft Library, University of
California, Berkeley. Photographs of the missions in the 19th century are from the
Margaret E. Schlichtmann collection.

Englehardt. *The Franciscans of California. Missions and Missionaries of California.*
Published in 1916, with contributions by Father Engelhardt (a researcher and author).

Faber & Lasagne. *Whispers Along the California Indian Trails* and *Whispers Along the California
Mission Trails.* Magpie Press, San Ramon, California. Student's Edition and Teacher's
Editions. 1983 and 1988. A history of the establishment of the mission chain.

Geiger, Maynard. *Life and Times of Father Junípero Serra.*
A classic resource written by a Franciscan.

Herbs — Mission San Antonia de Padua.
A booklet with pen and ink drawings of plants found in the missions.

Heizer & Elasser. *The Natural World of the California Indian.* Use for background reading.
This book is divided into topic areas which are then dealt with regionally. Adult Level.

Hoover, Mildred B., et al. *Historic Spots in California.*
Palo Alto, California: Stanford University Press, 1970.

Hutchinson, W.H. *California the Golden Shore by the Sundown Sea.*
A complete history of California.

Karney. *The Listening One.* John Day.
Set in the background of the Spanish-Mexican struggle over California, this is the story of a California mission Indian girl's struggles and victories in the California mission life.

Kuska, George and Linse, Barbara. *Live Again Our Mission Past.* Arts' Publications, 1992.
Craft projects and activities with a page for each mission.

Lowman, Hubert A. *The Old Spanish Missions of California.* Lawson Mardon Group.
Beautiful color photos taken by the author show the missions as they are today. A brief history and map are included.

Martin, Carol O. *Exploring the California Missions: Activity Cards.* Bay Area Explorers. 1984, 1991.
A practical and informative guide to the California missions.

Newcomb, Rexford. *The Old Mission Churches and Historic Houses of California.* Lippincott.
Adult Level. An excellent reference of mission and mission style architecture.

Palver, Francisco. *Founding the First California Mission.* Nurvena California Press. Adult Level.
A first-hand account of the founding of the early missions.

Scott. *Junípero Serra—A Pioneer of the Cross.* Valley Publications.
This is the story of the boy who would grow to become the man who started the California mission system.

Spizzirri, Linda, editor. *An Educational Coloring Book of California Missions.* Bellerophon Books.
A paragraph of facts for each mission with line drawings.

Sunset. *The California Missions: A Pictorial History.* Lane Publishing, 1979.
Use this as a general reference book. It contains many historical photos and sketches. The text covers the missions from exploration to secularization.

Townendolly, Grant (tales told to) Masson, Marcelle. *A Bag of Bones.* Naturegraph.
This retells many of the legends of the Wintu Indian Nation of Northern California.

World Book Encyclopedia. World Book, Inc. A Scott Fetzer Co.

Wright, Ralph B. (editor). *California's Missions,* Hubert A. Lowman, 1978.
The story of the Spanish conquest and the courageous padres who brought Christianity to the Pacific Coast. Pencil illustrations by Herbert C.Hahn.

Young, Stanley. *The Missions of California.* Chronicle Books, 1988.
Beautiful color photos depicting present-day buildings, grounds, and furnishings of the missions.

Note: *Most of the missions have informative brochures, pictures, and postcards available in the mission gift shop. Use the information on page 192 of this book for individual mission addresses and phone numbers.*

California Missions

Glossary

Glossary of New Words to Learn A to Col

Name ____________________

Date ____________________

abalone: A marine mollusk lined with mother of pearl.
acre(s): A measure of land 43,560 square feet.
adjacent: Near or close to something.
adobe: Sun dried bricks used in building.
affluent: Plentiful, abundant or wealthy.
allegiance: Loyalty or devotion to a cause.
altar: A table or stand used for sacred purposes in a place of worship.
annual: An event which happens once yearly.
antagonism: Being opposed or hostile to a group or people.
aqueduct: A large pipe or conduit made for bringing water from a distant source.
arbor(s): A place shaded by trees or shrubs.
armory: A store house for weapons.
artisan(s): A skilled workman or craftsman.
asinine: Acting stupid or silly.
authentic: Trustworthy; accepted; reliable.
authoritarian: Unquestioning obedience to authority (a dictator rather than person with freedom).
awe: Mixed feelings of fear, wonder, and reverence.

backslide: Sliding backward in morals or religious enthusiasm.
baptism: Submerging or dripping water on a person as a symbol of washing away sin.
barracks: A building or group of buildings used for housing soldiers.
barricade: A barrier or obstruction used for defense.
basilica: A Christian church built in the style of ancient Roman courtrooms.
belfry: A bell tower, usually one that is part of a building and placed on top.
bleak: Not promising or hopeful.

This is a picture of the altar at Carmel Mission.

candelabra: A large branched candlestick.
chastity: Not having sex (abstinence); celibacy.
cistern: A large tank for holding water, normally underground.
civilian: A person not in the military or police force.
cobblestone: A round stone mainly used for paving streets.
colleague: A fellow worker with the same profession.
colonist(s): Any original settlers or founders of a colony.

Glossary of New Words to Learn
Com to Ema

Name ___________________________

Date ___________________________

compromise: A settlement in which each side gives up something it wants.
conical: Resembling or shaped like a cone.
conventional: Following normal or accepted standards. Not unusual or extreme.
cornerstone: A stone that forms the corner of a building.
corrupt: Changed from a good condition to an unsound one.
creole: A person or the descendant of a person of European heritage born in the Gulf States.
cruciform: Shaped like a cross.
crusade: A Christian supported expedition that takes action for a cause or idea.
crux: A cross. Also a difficult problem.
cupola: A small dome on a roof. (See photo on page 157, San Luís Rey de Francisco.)
curtail: To cut short or reduce.

debate: To talk about opposing reasons; argue.
decree(s)**:** An official order or decision from a church or government.
defy (defiance)**:** Resisting or opposing boldly or openly.
degrade(ing)**:** Lowering in rank or status as punishment.
deject: To be depressed or cast down in spirit.
deplete(tion)**:** Gradually using up resources or supplies.
desolate: Left alone, uninhabited or deserted.
devastate(d)**:** Destroying or making empty.
devote(d)**:** To give up yourself or time for a special service.
dialect(s)**:** The way a language is spoken by a certain group of people.
dilapidate(d)**:** Partially ruined or needing repair as if neglected.
discretion: The freedom and authority to make decisions and choices.
disintegrate(d)**:** To separate or break up into parts.
dispatch(ed)**:** To send off promptly. Normally on a specific errand or official business.
distinguish(ed)**:** To separate by differences.
domain: Land or area owned by one person.
domesticate(d)**:** To get used to home life.
dormitory: A room or building used for housing a number of people.
dwelling(s)**:** A place to live.

economy: The management of income for a household or community.
ellipse: An imperfect circle or falling short of a goal.
emaciate(d)**:** To lose weight by starvation or disease.
emancipate(tion)**:** To set free from bondage.

Glossary of New Words to Learn
Emb to G

Name ______________________

Date ______________________

embellish: To improve or decorate by adding detail.
emigrant(s)**:** A person who has left their country or area to live in another.
encroach(ing)**:** To trespass or intrude past normal limits.
enterprise: A project or undertaking.
envy (envied)**:** Wanting something or a position someone else has.
epidemic: The rapid spread of a disease.
era: An event or date that marks the beginning of a new or important part of history.
erosion: Eroding or being eroded.
evade: To avoid or escape from something by being clever or deceitful.
expedition(s)**:** A journey or exploration.
expel: To drive out by force; eject.
exterminate(d)**:** To completely get rid of by killing.

facade: The front of a building or the part of a building facing the street.
fault: Fractures in rock strata (layers) that have movement against each other.
feeble: Weak or easily broken and frail.
fertile: Produces abundantly or is rich in resources.
flank(ed)**:** To be on the side or at the side of.
flora: A flower, or the plants of a specific region.
flourish: To blossom or grow rapidly.
font: A bowl, usually of stone, to hold the water used in baptismal services.
forerunner: A person sent early to prepare the way for another.
foray(s)**:** A sudden attack or raid in order to steal things.
Franciscan: Having to do with Saint Francis of Asís or the religious order founded by him.
friar(s)**:** Normally a person of the Augustinian, Carmelite, Dominican, or Franciscan belief.

garland: A wreath of flowers or leaves worn on the head, usually to show victory.
garrison: A secured place with troops and/or guns.
gentile(s)**:** Any person not a Jew, often a Christian. Among Christians, a heathen or pagan.
gild(ed)**:** To apply a thin layer of gold or make to appear more attractive than it is.
granary: A building used for storing threshed grain.

The weather vane on Mission San Juan Capistrano was a guilded rooster.

Glossary of New Words to Learn
H to Mea

Name ______________________________

Date ______________________________

harbor: To cling to; to hold in the mind.
(A place providing safety and shelter, i.e. where ships anchor.)
haven: Any sheltered, safe place.
hemisphere(s)**:** The half of a sphere or globe.
hospice: A home for the sick and poor; shelter for travelers.
hostage: Taken prisoner, usually by an enemy.
hostilities: Open acts of war or unfriendliness.

immaculate: Perfectly clean; with out flaw; innocent.
immunity(ies)**:** Resistance or protection against a disease or infection.
impede(d)**:** To stop or hinder the progress of.
industrious: Hardworking with a good, steady effort.
infirmary: A place used to care for the sick, often located in just one room.
ingenious: Gifted with genius; natural quality or ability; original and inventive.
institution: An organization with social, educational or religious purposes.
integrity: Having sound moral principal, honest and sincere.
intrusion: Illegally entering ones property with out ownership or permission.
invalid: Someone not well; weak and sickly.
irony (ironically)**:** A series of events that happen in a way opposite to what is expected.

Jesuit(s)**:** A member of the Society of Jesus, a Roman Catholic religious order.
jurisdiction: The area or boundaries set for a power or authority.

kiln: A furnace or over used for drying, burning or baking something.

limestone: Rock consisting mainly of calcium carbonate.
liquidate(d)**:** To settle an amount by agreement or legal process.
logic(ally)**:** Correct reasoning; valid induction or deduction.

manuscript: A written document or paper.
Mass: A Roman Catholic church service, consisting of many prayers or ceremonies.
massacre: Merciless, random killing or slaughter.
meager: Thin or lean; of poor quality or small amount.

Glossary of New Words to Learn
Mer to Phi

Name ______________________________

Date ______________________________

merchant: A person whose business is buying and selling goods for profit.
mezcla(s): A type of mortar used to hold stone and brick together.
missal(s): The official Roman Catholic book used in Mass containing prayers, rites, and so on.
missionary(ies): A person sent on a mission often by a church.
monastery: A place occupied by a group of people, often times monks.
monogamy: Being married to only one person at a time.
Moor(ish): A member of a Moslem people of mixed Arab and Berber descent.
moral(ly): Good or right in conduct and character.
mortar: A very hard bowl where softer substances are ground to powder.
motif: A main theme or subject; a repeated feature in design.
mourn: To feel or express sorrow; to grieve for someone who died.
mourning: The actions or feelings of someone who mourns; a sign of grief for the dead.
mural(s): A large picture painted on a wall or ceiling.

nave: The part of a church between the aisles, the altar and main entrance.
neophyte: Any new convert to the early Christian Church.
noble: Having inherited rank or title; High moral qualities or ideals.
nun: A woman devoted to religious life.

octagon: A figure with eight sides and eight angles.
optimism: The belief or doctrine that believes good wins over evil.
outlandish: Very odd, strange; fantastic; bizarre.

padre: Father; a priest or chaplain.
pagan: A person who is not a Christian, Muslim or Jew.
pageantry: Grand spectacle; gorgeous display.
pardon: To release from further punishment for a crime.
parish: The members of the congregation of any church.
patronage: A showing of support and encouragement to somebody else.
peer(s): A person or thing of the same rank or value.
peninsula: A land area surrounded by water on three sides.
perpendicular: Exactly upright; vertical; straight up or down.
philanthropy: A desire to help mankind, usually shown by gifts to charitable organizations.
philosophy: The search for wisdom or knowledge.

This bench, at Mission San Antonio, is made from adobe bricks and held together by mortar. (It's as uncomfortable as it looks!)

Glossary of New Words to Learn
Pla to Sem

Name ______________________

Date ______________________

plague: Any contagious epidemic disease that is deadly.
plantation: An area growing cultivated crops.
plunder(ed)**:** To steal property by force or fraud.
political(ly)**:** Concerned with government, the state or politics.
prank: A mischievous trick or practical joke.
predominant(ly)**:** Acting with authority or superiority; most frequently.
presidio(s)**:** A fortified place or military post.
primitive: Crude, simple, rough, uncivilized.
prominent: Sticking out; widely and favorably known.
proportion: The relation between parts or things relating to size, amount or degree.
province: A territorial district; territory
pueblo: In Spanish America, a village or town. An Indian village.

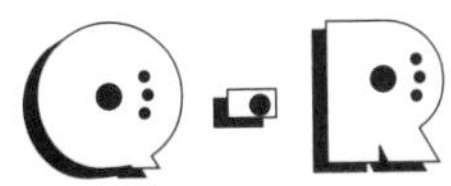

quadrangle: An area surrounded by buildings on four sides.

regime: A form of government or rule.
reign(ed)**:** Royal power, authority or rule.
remote: Far off or hidden away; secluded.
rendezvous: A place designated for meeting or assembling.
rendition: A version, translation, or interpretation of something else.
renounce: to give up; to cast off or disown.
renown(ed)**:** Famous; much talked about; very good.
replicate(ing)**:** To duplicate or copy as closely as possible.
republic: A group whose members have equality or common goals.
reservoir(s)**:** A natural or artificial lake or pond where water is stored for use.
retaliate(tion)**:** To pay back like for like; to return an injury for an injury.
retreat(s)**:** Withdrawing in the face of opposition.
rheumatism: A popular term used to describe many aches and pains in joints.

sandstone: A rock used mainly in building made mostly of sand grains.
sanitarium: An institution that takes care of sick people, or those who have certain diseases.
sarcasm (sarcastic)**:** A taunting or cutting remark, usually uses irony.
scaffold: A temporary wooden or metal framework.
scurvy: A disease resulting from a vitamin C deficiency.
secular: Living in the outside world, not bound by religious views.
seize: To forcibly take legal possession of.
seminary: A school where priests, ministers and rabbis are trained.

Glossary of New Words to Learn
Ser to Z

Name ______________________

Date ______________________

serape(s): A brightly covered woolen blanket.
shale: A kind of fine-grained, thinly bedded rock formed mostly by the hardening of clay.
slave (enslaved)**:** A human being who is owned by another and subject to his will.
solitude: Seclusion, isolation or remoteness.
squatter: A person who settles on public or unoccupied land.
strata (stratum)**:** A layer of rock material that lays on top of another.
successor: One who succeeds or follows another into a position.
susceptible: Having a sensitive nature or feelings.
symmetry (symmetrically)**:** Balanced in size shape and proportion.

T

tallow: The nearly colorless and tasteless solid fat from a cow or sheep used to make soap.
terrain: The ground or a piece of ground described with its geographical features.
thatch(ed)**:** A roof made of straw, leaves, palm branches, and so on.
trademark: A symbol, design, word, and so on used by a manufacturer to distinguish a product.
transept: The part of a cross shaped church at right angles to the long main section, or nave.
transparent: Capable of being seen through.
thresh(ed)**:** To beat out grain from its husk (outer shell).
trestle: A frame with one horizontal beam fastened to two pairs of spreading legs, often used in bridge building.
trough(s)**:** A long, narrow, open container used for holding water or food for animals.
turmoil: Commotion; uproar; confusion.

Vatican: The Pope and Roman Catholic Church (papal) palace or government.
vault: An arched roof, ceiling, or covering of masonry.
viceroy(s)**:** A person ruling a country, province or colony as the deputy to the leader.
viol(s)**:** Any of an early family of stringed instruments played with a curved bow.
virgin: A person who has not had sexual intercourse.
vow(s)**:** Dedicating oneself to an act service or way of life.

(un)**warrant**(ed)**:** An assurance or guarantee of some event or result.

yard: *Nautical.* The cross member of a mast which supports the sails.

zeal: Intense enthusiasm; devotion.

A yard supports the sail.

Notes & Doodles

Notes & Doodles